W9-AVL-230

PRAISE FOR

THE END OF MEN

"Rosin is a gifted storyteller with a talent for ferreting out volumes of illustrative data, and she paints a compelling picture of the ways women are ascendant."
—*Time*

"Fascinating." —David Brooks, *The New York Times*

"Pinpoints the precise trajectory and velocity of the culture . . . Rosin's book, anchored by data and aromatized by anecdotes, concludes that women are gaining the upper hand." —*The Washington Post*

"A persuasive, research-grounded argument . . . The most interesting sections in *The End of Men* show that in the portions of the country where, through culture and money, something like equality between the sexes is being achieved, the differences between them collapse."
—*Esquire*

"Heralds the ways current economic and societal power shifts are bringing 'the age of testosterone' to a close, and the consequences."
—*Vanity Fair*

"Refreshing . . . Rosin's book may be the most insightful and readable cultural analysis of the year, bringing together findings from different fields to show that economic shifts and cultural pressures mean that in many ways, men are being left behind. . . . *The End of Men* is buttressed by numbers, but it's a fascinating read because it transcends them. . . . Rosin's genius was to connect these dots in ways no one else has for an unexpected portrait of our moment. *The End of Men* is not really about a crisis for men; it's a crisis of American opportunity."
—*Los Angeles Times*

"Makes us see the larger picture. . . . This provocative book is not so much about the end of men but the end of male supremacy . . . The great strength of Ms. Rosin's argument is that she shows how these changes in sex, love, ambition, and work have little or nothing to do with hard-wired brain differences or supposed evolutionary destiny. They occur as a result of economic patterns, the unavailability of marriageable men, and a global transformation in the nature of work."   —*The Wall Street Journal*

"Especially timely . . . Rosin has her finger squarely on the pulse of contemporary culture . . . Fresh and compelling."   —*USA Today*

"Ambitious and surprising . . . [*The End of Men* is] solidly researched and should interest readers who care about feminist history and how gender issues play out in the culture. . . . A nuanced, sensitively reported account of how cultural and economic forces are challenging traditional gender norms and behavior."   —*The Boston Globe*

"Backed by workforce stats, [Rosin's] stories forge a convincing case that modern female aptitudes give women the advantage."   —*Mother Jones*

"[Rosin's] thorough research and engaging writing style form a solid foundation for a thoughtful dialogue that has only just begun. . . . It's not the final word on gender roles in the twenty-first century, but it's a notable starting point for a fascinating conversation."

—*Minneapolis Star Tribune*

"In this bold and inspired dispatch, Rosin upends the common platitudes of contemporary sexual politics with a deeply reported meditation from the unexpected frontiers of our rapidly changing culture."

—Katie Roiphe, author of *The Morning After* and
Uncommon Arrangements

"*The End of Men* describes a new paradigm that can, finally, take us beyond 'winners' and 'losers' in an endless 'gender war.' What a relief! Ultimately, Rosin's vision is both hope-filled and creative, allowing both sexes to become far more authentic: as workers, partners, parents . . . and people."   —Peggy Orenstein, author of
Cinderella Ate My Daughter and *Schoolgirls*

THE
END
OF
MEN

AND THE

RISE

OF

WOMEN

HANNA ROSIN

RIVERHEAD BOOKS
New York

RIVERHEAD BOOKS
Published by the Penguin Group
Penguin Group (USA)
375 Hudson Street, New York, New York 10014, USA

USA I Canada I UK I Ireland I Australia I New Zealand I India I South Africa I China

Penguin Books Ltd., Registered Offices: 80 Strand, London WC2R 0RL, England
For more information about the Penguin Group, visit penguin.com.

Grateful acknowledgment is made to *The Atlantic*, where portions of this book previously
appeared in slightly different form.

The Library of Congress has catalogued the Riverhead hardcover edition as follows:

Rosin, Hanna.
The end of men : and the rise of women / Hanna Rosin.
p.   cm.
Includes bibliographical references and index.
ISBN 978-1-59448-804-7
1. Women—Social conditions—21st century.   2. Women—Economic conditions—
21st century.   3. Feminism.   I. Title.
HQ1155.R67   2012   2012018005
305.42—dc23

First Riverhead hardcover edition: September 2012
First Riverhead trade paperback edition: September 2013
Riverhead trade paperback ISBN: 978-1-59463-183-2

PRINTED IN THE UNITED STATES OF AMERICA

10 9 8 7 6 5 4 3 2 1

Cover design by Darren Haggar
Book design by Nicole LaRoche

To Jacob, with apologies for the title

CONTENTS

INTRODUCTION *1*

HEARTS OF STEEL
SINGLE GIRLS MASTER THE HOOK-UP *17*

THE SEESAW MARRIAGE
TRUE LOVE (JUST FOR ELITES) *47*

THE NEW AMERICAN MATRIARCHY
THE MIDDLE CLASS GETS A SEX CHANGE *79*

PHARM GIRLS
HOW WOMEN REMADE THE ECONOMY *113*

DEGREES OF DIFFERENCE
THE EDUCATION GAP *145*

A MORE PERFECT POISON
THE NEW WAVE OF FEMALE VIOLENCE *167*

THE TOP
NICE-ISH GIRLS GET THE CORNER OFFICE

191

THE GOLD MISSES
ASIAN WOMEN TAKE OVER THE WORLD

229

CONCLUSION

257

AFTERWORD *269*

ACKNOWLEDGMENTS *283*

NOTES *287*

INDEX *315*

INTRODUCTION

*This world has always belonged to males, and none of
the reasons given for this have ever seemed sufficient.*

—Simone de Beauvoir, *The Second Sex*

In 2009, in a beach town in Virginia where my family had been
vacationing for several years, I noticed something curious.
Every time I ventured away from the houses rented by the
vacationers—to the supermarket, say, or the ice cream store—I
almost never saw any men. Hardly any showed up at the fairgrounds
Saturday evenings, nor did many climb out of the cars in the church
parking lots on Sunday mornings, as they had in previous years.
This was a prosperous working-class town, and one of its main businesses had always been construction. I recalled in earlier years seeing groups of men riding in pickup trucks down the main streets,
even on Saturdays. But this time, there weren't all that many pickup
trucks; mostly Chevys and Toyotas filled with women and children
going about their weekend business.

On a food run one afternoon, I accidentally slammed my cart into
another woman's and knocked out of it some granola bars that had
been balanced on a giant box of Cheerios. I apologized and she was

forgiving, and in fact she turned out to be the kind of stranger who is open to conversation. Her name was Bethenny, she told me. She was twenty-nine and ran a day care out of her house (hence, the Cheerios). She was also studying to get a nursing degree and raising her daughter, who was ten. Because she was so forthcoming I thought I'd edge closer to the heart of the matter. Was she married? I asked. No. Did she want to be? Kind of, she said, and spun me a semi-ironic fantasy of a Ryan Reynolds look-alike swooping in on a white horse, or maybe a white Chevy. Was there any mortal male who might qualify for the role? I asked. "Well, there's Calvin," she said, meaning her daughter's father. She looked over at her daughter and tossed her a granola bar and they both laughed. "But Calvin would just mean one less granola bar for the two of us."

Bethenny seemed to be struggling in the obvious ways. Later I saw her at checkout, haggling over coupons. But she did not exactly read as the pitiable single mother type. There was genuine pleasure in that laugh, a hint of happy collusion in hoarding those granola bars for herself and her daughter. Without saying as much, she communicated to me what her daughter seemed already to understand and accept: By keeping Calvin at arm's length, Bethenny could remain queen of her castle, and with one less mouth to feed, they might both be better off.

How is it that the father of her only child had so little hold on her? How could his worth be measured against the value of a snack? I got up the courage to ask her if I could contact Calvin, and she readily gave me his phone number.

Over the next few months Calvin and I talked every few weeks, me always trying to figure out how he had become so invisible. He was a gentle, earnest type and hard not to like. He talked about all the jobs he'd held and hated and I gave him advice, about work and other important matters (such as how to operate the microwave at the 7-Eleven, a source of constant frustration during his midafternoon food runs). I had an idea that I might write a story about what was happening to guys like Calvin in the post–manufacturing age, that Calvin might help me solve the mystery of those missing men.

The terms "mancession" and "he-cession" featured prominently in headlines that year, their efforts at cuteness meant to soften the painful reality that the primary victims of our latest economic disaster had been men like Calvin, the ordained breadwinners. If these men had already been laid low by the recession of the 1990s, I wondered, where were they now, nearly twenty years later, after this last series of blows? And how would they find their way back? My hope was to stay in touch with Calvin long enough that he would start earning enough money to pick up the grocery bill again, that he would find his way home. Part of me kept imagining some distant point in the future when, like in the old *Ladies' Home Journal* "Can This Marriage Be Saved?" series, Calvin and Bethenny would get back together and forge a happy trio, and in the dramatic crescendo of any imaginary reality series, the streets of the town would once again become peopled with men.

But as I spent time with Calvin and dug into the research, I discovered that I had started with the wrong questions. Calvin and his friends were not really trying to get back the lives they'd once had, because those lives were no longer there to get back. I began to understand that something seismic had shifted the economy and the culture, not only for men but for women, and that both sexes were going to have to adjust to an entirely new way of working and living and even falling in love. Calvin was not going to drive up in a Chevy and take his rightful place at the head of the table one day soon, because Bethenny was already occupying that space, not to mention making the monthly payments on the mortgage, the kitchen renovation, and her own used car. Bethenny was doing too much but she was making it work, and she had her freedom. Why would she want to give all that up?

The story was no longer about the depths men had sunk to; that dynamic had been playing out for several decades and was more or less played out. The new story was that women, for the first time in history, had in many ways surpassed them. The Calvins and Bethennys—all of us—had reached the end of two hundred thousand years of human history and the beginning of a new era, and there was no going back. Once I opened my eyes to that possibility, I realized that the evidence was everywhere, and it was only centuries of habit and history that prevented everyone from seeing it.

With a lot more reporting and research, I was able to put a clear story together. In the Great Recession, three-quarters of the 7.5 million jobs lost were lost by men. The worst-hit industries were overwhelmingly male, and deeply identified with macho: construction, manufacturing, high finance. Some of those jobs have come back, but the dislocation is neither random nor temporary. The recession merely revealed—and accelerated—a profound economic shift that has been going on for at least thirty years, and in some respects even longer.

In 2009, for the first time in American history, the balance of the workforce tipped toward women, who continue to occupy around half of the nation's jobs. (The UK and several other countries reached tipping point a year later.) Women worldwide dominate colleges and professional schools on every continent except Africa. In the United States, for every two men who will receive a BA this year, for example, three women will do the same. Of the fifteen job categories projected to grow the most in the United States over the next decade, twelve are occupied primarily by women. Indeed, the US economy is becoming a kind of traveling sisterhood: Professional women leave home and enter the workforce, creating domestic jobs for other women to fill. Our vast and struggling middle class, where the disparities between men and women are the greatest, is slowly turning into a matriarchy, with men increasingly absent from the workforce and from home, and women making all the decisions.

In the past, men derived their advantage largely from size and strength, but the postindustrial economy is indifferent to brawn. A service and information economy rewards precisely the opposite qualities—the ones that can't be easily replaced by a machine. These attributes—social intelligence, open communication, the ability to sit still and focus—are, at a minimum, not predominantly the province of men. In fact, they seem to come more easily to women.

Women in poor parts of India are learning English faster than men, to meet the demands of new global call centers. Women own more than 40 percent of private businesses in China, where a red Ferrari is the new status symbol for female entrepreneurs. In 2009, Icelanders made Johanna Sigurdardottir prime minister, electing the world's first openly lesbian head of state. Sigurdardottir had campaigned explicitly against the male elite she claimed had destroyed the nation's banking system, vowing to end the "age of testosterone."

Economic changes can shift and warp the culture, and in some countries the new breed of power women has landed as a shock. Japan is in a national panic over "herbivores," the cohort of young men who are refusing to date or have sex, and instead are spending their time gardening, organizing dessert parties, and acting cartoonishly feminine. The power women they are presumably too scared to date are known as "carnivores," or sometimes "hunters." In Brazil, church-based groups known as "Men of Tears" have proliferated to console the growing number of men whose wives make more money than they do.

These changes have reached deep into the intimate lives of couples, shifting the way men and women worldwide think about marriage, love, and sex. In Asia, as women gain more economic power and retreat further from the culture's long-standing ideal of a perfect wife, the average age of marriage for women is thirty-two, and divorce in many Asian countries is skyrocketing. The mismatch between tradition-minded men and forward-marching women has given rise to an international market for spouses, as men around the world seek out brides with values (for now) more consonant with their own. In the West, meanwhile, women behave in sexually aggressive ways that would have been unimaginable even twenty years ago.

In the United States, the relationship changes are playing out in vastly different, almost opposite ways in different classes. This point almost always gets confused, which is why I ended up writing two chapters on marriage rather than one. Our nation is splitting into two divergent societies, each with its own particular marriage patterns. One is made up of the 30 percent of Americans who have a college degree and the other is made up of everyone else—the poor, the working class, and what sociologists are calling the "moderately educated middle," meaning high school graduates who might have some technical training or college experience but not a full degree.

In this large second group, the rise of women is associated with the slow erosion of marriage and even a growing cynicism about love. As the women in this second group slowly improve their lot, they raise the bar for what they want out of marriage—a Ryan Reynolds look-alike, a white Chevy. But the men of their class are failing to meet their standards. The men may cling to traditional ideals about themselves as providers, but they are further than ever from being able to embody those ideals. This is the class from which we draw our romantic notions of manhood, which inspired generations of country music and political speeches. But now the rising generation has come to think of lasting love as a fiction that lives on only in those speeches and pop songs.

Among the educated class, women's new economic power has produced a renaissance of marriage. Couples in possession of college degrees are much more fluid about who plays what role, who earns more money, and, to some extent, who sings the lullabies. They have gone beyond equality and invented whole new models of marriage. I call these "seesaw marriages," where the division of earnings might be forty-sixty or eighty-twenty—and a year or two later may flip, giving each partner a shot at satisfaction. More wives at the top are becoming the main breadwinners for some period of time, and, as a result of this new freedom, more couples are describing their marriages as "happy" or "very happy." But even "happy" can hide complications. As I interviewed such couples, I realized that men, even if they check the "happy" box, are not nearly so quick or eager to inhabit these new flexible roles as women are.

In fact throughout my reporting, a certain imaginary comic book duo kept presenting themselves to me: Plastic Woman and Cardboard Man. Plastic Woman has during the last century performed superhuman feats of flexibility. She has gone from barely working at all to working only until she got married to working while married and then working with children, even babies. If a space opens up for her to make more money than her husband, she grabs it. If she is no longer required by ladylike standards to restrain her temper, she starts a brawl at the bar. If she can get away with staying unmarried and living as she pleases deep into her thirties, she will do that too. And if the era calls for sexual adventurousness, she is game.

She is Napoleonic in her appetites. As she gobbles up new territories she hangs on to the old, creating a whole new set of existential dilemmas (too much work *and* too much domestic responsibility, too much power *and* too much vulnerability, too much niceness *and* not enough happiness). Studies that track women after they get their MBAs have even uncovered a superbreed of Plastic Women: They earn more than single women and just as much as the men. They are the women who have children but choose to take no time off work. They are the mutant creature our society now rewards the most—the one who can simultaneously handle the old male and female responsibilities without missing a beat.

Cardboard Man, meanwhile, hardly changes at all. A century can go by and his lifestyle and ambitions remain largely the same. There are many professions that have gone from all-male to female, and almost none that have gone the other way. For most of the century men derived their sense of manliness from their work, or their role as head of the family. A "coalminer" or "rigger" used to be a complete identity, connecting a man to a long lineage of men. Implicit in the title was his role as anchor of a domestic existence.

Some decades into the twentieth century, those obvious forms of social utility started to fade. Most men were no longer doing physically demanding labor of the traditional kind, and if they were, it was not a job for life. They were working in offices or not working at all, and instead taking out their frustration on the microwave at the 7-Eleven. And as fewer people got married, men were no longer acting as domestic providers, either. They lost the old architecture of manliness, but they have not replaced it with any obvious new one.

What's left now are the accessories, maybe the "mancessories"—jeans and pickup trucks and designer switchblades, superheroes and thugs who rant and rave on TV and, at the end of the season, fade back into obscurity. This is what critic Susan Faludi in the late 1990s defined as the new "ornamental masculinity," and it has not yet evolved into anything more solid.

As a result men are stuck, or "fixed in cultural aspic," as critic Jessica Grose puts it. They could move more quickly into new roles now open to them—college graduate, nurse, teacher, full-time father—but for some reason, they hesitate. Personality tests over the decades show men tiptoeing into new territory, while women race into theirs. Men do a tiny bit more housework and child care than they did forty years ago, while women do vastly more paid work. The working mother is now the norm. The stay-at-home father is still a front-page anomaly.

The Bem test is the standard psychological tool used to rate people on how strongly they conform to a variety of measures considered stereotypically male or female: "self-reliant," "yielding," "helpful," "ambitious," "tender," "dominant." Since the test started being administered in the mid-1970s, women have been encroaching into what the test rates as male territory, stereotypically defining themselves as "assertive," "independent," "willing to take a stand." A typical Bem woman these days is "compassionate" and "self-sufficient," "individualistic," and "adaptable." Men, however, have not met them halfway, and are hardly more likely to define themselves as "tender" or "gentle" than they were in 1974. In fact, by some measures men have been retreating into an ever-narrower space, backing away from what were traditionally feminine traits as women take over more masculine ones.

For a long time, evolutionary psychologists have attributed this rigidity to our being ruled by adaptive imperatives from a distant past: Men are faster and stronger and hardwired to fight for scarce resources, a trait that shows up in contemporary life as a drive to either murder or win on Wall Street. Women are more nurturing and compliant, suiting them perfectly to raise children and create harmony among neighbors. This kind of thinking frames our sense of the natural order.

But for women, it seems as if those fixed roles are more fungible than we ever imagined. A more female-dominated society does not necessarily translate into a soft feminine utopia. Women are becoming more aggressive and even violent in ways we once thought were exclusively reserved for men. This drive shows up in a new breed of female murderers, and also in a rising class of young female "killers" on Wall Street. Whether the shift can be attributed to women now being socialized differently, or whether it's simply an artifact of our having misunderstood how women are "hardwired" in the first place, is at this point unanswerable, and makes no difference. Difficult as it is to conceive, the very rigid story we believed about ourselves is obviously no longer true. There is no "natural" order, only the way things are.

LATELY WE ARE STARTING to see how quickly an order we once considered "natural" can be overturned. For nearly as long as civilization has existed, patriarchy—enforced through the rights of the firstborn son—has been the organizing principle, with few exceptions. Men in ancient Greece tied off their left testicle in an effort to produce male heirs; women have killed themselves (or been killed) for failing to bear sons. In her iconic 1949 book *The Second Sex*, the French feminist Simone de Beauvoir suggested that women so detested their own "feminine condition" that they regarded their new-born daughters with irritation and disgust. Now the centuries-old preference for sons is eroding—or even reversing. "Women of our generation want daughters precisely because we like who we are," breezes one woman in *Cookie* magazine.

In the 1970s, the biologist Ronald Ericsson came up with a way to separate sperm carrying the male-producing Y chromosome from those carrying the X. He sent the two kinds of sperm swimming down a glass tube through ever-thicker albumin barriers. The sperm with the X chromosome had a larger head and a longer tail, and so, he figured, they would get bogged down in the viscous liquid. The sperm with the Y chromosome were leaner and faster and could swim down to the bottom of the tube more efficiently. The process, Ericsson said, was like "cutting out cattle at the gate." The cattle left flailing behind the gate were of course the X's, which seemed to please him.

Ericsson had grown up on a ranch in South Dakota, where he'd developed his cowboy swagger and mode of talking. Instead of a lab coat, he wore cowboy boots and a cowboy hat, and doled out his version of cowboy poetry. The right prescription for life, he would say, was "breakfast at five thirty, on the saddle by six, no room for Mr. Limp Wrist." In 1979, he loaned out his ranch as the backdrop for the iconic Marlboro Country cigarette ads because he believed in the campaign's central image—"a guy riding on his horse along the river, no bureaucrats, no lawyers," he recalled when I spoke to him. "He's the boss." He would sometimes demonstrate the sperm-selection process using cartilage from a bull's penis as a pointer. In the late 1970s, he leased the method to clinics around the United States, calling it the first scientifically proven method for choosing the sex of a child.

Feminists of the era did not take kindly to the lab cowboy and his sperminator. "You have to be concerned about the future of all women," said Roberta Steinbacher, a nun turned social psychologist, in a 1984 *People* profile of Ericsson. Given the "universal preference for sons," she foresaw a dystopia of mass-produced boys that would lock women in to second-class status while men continued to dominate positions of control and influence. "I think women have to ask themselves, 'Where does this stop?'" she said. "A lot of us wouldn't be here right now if these practices had been in effect years ago."

Ericsson laughed when I read him these quotes from his old antagonist. Seldom has it been so easy to prove a dire prediction wrong. In the 1990s, when Ericsson looked into the numbers for the two dozen or so clinics that use his process, he discovered, to his surprise, that couples were requesting more girls than boys. The gap has persisted, even though Ericsson advertises the method as more effective for producing boys. In some clinics, he has said, the ratio of preference is now as high as two to one. Polling data on Americans' sex preference in offspring is sparse, and does not show a clear preference for girls. But the picture from the doctor's office unambiguously does. A newer method for sperm selection, called MicroSort, is currently awaiting clinical approval from the Food and Drug Administration. The girl requests for that method run at about 75 percent. The women who call Ericsson's clinic these days come right out and say, "I want a girl"; they no longer beat around the bush. "These mothers look at their lives and think their daughters will have a bright future their mother and grandmother didn't have, brighter than their sons, even," says Ericsson, "so why wouldn't you choose a girl?" He sighs and marks the passing of an era. "Did male dominance exist? Of course it existed. But it seems to be gone now. And the era of the firstborn son is totally gone."

Ericsson's extended family is as good an illustration of the rapidly shifting landscape as any other. His twenty-seven-year-old granddaughter—"tall, slender, brighter than hell, with a take-no-prisoners personality"—is a biochemist and works on genetic sequencing. His niece studied civil engineering at the University of Southern California. His grandsons, he says, are bright and handsome, but in school "their eyes glaze over. I have to tell 'em: 'Just don't screw up and crash your pickup truck and get some girl pregnant and ruin your life.'" Recently Ericsson joked with the old boys at his elementary school reunion that he was going to have a sex-change operation. "Women live longer than men. They do better in this economy. More of 'em graduate from college. They go into space and do everything men do, and sometimes they do it a whole lot better. I mean, hell, get out of the way—these females are going to leave us males in the dust."

The shift is apparent not only in the United States, but in many of the world's most advanced economies. For several centuries South Korea constructed one of the most rigid patriarchies on the planet. Many wives who failed to produce male heirs were abused and treated as domestic servants; some families prayed to spirits to kill off girl children. Now that preference for firstborn sons—or any sons—has vanished. Over the last few years the government has conducted a national survey of future parents, asking, "If you found out you were pregnant, what sex would you want your child to be?" In 2010, 29.1 percent of women said they preferred a boy as their firstborn child, and 36.3 percent said a girl (the rest answered "no preference"). For men, the gap was even higher, with only 23 percent choosing a boy and 42.6 percent a girl. It took an imaginary third child, after two hypothetical daughters, for people to say they'd prefer a boy, and then by only a tiny margin.

From a feminist standpoint, the recent social, political, and economic gains of women are always cast as a slow, arduous form of catch-up in the continuing struggle for gender equality. But a much more radical shift seems to have come about. Women are not just catching up anymore; they are becoming the standard by which success is measured. "Why can't you be more like your sister?" is a phrase that resonates with many parents of school-age sons and daughters, even if they don't always say it out loud. As parents imagine the pride of watching a child grow and develop and succeed as an adult, it is more often a girl than a boy that they see in their mind's eye.

Yes, the United States and many other countries still have a gender wage gap. Yes, women still do most of the child care. And yes, the upper reaches of power are still dominated by men. But given the sheer velocity of the economic and other forces at work, these circumstances are much more likely the last artifacts of a vanishing age rather than a permanent configuration. Dozens of undergraduate women I interviewed for this book assumed that they very well might be the ones working while their husbands stayed at home, either minding the children or simply looking for work. Guys, one college senior remarked to me, "are the new ball and chain." It may be happening slowly and unevenly, but it's unmistakably happening: The modern economy is becoming a place where women hold the cards.

In the year since I wrote the story in *The Atlantic* magazine that inspired this book, I have been called a radical feminist for trumpeting women over men and an antifeminist for suggesting that the struggles are over for women. I am neither of those things, but my findings do herald both straightforward progress for women on some fronts and tremendous headaches on others. Women like Bethenny—my friend from the town of vanishing men—have a kind of ambiguous independence right now. They are much less likely to be in abusive relationships, much more likely to make all the decisions about their lives, but they are also much more likely to be raising children alone. It's a heavy load. One reporting experience that lingers with me is waking up a woman in the elevator at a community college in Kansas City. Between floors one and four she had fallen asleep, so hard had she been working to get her degree, hold down a night job, and raise three kids.

Among the college-educated class, ambivalence comes in the form of excess choice. Educated women take their time finding the perfect partner, seeking out creative, rewarding jobs, and then come home and parent their children with homeschooling intensity. Their lives are rich with possibilities their mothers never dreamed of. And yet in most surveys women these days are not more likely to rate themselves happier than women did in the 1970s. Choice creates its own set of anxieties—new spheres to compete in and judge yourself wanting, a constant fear that you might be missing out.

Men today, especially young men, are in a transition moment. They no longer want to live as their fathers did, marrying women they can't talk to, working long hours day after day, coming home to pat their kids on the head absentmindedly. They understand that the paternal white boss, like the one on *The Office*, has now become a punch line. But they can't turn away from all that because they fear how power and influence could be funneled away from them: by wives who earn more money than they do, jobs with less prestige, tedious Tuesday afternoons at the playground. There are plenty of opportunities for men. Theoretically, they can be anything these days: secretary, seamstress, PTA president. But moving into new roles, and a new phase, requires certain traits: flexibility, hustle, and an expansive sense of identity.

I started this book thinking that we were heading into a woman's world, and that this world would reflect some set of "womanly values" as defined by the Bem test—"tender," "yielding," "compassionate." But by the end of my research I became less convinced that what has happened to women and men reveals or is the result of any such fixed values or traits. Assuming a world run by women is more "tender" seems to me, again, just a story we tell ourselves to make the current massive upheavals in gender roles seem tamer and more predictable, when they are anything but: more like revolutionary, potentially exhilarating, and sometimes frightening, but altogether inevitable. So the least we can do is to see them clearly.

HEARTS
OF STEEL

SINGLE GIRLS MASTER
THE HOOK-UP

O n a mild fall afternoon in 2011, I sat in a courtyard with some students at Yale to ask about their romantic lives. I had read many accounts of how hook-up culture in college unravels women, and Yale seemed like a good place to explore. A few months earlier, a group of mostly feminist-minded students had filed a Title IX complaint against the university for tolerating a "hostile sexual environment on campus." The students specifically cited an incident in 2010 when members of the fraternity Delta Kappa Epsilon stood outside freshman dorms chanting, "No means yes! Yes means anal!" The week before I arrived, a letter ran in the paper complaining that the heart of the problem was "Yale's sexual culture" itself, that the "hook-up culture is fertile ground for acts of sexual selfishness, insensitivity, cruelty, and malice."

Tali, a junior and a sorority girl with a beautiful tan, long dark hair, and a great figure, told me that freshman year she, like many of her peers, was high on her first taste of the hook-up culture and didn't want a boyfriend. "It was empowering, to have that kind of control," she recalls. "Guys were texting and calling me all the time, and I was turning them down. I really enjoyed it!" But sometime during sophomore year, she got tired of relationships just fading away, "no end, no beginning." Guys would text her at eleven P.M., "wanna hang out?" but never during the day. Like many of the college women I talked to, Tali and her friends seemed much more sexually experienced and knowing than my friends at college. They were as blasé about blow jobs and anal sex as the one girl I remember from my freshman dorm whom we all judged as destined for tragic early marriage or a string of abortions. But they were also more innocent. When I asked Tali what she really wanted, she said, "Some guy to ask me out on a date to the frozen yogurt place."

Given the soda-fountain nostalgia of such an answer, a follow-up occurred to me: Did they want the hook-up culture to change? Might they prefer the mores of an earlier age, with formal dating and slightly more obvious rules? This question, each time, prompted a look of horror. Reform it, maybe, teach women to "advocate for themselves"—a phrase I heard many times—but end it? Never. Even one of the women who had initiated the Title IX complaint, Alexandra Brodsky, felt this way. "I would never come down on the hook-up culture," she said. "Plenty of women enjoy having casual sex." Or as Claire Gordon, a Yale graduate and lawsuit supporter, put it when I asked if she'd like to turn back the clock on the hook-up culture, "Compared to an egalitarian sexual wonderland, the situation is not good. But compared to when girls are punished for any sexual experience before marriage, it's much better." Gordon was already out of college and working so could see her way to the future: "Women just need a little time, to figure out what they want and how to ask for it."

The young women seemed instinctively to understand a remarkable fact about the age they were living (and sometimes suffering) in: Despite the particular heartaches of the college dating scene, despite the hand-wringing about our oversexualized culture and our saturation in porn, despite the warnings conveyed by reality shows such as *Teen Mom* and *16 and Pregnant*, the underlying dynamics between men and women these days point to a different story. Young women are more in control of their sexual destinies now than probably ever before. The sexual revolution of the 1960s and 1970s transformed women's behavior, but in some ways the changes of the last thirty or so years have been just as profound.

The era has little in common with the free love, naked in Central Park kind of sexual abandon. Instead, what makes it stand out is the new power women have to ward off men if they want to. By certain measures young people's behavior can even look like a return to a more innocent age. Teenagers today are far less likely than their parents were to have sex or get pregnant. In 1988, half of boys aged fifteen to seventeen reported having sex; by 2010 that number fell to just under a third. For teenage girls, the numbers dropped from 37.2 to 27 percent, according to the latest data from the US Centers for Disease Control and Prevention. Teen pregnancy rates dropped 44 percent after peaking in 1991, and reached a record low in 2010.

One of the great crime stories of the last twenty years, meanwhile, is the dramatic decline of rape and sexual assault. Between 1993 and 2008, the rate of those crimes against females declined by 70 percent. "Women in much of America might as well be living in Sweden, they're so safe," says criminologist Mike Males, a researcher at the Center on Juvenile and Criminal Justice. The most dramatic declines occurred in acquaintance rape. Those changes particularly are directly related to women's recent economic success. When women were financially dependent on men, it was much harder for them to leave an abusive relationship or situation. But now women who in earlier eras might have stayed in such relationships can leave or, more often, kick men out of the house. Women, says Males, "have achieved a great deal more power. And that makes them a lot harder to victimize."

At a time when people stay single longer, independent, college-educated women such as Tali run through a long sexual arc. The early years can be a struggle—more so than they were when chivalry prevailed. With marriage on the far-distant horizon, both men and women are less likely to commit and therefore less likely to behave (or even pretend) like they might want to. At some point in my interviews with college students, I always asked the women, "If a man sleeps with you and then doesn't acknowledge you the next day in class, is he a jerk?" (That was the understanding when I was in college.) But most of the women I spoke with just laughed, or gave me a puzzled look, as in, *Don't lots of guys do that?*

Books about the hook-up culture tend to emphasize the frustration that results from such a dynamic: "A lot of them just want to hook up with you and then never talk to you again . . . and they don't care!" one woman complains to Kathleen Bogle in *Hooking Up: Sex, Dating, and Relationships on Campus.* "That might not stop you from [hooking up] because you think 'This time it might be different.'" From her interviews with seventy-six college students, Bogle also deduces that the double standard is alive and well. Men tally fuck points on the bulletin board of their frat houses. Women who sleep with too many men are called "houserats" or "lacrosstitutes" (a term derived from women who sleep with several guys on the lacrosse team) or are deemed "HFH," meaning "hot for a hook-up" but definitely not for anything more. Hook-up culture, writes Bogle, is a "battle of the sexes" in which women want relationships and men want "no strings attached."

But it turns out that this is one of those cases where spotlight interviews can be misleading. An individual nineteen-year-old woman may give you an earful of girl trouble. But as her girlfriend might tell her after a teary night, you have to get some perspective. Zoom out and you see that for most women the hook-up culture is like an island they visit mostly during their college years, and even then only when they are bored or experimenting or don't know any better. But it is not a place where they drown. The sexual culture may be more coarse these days, but young women are more than adequately equipped to handle it, because unlike in earlier ages they have more important things going on, such as good grades and internships and job interviews and a financial future of their own to worry about. The most patient and thorough research about the hook-up culture shows that over the long run, women benefit greatly from living in a world where they can have sexual adventure without commitment or all that much shame, and where they can enter into temporary relationships that don't derail their careers.

To put it crudely, now feminist progress is largely dependent on hook-up culture. To a surprising degree, it is women—not men— who are perpetuating the culture, especially in school, cannily manipulating it to make space for their success, always keeping their own ends in mind. Today's college girl likens a serious suitor to an accidental pregnancy in the nineteenth century: a danger to be avoided at all costs, lest it thwart a promising future.

IN 2004, Elizabeth Armstrong, then at the University of Indiana, and Laura Hamilton, a young graduate student, set out to do a study on sexual abuse in college students' relationships. They applied for permission to interview women on a single floor of what was known as a "party dorm" at a state university in the Midwest. About two-thirds of the students came from what they called "more privileged" backgrounds, meaning they had financial support from their parents, who were probably college educated themselves. A third came from less privileged families; they supported themselves and were probably the first in their family to go to college. The researchers' first day of interviewing proved so enlightening that they decided to ask the administration if they could camp out at the dorm for four years and track the fifty-three women's romantic lives.

Girls in the dorm complained about the double standard, about being called sluts, about not being treated with respect. But what emerges over the four years is the sense of hooking up as part of a larger romantic strategy, a phase of what Armstrong came to think of as a "sexual career." Hook-ups functioned as a "delay tactic," Armstrong writes, because the immediate priority, for the privileged women at least, was setting themselves up for a career. "If I want to maintain the lifestyle that I've grown up with," one woman told Armstrong, "I have to work. I just don't see myself being someone who marries young and lives off of some boy's money." Or from another woman: "I want to get secure in a city and in a job. . . . I'm not in any hurry at all. As long as I'm married by thirty, I'm good."

The women still had to deal with the old-fashioned burden of protecting their personal reputations, but in the long view, what they really wanted to protect was their future professional reputations. "Rather than struggling to get into relationships," Armstrong found, women "had to work to avoid them," she reports. They often lied to interested guys, telling them they were "too conservative" to date or had a boyfriend back home, when the truth was that they did not want relationships to steal time away from studying.

Armstrong and her researchers had come looking for sexual victims and instead found the opposite: women who were managing their romantic lives like savvy headhunters. "The ambitious women calculate that having a relationship would be like a four-credit class, and they don't always have time for it so instead they opt for a lighter hook-up," Armstrong told me.

The women described relationships as "too greedy" or "too involved." One woman "with no shortage of admirers" explained, "I know this sounds really pathetic and you probably think I am lying, but there are so many other things going on right now that it's really not something high up on my list." The women wanted to study or hang out with friends or just be "a hundred percent selfish," as one said. "I have the rest of my life to devote to a husband or kids or my job." Some even purposely had "fake boyfriends" whom they considered sub-marriage quality: "He fits my needs now because I don't want to get married now. I don't want anyone else to influence what I do after I graduate," one said. Or: He "wants to have two kids by the time he's thirty. I'm like, I guess we're not getting married."

The most revealing portions of the study emerge from the interviews with the less privileged women. They came to college mostly with boyfriends back home and the expectation of living a life similar to their parents', piloting toward an early marriage. They were still fairly conservative and found hook-up culture initially alienating ("Those rich bitches are way slutty" is how Armstrong summarizes their attitude). They felt trapped between the choice of marrying a kind of hometown guy they called "the disaster"—a man who never gets off the couch and steals their credit card—or joining a sexual culture that made them uncomfortable. The ones who chose option A were considered the dorm tragedies, women who had succumbed to some Victorian-style delusion. "She would always talk about how she couldn't wait to get married and have babies," one woman said about her working-class friend. "It was just like, Whoa. I'm eighteen. . . . Slow down, you know? Then she just crazy dropped out of school and wouldn't contact any of us. . . . The way I see it is that she's from a really small town, and that's what everyone in her town does . . . get married and have babies."

Success meant seeing the hook-up culture for what it is: a path out of a dead-end existence, free from a life yoked to the "disaster." "Now I'm like, I don't even need to be getting married yet [or] have kids," one of the less privileged women told the researchers in her senior year. "All of [my brother's] friends, seventeen- to twenty-year-old girls, have their . . . babies, and I'm like, Oh my God. . . . Now I'll be able to do something else for a couple years before I settle down . . . before I worry about kids." The hook-up culture opened her horizons. She could study and work and date and live off temporary intimacy for a few years before getting married.

The broad, shallow research also confirms the idea that heartaches have been vastly exaggerated. Over the last decade, sociologist Paula England at New York University has been collecting data from an online survey about hook-ups. She is now up to about twenty thousand responses—making hers the largest sample to date. In her survey, seniors report an average of 7.9 hook-ups over 4 years but a median of only 5. This confirms what other surveys have found: Some people at either end of the scale are skewing the numbers. Researchers guess that about a quarter of college kids skip out of the hook-up culture altogether while a quarter participate with gusto—about ten hook-ups or more (the lacrosstitutes?). For the majority in the middle, hook-up culture is a place to visit freshman year, or whenever you feel like it, or when you've broken up with a boyfriend, says England. Most important, hook-ups haven't wrecked the capacity for intimacy. In England's survey, 74 percent of women and about an equal number of men report having had a relationship that lasted at least six months in college (which means Tali is very unlucky, or due to get lucky her senior year).

When they do hook up, the weepy woman stereotype doesn't exactly hold. Men are more likely to have an orgasm during a hook-up, maybe because men in college are not all that experienced yet and don't know how to please their partners, or because women don't always insist on having their sexual needs attended to. Still, equal numbers of men and women—about half—report to England that they enjoyed their last hook-up "very much," implying that women are getting something out of their encounters—maybe pleasure (even without an orgasm), experience, the thrill of turning someone else on, or just a good story. About 66 percent of women say they wanted their last hook-up to turn into something more, and 58 percent of men say the same—not a vast difference considering the cultural panic about the demise of a chivalrous age and its consequences for women.

Almost all of the women Armstrong and Hamilton interviewed in the dorm assumed they would get married, and looked forward to it. In England's survey, around 90 percent of the college kids, male and female, said they wanted to get married. The men picked an ideal marrying age that was two years older than the women, which is how marriages typically work out anyway. The whole picture suggests that for most of the young women, they could have their dalliance with the hook-up culture and life would eventually smile on them. They would have a few years of working and playing, and by thirty they would probably get married and eventually make their way to the happy ending.

Of course, most of them still had a decade left in their "sexual career," a decade in which the conflicting strains in the new sexual culture would get even more intense, when the women would gain even more sexual confidence and financial stability, but would feel a new kind of vulnerability as they approached marrying age.

THE PORN PIC being passed around on the students' cell phones at this Ivy League business school party was more prank than smut: a woman in a wool hat with a pom-pom giving a snowman with a snow penis a blow job. Snowblowing, it's called, or snowman fellatio, terms everyone at this midweek happy hour seemed to know (except me). The men at the party flashed the snapshot at the women and the women barely bothered to roll their eyes, much less use words like "hostile sexual environment" or "Title IX." These were not Yale women's studies types for sure; they were already several years out of college and hook-up veterans.

One of the women had already seen the photo five times by the time her boyfriend showed it to her, so she just moved her pitcher of beer in front of his phone and kept on talking. He'd already suggested twice that night they go to a strip club, and when their mutual friend had asked if the two of them were getting married, he had given the friend the finger and made sure his girlfriend could see the finger, so she didn't get any ideas about any forthcoming ring. She was used to her boyfriend's "juvenile thing," she told me. She had three little brothers. It barely registered.

I first saw the image when I moved out to the balcony, opting for cold instead of loud music. My viewing was interrupted by an ex-military guy who yelled, "Party like a rock star!" and then bent over so two women in tube tops could pat his ass. For these official school-sponsored parties held on campus, corporate sponsors paid for the minimal food and limitless beer, which flowed from kegs directly into handheld pitchers. ("Head, brought to you by Credit Suisse," one bartender joked with every generous pour, high-fiving anyone who wasn't too drunk to catch his double meaning.) The parties were not an illicit distraction from studying; quite the opposite. The students were supposed to pick up the official message: For their future success, networking, aided by social lubricants, was just as important as studying—maybe more important.

At this party, the phrase "No means yes! Yes means anal!"—the phrase that prompted the lawsuit at Yale—also came up, only this time as a fond memory. Some students were recalling a game they had played when they went on a spring break trip together called "dirty rounds"—something like charades, except instead of acting out movie or book titles they acted out sex terms, like "pink sock" (what your anus looks like after too much anal sex) or "snowblowing."

The ambiance was frat party, only a frat party for students several years out of college, who had already tasted the work world and were happy to regress for a couple of hours. They had the confidence and the money of almost-adults, and they flaunted it. Guys in expensive fitted jackets flirted with women in four-inch heels and negged one another about job offers and sexual conquests. Sometimes the two were mixed up in the same sentence: "Goldman plus HSBC," one woman bragged. "Now will you do me those sexual favors?" In a corner, a beautiful Asian woman was entertaining the six guys around her with her best imitation of an Asian prostitute—"Oooo, you so big. Me love you long time"—winning the Tucker Max showdown before any of the guys had even tried to make a move on her.

(She eventually chose the shortest guy in the group to go home with because, she later told me, he seemed like he'd be the best in bed.)

I had gone to the Ivy League business school because a friend had described the women there as so sexually aggressive, they were scary. Many of them had been molded on trading floors or in investment banks with male-female ratios as terrifying as fifty to one, so they learned to keep up with the boys. (At this business school, the ratio was a piece-of-cake seven to three.) Women told me stories of being hit on at work by "FDBs" (finance douche bags) who hadn't even bothered to take off their wedding rings, sitting through Monday morning meetings that started with stories about who had banged whom (or what) that weekend. They'd been routinely hazed by male colleagues showing them ever more baroque porn downloaded on cell phones. Snowman fellatio was nothing to them. In general, their response was not to call in the lawyers, but to rise—or maybe stoop—to the occasion.

In college, the average freshman might have been shell-shocked by the speed and crudeness of come-ons, but here I barely found anyone who even *noticed* the vulgarity anymore until I came across a new student. She had just arrived two weeks earlier from Argentina, and found herself stunned by the party scene around her. "Here in America, the girls, they give up their mouth, their ass, their tits," she said, punctuating each with the appropriate hand motion, "before they even know the guy. It's like, 'Hello.' 'Hello.' 'You wanna hook up?' 'Sure.' They are so aggressive! Do they have hearts of steel or something? In my country, a girl like this would be desperate. Or a prostitute."

But maybe these women consider a heart of steel a fair price to pay for their new high ranking in this social hierarchy. In eras past, the pretty women in such a corporate setting would have been imports brought in to liven up the party, secretaries maybe, or paid escorts, in the early Playboy Club days. But here the women floating around in their feather earrings, thigh-high boots, and knowing smiles were social equals, at least. These twenty-eight-year-old women halfway to an elite MBA, with five years of finance experience behind them and enough money to shop at Barneys, were using their sex appeal not just to catch the man or dazzle him with some girls-gone-wild striptease, but to challenge him in his most important domain, the workplace.

When I watched the business school women flirt at the bar, it seemed to me they were testing themselves. If they could ignore the porn jokes, they could hold their own on the trading floor. If they could make the first move, then they could also beat the guys at a negotiation. This was their way of psyching the men out, by refusing to back down in any game where, in another era, they would have been assumed to be the weaker opponent.

It's even possible that women their age are using their sex appeal not just to keep up with the men, but to surpass them. If in college sex appeal is something you have to rein in to focus on your career, after college it might actually be a career-booster. For the last few years, economists have tried to measure the tangible marketplace value of various amorphous traits—social skills, for example, or cultural capital, or "soft power"—all of which refer to something other than concrete assets or skills. Recently, British economist Catherine Hakim has identified a new potential asset she called "erotic capital." The term refers not to beauty or sexiness, exactly, but more to charm and charisma. People who have it (Michelle Obama, Ségolène Royal) reap financial gains, because they can attract other people to them and be seen as potential leaders. "Properly understood, erotic capital is what economists call a 'personal asset,' ready to take its place alongside economic, cultural, human, and social capital. It is just (if not more) as important for social mobility and success," Hakim writes.

In Hakim's view, erotic capital has always been an obvious asset, but not considered to have any measurable value in the workplace. Men in charge trivialized it because it was something women had mastered. And feminists disdained the idea of claiming it as a real source of empowerment. But now those dynamics are changing, Hakim writes. Instead of being done in by a highly sexualized culture, women are learning to manipulate it to their advantage. In an economy that values social skills and a more charismatic style of leadership, attractiveness gives you a genuine edge. Economists have even begun to measure the "beauty premium," or the idea that magnetism has a direct connection to earning power. In the United States, for example, a large national study showed that people labeled "attractive" earned 12 to 17 percent more than those labeled "plain." The bump applies to both men and women, but women have been playing on this turf a lot longer.

Men, by necessity, have been playing catch-up. The recent rise in plastic surgeries is fueled by men—especially middle-aged men— who have been lining up for face-lifts, Botox, and liposuction. In 1986, *People* magazine's Sexiest Man Alive was the actor Mark Harmon, who had so much back hair it was visible from the front. Now the new standards for male waxing and trimming are as stringent as they are for women. The new men's magazines crib directly from *Cosmopolitan*: WHAT SEXY WOMEN LOVE! and SIX-PACK ABS calls the cover of *Men's Health* in headlines recycled every few months. Designers are starting to peddle "mancessories," feather bracelets and metal cuffs and even makeup for men.

Of course, these shifts in the power dynamic do not mean that men and women just cleanly switch roles on the dating scene. In the very first episode of *Sex and the City*, aired in 1998, Carrie Bradshaw asks in her column if a woman can get laid like a man. The answer, delivered barely ten minutes into the episode, is not exactly, and that is still largely true. With sex, as with most areas of life, women tend to preserve a core of their old selves—romantic, tender, vulnerable— even while taking on new sexual personas. The women at business school no longer *needed* a man to support them, but that didn't mean they didn't *want* one. And years of practice putting up their guard made it hard for them to know when to let it down. As Meghan Daum writes in *My Misspent Youth*, her memoir of single woman-hood, the "worst sin imaginable was not cruelty or bitchiness or even professional failure but vulnerability."

I arrived at the business school during recruiting week, and I could see the strain it was causing the women who were already in relationships. One woman was dating a man who'd just gotten a job offer in London. She was willing to go to London, but he hadn't asked her yet, and she wasn't going to bring it up for fear of seeming too needy. In the meantime, she was putting off her own job offer to see how it all sorted out. This same situation was playing out between other couples, with Tokyo and San Francisco as potential backdrops. For these tough, ambitious women, the challenge was how to hang on to their hearts of steel for long enough that they seemed invulnerable, but not for so long that they missed their chance at happiness.

I FIRST HEARD about Sabrina from her ex-boyfriend of nine months, a fellow business school student I met on the balcony at the party. I trusted him immediately because he did not resort to the kind of jerkoff party swagger I'd heard from some of his classmates: "I just don't want to be tied down right now" or "Fuck marriage." He was at least willing to entertain the theater of romance. "I've already found my dream girl," he told me. "Six different times." He was in love with Sabrina from the first night they hung out after a business school happy hour, he told me, although they didn't sleep together, not for another two weeks. Once they did, he told me, it was a whole new experience for him. In bed she was her sublime, adventurous self: confident, aggressive, and totally comfortable asking for what she wanted; nimble and responsive and full of surprises, suggesting things he wouldn't have thought to ask. She seemed to want it more than he did. "I was always the one to be in control in that scenario, so I wasn't used to it," he said. He kept describing her as "unique" and "one of a kind," although they had broken up several months earlier. "You'll see when you meet her," he said, and so I sought her out.

I tracked her down several days later in a classic single-girl-in-a-sitcom pose. Sabrina, who is thirty-one, was hanging out with a girlfriend, drinking wine and not eating the crackers and cheese on the table. In a few hours she was going to meet a guy she had just texted with, a trader they refer to as "the hot guy" she'd met at work that summer and slept with a couple of times. (After the second time, she'd texted him, "I'm just not feeling it" and—miracle—"he was cool with it. He didn't take it personally." So they still hang out occasionally as friends, even though they don't have sex anymore.)

But for the moment, the two women were talking about things they like: red wine, Lady Gaga concerts, Angela Merkel, and their favorite advice book of the moment, *Nice Girls Don't Get the Corner Office*, which advises women how to stop sabotaging their careers by being excessively deferential. Things they don't like: short men; FDBs; men who, when you reject them, send texts saying "shouldn't you be thinking about your eggs?" Also, their friend Anna, "who sits on the couch all day obsessing about finding *The One*"—that last phrase drips with sarcasm.

Sabrina had met her share of Annas in business school, the girls who microanalyze every text and phone call, who wait, wait for the phone to ding or beep or pirouette out of their hands or whatever it does when they get a text from a boy. And who, when it doesn't, when it just sits in their lap obstinately like a permanent stain, moan, "Why isn't he texting me? What's going on?" (this she says in a mock idiot-girl-who-reads-*Cosmo* voice). "Well, because we all need affection sometimes, and he just happened to get it from you that night," she barked at the imaginary Annas. "Retard."

Did she ever wait by the phone? "Never. *Never.*" At least not since college, when she was not as good at reading the signals. "I started to think about it," she said, lounging back on her friend's couch, putting her socked feet up on the coffee table. "What do I need a man for? I don't need him financially. I don't need him to do activities. I have lots of friends here. So fuck it."

One problem I had with our conversation was the cognitive dissonance produced by the difference between the voice and the person: The distinctive thing about Sabrina is her effortless, natural beauty. It's hard to describe her physically without resorting to Nancy Drew–era clichés such as "youthful" and "fresh." She is half Asian, with creamy skin and long black hair and clear green eyes. On the day I met her she was wearing an outfit that Katniss, the heroine from *The Hunger Games*, might wear to go hunting: jeans and what looked like a boy's flannel checked button-down shirt, with no makeup. (She made no wardrobe adjustments at all when it was time to meet "the hot guy" at the bar.) "In both cases I think I'm a hunter, a killer," she said, musing on how her dating style echoed her favorite negotiating tactics.

But my larger problem was my inability to judge how much of what she said was bluster and how much was real. And even if it was all real, whether Sabrina was an unusual case, or whether there was a little bit of Sabrina in every woman of this generation. I couldn't say. But what I wanted to know was whether her years in the hook-up culture and on Wall Street had landed her in an extreme and untenable place.

We've been taught that acting like a girl—even when we're grown up—isn't such a bad thing. Girls get taken care of in ways boys don't. Girls aren't expected to fend for or take care of themselves—others do that for them. Sugar and spice and everything nice—that's what little girls are made of. Who doesn't want to be everything nice?

This is the diagnosis Lois Frankel makes in *Nice Girls Don't Get the Corner Office*, one of Sabrina's favorite books. The cautionary examples in Frankel's book—the Susans and Rebeccas and Jills—are polite and accommodating. They work hard and they don't play the office politics game. Mostly they wait around at work to be *given* what they want, just as Anna waits around for her phone to ring. *Nice Girls* is a business advice book, but Sabrina uses it as a dating guide, too, a primer on how to play in the big-city dating scene and never lose.

Sabrina was twenty-three and just finishing college when she met a guy who looked like Justin Timberlake and "I totally lost my head. I was obsessed." After less than a year they got engaged, and then he cheated on her. She was "miserable. Totally out of control, and I hated feeling totally out of control." She vowed that she would never be "that sad miserable crawling thing again." How did she do it? She put some distance between herself and sex. Sex was something apart from her, something "I could step back from and put in a box so I would never be overwhelmed again. It's like, 'I can't be obsessing, I have shit to get done.'"

From then on, Sabrina has scrutinized herself for any vulnerability and rooted it out. "We have sex, there's that oxytocin floating around, we get attached, blah blah blah." Or maybe it's the way she was raised, by a Japanese mother who convinced her that she was supposed to make herself "easy to be around" and not talk too much around men. "There is always this little voice in your head saying, 'This is not ladylike. This is not normal. Nice girls don't do that. Nice girls don't ask for raises.' But then it's like BAM! Smash it! 'Nice girls don't ask guys out on dates.' BAM. Clear that! And then it's gone."

After her disastrous college engagement to the Timberlake look-alike, Sabrina took a safer route. She picked someone with whom she had less sexual chemistry but who was her friend, and within a year they got engaged. One day, at twenty-eight, she found herself sitting next to her fiancé, on a plane that was experiencing massive turbulence. As the plane shook she thought to herself, "I am not living the life I want to live. I am not dating the guy I want to date. I am engaged to a guy I don't want to be engaged to." She had by that time been working at banks for several years and had traveled all over the world and experienced turbulence dozens of times. But this time the plane was shaking so hard, she had imminent death on her mind. And she wasn't thinking about the nice life she and her fiancé could have enjoyed together. She was thinking about herself in a house in Darien, Connecticut, cooking in the kitchen with kids at her feet, and feeling like a plane crash might be preferable. The plane landed safely, and shortly thereafter Sabrina broke off an engagement for the second time in her life. In the marriage market, twice fleeing the altar makes you the equivalent of the person who's had a near-death experience and seen the white light. In other words, it makes you free, to text cute guys at eleven P.M. yourself and tell them to fuck off if you want to and forget about *The One.*

Or does it? When I met her a few days later, Sabrina was in a different mood and thinking more about what she wanted from life. That business school boyfriend—the one I'd met at the party—had inspired a breakthrough for her. Before business school he'd lived in Thailand for almost a decade, and this part of his sexual history had become a source of anguish for her in the relationship. In Thailand, she figured, sex was so ubiquitous that "it becomes just like Burger King. 'I'll have a blow job with a side of sex, and an extra order of massage my balls.'" After they broke up, she had begun to wonder if his attitude about sex echoed her own at all, and whether she'd better start worrying about whether a certain kind of cheap sex wipes out the ability to be intimate.

Her second inspiration came from an older woman she knew from an investment bank where she used to work, a woman she considered her mentor. She and this woman sat together at the computer one afternoon between trades, shopping for bags, chatting about their families—their families of origin, as the woman, though in her forties, had yet to marry. This was a woman Sabrina idolized, an incredibly successful trader who oozed erotic capital. "She is elegant, charming, and had a smooth, rich voice," Sabrina says. Another young trader came over and asked about a certain bond, a bond they had already discussed. "Her eyes just hardened," Sabrina recalls. "It was almost like they turned a different color. Her voice turned sharp and almost ugly. 'Do not come over here wasting my time,' she said to the guy. 'We have already been over this.' And then she turned to me, got all soft again, and kept chatting!"

Lately Sabrina had been thinking about that insta–personality switch, about the dangers of being so plastic and malleable that you never settle into something solid and knowable. If you can move in the span of a head turn from bitchy to seductive, if you can turn your erotic capital on and off like an actress on a stage, "then maybe you don't know how to stop acting. And that can't be good for a relationship." That's when she decided that she did not want to be her idol exactly, if being her meant being forty and alone.

THEORETICALLY, a twenty-seven- or twenty-eight-year-old woman with no children is at the top of the game. She is, on average, more educated than the men around her, and making more money. She is less restricted by sexual taboos than at any other time in history. None of her peers judge her for not being a mother; in fact, they might pity her if she were. In 2011, psychologist Roy Baumeister measured whether more gender equality matched up with less restrictive sexual norms. In a study of thirty-seven nations, the hypothesis proved true. More sex means a more feminist-minded country. As the authors of the 2010 *Sex at Dawn: The Prehistoric Origins of Modern Sexuality* put it, "Societies in which women have lots of autonomy and authority tend to be decidedly female-friendly, relaxed, tolerant, and plenty sexy." Empowerment! Sexiness! What could be better? Sounds like an Erica Jong fantasy come to life! Neo-Amazonia, played out on soft memory foam instead of the jungle floor!

And yet the single-girl memoirs of such high-achieving women are not exactly ringing with triumph. Eventually, they come to the same realization Sabrina did. "At twenty-seven and counting, we're not really old old, but damn it, tell that to our uteruses (uterun, uteri?)," writes Helena Andrews in *Bitch Is the New Black*. "Tell it to our mothers, who want grandchildren so badly they can catch a whiff of dirty diapers in the night air. . . . Tell it to our hearts that are so tired of being broken that they'd rather stay that way than be fixed for a better smashing later. I'm telling you, it's been rough—sorta."

Why is it so rough when it should be so good? The story is not the usual one, about women always at the mercy of men. These days the problem in the dating market is caused not by women's eternal frailty but by their new dominance. In a world where women are better educated than men and outearning them in their twenties, dating becomes complicated. Men are divided into what the college girls call the players (a smaller group) and the losers (a much larger group), and the women are left fighting for small spoils. The players are in high demand and hard to pin down. The losers are not all that enticing. Neither is in any hurry to settle down.

In the dating market, erotic capital works in a slightly different way. A woman's sexuality has social value, and she trades it for other things she wants. In the old days the exchange was fairly obvious. Women traded sex for security, money, maybe even social and political influence. Because they had no other easy access to these things, it was imperative they keep the price of sex high so they had something to bargain with. Now women no longer need men for financial security and social influence. They can achieve those things by themselves. So they have no urgent incentive to keep the price of sex high. The result is that sex, by the terms of sexual economics, is cheap, bargain-basement cheap, and a lot more people can have it.

When sex is cheap, something funky happens to the men. More of them turn into what sociologist Mark Regnerus calls "free agents." They sleep with as many women as possible, essentially because they can. They become allergic to monogamy. "What motivation exists for men to be anything besides the stereotypic 'take what you can get' kind of man?" asks Regnerus in *Premarital Sex in America.* "Not a lot." The new equation doesn't leave women vulnerable exactly, but it may leave them less than satisfied. "Erotic capital," Regnerus writes, "can be traded for attention, a job, perhaps a boyfriend, and all the sex she wants, but it can't assure her love and lifelong commitment. Not in this market." It's no accident that the girls-gone-wild culture rose up at the same time women started to dominate college campuses. Katie, one of the interviewees in Regnerus's book, summarizes her experience in the new marketplace thus: "I felt like I was dating his dick."

What exaggerates this dysfunction and gives it a grand scale is the chronic oversupply problem. In their 1983 book *Too Many Women? The Sex Ratio Question*, two psychologists developed what has become known as the Guttentag-Secord theory, which explains what happens when gender ratios are skewed. Societies where men outnumber women tend to be less egalitarian, but women are held in high esteem. The roles of mother and wife are highly respected, and rates of divorce and out-of-wedlock childbirth are low. In societies with more women, men have the candy-store attitude. They want the Twizzlers and the Jujubes. They become promiscuous and can't be relied on to settle down. The women, in turn, stop relying on them, and focus on making their own way. In our society overall we don't have more women than men, but in certain segments of society it plays out that way—the average state school, the rising middle class. In those places the women can be ready for marriage while the men are still playing video games. Thus the cycle continues, and *Cosmo* sells magazines in perpetuity.

The result is that the women suffer through a lot of frustrating little dating battles. But it's the men who are losing the war. On the cover of *Guyland*, Michael Kimmel's 2008 anthropology of the new young American man, the four guys seem to be caught in the midst of some delirious frat boy cheer. The four hundred boys/men he interviews, all between the ages of sixteen and twenty-six, tell Kimmel that they party hard and hook up with lots of women. The three pillars of their lives are "drinking, sex, and video games." They watch a lot of Spike TV and a lot of porn, on their laptops, their desktops, and their phones. They mostly hang out with one another. At frat parties they hook up with actual women, but for the most part, the women represent a threat to their way of existence. The recurring anthem he comes across is "Bros before hos." The difference between them and the women, though, is that they are more likely to get stuck in Guyland, fail to graduate, and then never move on. So entrenched is this universal frat boy culture that Stanford psychology professor Philip Zimbardo is coining a new disease to describe it: "social intensity syndrome." Many young men these days, Zimbardo argues, are so awash in video games and porn that they cannot cope with face-to-face contact. Their brains, he says, become "digitally rewired" and no longer suitable for stable romantic relationships, especially relationships with "equal status female mates."

THE SEXUAL REVOLUTION did radically transform women's attitudes and behaviors. The bedroom worked much like the workplace— women experimented, took on new roles, became more aggressive. They took advantage of whatever liberties society offered them. The problem is, it did very little to change men, who measure about the same in their sexual preferences and desires as they did in the early

1960s. This is the argument feminist Barbara Ehrenreich proposes in her 1986 book *Re-Making Love*. More recently, Baumeister put that theory to the test, but on a grander scale: Is female sexuality more transformable than male sexuality, or, in psychology speak, do women have more "erotic plasticity"? In a 2000 review of fifty years of literature, Baumeister concludes that they do. Male sexuality, he concludes, is "relatively constant and unchanging," which suggests it is ruled by factors that are "rigid" and more "innate." Female sexuality, by contrast, is "malleable and mutable: It is responsive to culture, learning, and social circumstances."

Individual women tend to become more sexually adventurous as they date more. They adapt their behavior quickly to match the expectations of family, peers, church groups, a move to a new country where sexual mores are different. Studies of older women show small cohorts that masturbate much more with age, whereas men's masturbation rates almost always stay constant over a lifetime. Women can go cold after a breakup and then become passionate when they meet someone new. Men's sexual desire is defined by what Alfred Kinsey called "no discontinuity in total outlet." Their appetite stays constant. If they do not have a girlfriend, they masturbate to make up the difference. Women fall in love with women, and then with men again. Studies of swinger culture in the 1970s, for example, showed that women entered the subculture with gusto, and were much more experimental in it than men.

The modern-day index to women's sexual plasticity is anal sex. More women have tried it, and tried it repeatedly, than ever before. In 1992, 16 percent of women aged eighteen to twenty-four said they had tried it, and now, at the upper end of that bracket, the number is 40 percent. Many people would assume that this increase reflects new lows in the chivalrous standards as men force their porn fantasies on real live mates. But as *Slate* writer William Saletan points out, the data doesn't support that view. Women who had anal sex were far more likely to report having had an orgasm during their sexual encounter—more even than those who received oral sex. There are lots of possible explanations—women who are willing to try anal sex trust their partners more; orgasms relax women, so they are willing to try anal sex; sexually adventurous women are willing to try anything. But whatever the explanation, the general conclusion is that advances in sexual openness are, in fact, advances.

Baumeister, who teaches at Florida State University, is prone to brilliant, sweeping theories on an unusually wide range of subjects. In this case he traces the implications of his findings across global cultures and back in time. In years past, and in many cultures still, women's sexual malleability has made them vulnerable to coercion and control, either by an individual man or a patriarchal culture; say, mullahs in Afghanistan. But it also makes women adaptable to changing circumstances, and able to take advantage when sexual mores change. When a space opens up for them to do something new—like a fifteen-year space when they are no longer required to get married or have children or otherwise live at the mercy of men but can live as they please—they will move into it.

Thus we have landed in an era that's produced a new breed of female sexual creature the world has never witnessed before, one who acknowledges the eternal vulnerability of women but, rather than cave in or trap herself in the bell jar, instead looks that vulnerability square in the face and then manipulates it in unexpected, creative, or crazy ways. It's no accident that the most popular fictional heroine of the last decade is Lisbeth Salander—The Girl with the Dragon Tattoo—a pale waif who was sexually abused as a child but, instead of cowering or attending support groups, spends her adulthood beating up scary men.

Sometimes the new kind of woman takes her revenge not with a knife but with excellent comic timing. In the fall of 2010, Duke senior Karen Owen became momentarily famous when her friends leaked her pornographic PowerPoint presentation, which described her sexual exploits with thirteen Duke athletes, whom she identified by name, skill, and penis size. ("While he had girth on his side, the subject was severely lacking in length.") In Owen's hands, scenes of potential humiliation got transformed into punch lines. ("Mmm tell me about how much you like big, black cocks," number six, a baseball player told her. "But, I've never even hooked up with a black man!" she told him. "Oh . . . well, just pretend like you have," he responded. "Umm ok . . . I like big, black . . . cocks?")

The 2012 successor to *Sex and the City* is *Girls*, a new HBO show created by indie actress/filmmaker Lena Dunham, who plays the main character, Hannah. When Hannah has sex, she is not wearing a Carrie Bradshaw–style $200 couture bra and rolling in silk sheets, but hiking her shirt up over belly flesh loose enough that her boyfriend, Adam, can grab it by fistfuls. In one scene they have failed anal sex. "That feels awful." In another, Adam spins a ridiculously degrading fantasy about Hannah being an eleven-year-old hooker with a "fucking Cabbage Patch lunchbox." Hannah plays along, reluctantly. But when she's done she doesn't feel deep remorse or have to detox with her girlfriends or call the police. She makes a joke about the eleven-year-old, which he doesn't get. Our enduring image of Hannah is of her rocking out with her roommate to Swedish pop star Robyn's "Dancing on My Own."

In Hannah's charmed but falling-apart life, her encounters with

Adam count as "experience," fodder for the memoir she half jokingly tells her parents will make her the "voice of this generation." She is our era's Portnoy, entitled and narcissistic enough to obsess about precisely how she gets off and how she will later write about it. (Adam plays the role of the Pumpkin or the Monkey from *Portnoy's Complaint*, so many props in Portnoy's long and comical sexual journey.)

The suspense in *Girls* is not driven by the usual rom-com mystery—Will Hannah get her man? She snags him pretty early on. Instead it's driven by the uncertain outcome of her career—Will she fulfill her potential and become a great writer? When in the season finale Adam asks to move in, she rejects him because she's afraid he might hinder her bigger plans.

There is no retreating from the hook-up culture to a more innocent age where young men showed up at your father's door with a box of chocolates. This is why the "war on women" that popped up in the 2012 primary season and centered on contraception played as absurd. The most appropriate responses to the bombast were those that asked some version of, "Are you serious?" A society that has become utterly dependent on the unfettered ambition of women cannot possibly, with a straight face, reopen the debate about contraception.

Even the women most frustrated by the hook-up culture don't really want that. The hook-up culture is too bound up with everything that's fabulous about being a young woman in 2012—the freedom, the independence, the knowledge that you can always depend on yourself. The only option is to do what Hannah's friends always tell her—stop doing what feels awful, and figure out what doesn't. And take some comfort in the notion that for most people who make it through the rocky years, it ends well. Young women may be less vulnerable than ever but that does not mean they experience that as empowerment. As the young woman from Yale told me, it will take time for them to figure out what they want and how to ask for it. A gay friend of mine once made this astute observation: The college hook-up culture right now is at the same phase as gay sex was in the 1970s. Young men and women have discovered a sexual freedom unbridled by the conventions of marriage, or any conventions. But that's not how the story ends. Ultimately the desire for a deeper human connection always wins out, for both men and women.

THE LAST TIME I saw Sabrina, she was just back from a Buddhist retreat in Vermont and still had a bit of what she called the "luminous glow." From this vantage point, she found it hard to relate to her old stressed-out trading floor self, "nasty and short and only wanting everyone around me to talk in bullet points." She was softer and more contemplative about love, too. "I don't need a man to survive and I don't need him to pay the bills, but people still need each other. That's just how we're built." She was starting to face up to what she calls her addiction—the particular disease that afflicts women in an era when love and sex are sped up and confusingly mixed together: "I guess what I want is the candy. I need the love to feel the passion, and I need the passion to feel sexually into it. My last boyfriend told me I'm the kind of person who creates the weather. I bring on the sun, and then one day, I let the rain clouds in. Fuck. I just get bored. I want the candy—the first few months of the relationship, the passion, the puppy love, getting to know someone. That's what makes the sex good! I know that's a game, that's not a real relationship. I don't even know the person! But fuck. I don't want to eat my veggies."

Sabrina had a few new boyfriends during the time I knew her, and always she was half in love. The last I heard, she was planning to move with one of them to California. "He's really amazing! Glad I held out for the right one," she wrote me. "So many people settle." A good friend of hers had recently gotten married, to Sabrina's surprise. She thought her friend had always been keeping the guy at a distance, never really letting him in. After the wedding, Sabrina asked her friend about that. "You get married," her friend told her, "and you stop keeping the guy at bay." For the moment this seemed like a reasonable goal to aim for.

A few months later she wrote me that she was "very well and happy—planning a wedding actually :) and the best part, it's mine!" Sabrina had met a guy from the Midwest who'd come to New York and been shocked that "smart, educated people were hooking up left and right with people they wouldn't share a cereal bowl with." In dating him she had realized that men and women want largely the same things, but men are afraid to admit it for fear of losing their "man-cred." "I think NYC is full of people who want sublime connection but can't find it so rationalize useless hookups to bide the time . . . I think the solution is really knowing oneself and being honest/genuine in one's value."

THE SEESAW
MARRIAGE

TRUE LOVE
(JUST FOR ELITES)

Perhaps the most famous TV sitcom scene ever comes from a 1952 episode of *I Love Lucy* called "Job Switching." The antics are set in motion by a tiff over money. "Do you realize how tough it is for a guy to make a buck these days?" asks Ricky. "Do you think that the money grows on trees?" And thus the game is on. Ricky and Fred will play the housewives for the day while Lucy and Ethel go out and look for a job. The resulting pandemonium illustrates the absurdity of such a reversal of roles. Ricky and Fred dress essentially in drag, with flowered aprons and do-rags on their heads. For dinner they produce two exploding chickens, a volcanic eruption of rice, and a seven-layer cake as flat as a pancake, leaving the kitchen a disaster. The ladies fare no better. They get jobs at a chocolate factory, which produces the famous scene: the chocolate bonbons racing down the conveyor belt as Lucy and Ethel, overwhelmed by the pace and terrified of the boss, stuff them in their mouths, chef hats, and shirts. The girls return home hoarse and exhausted and eager to restore the natural order of things. "We're not so good at bringing home the bacon," Lucy confesses, and Ricky suggests, "Let's go back to the way we were."

Barely two generations later, the housewife is a rare breed on American television, unless you count the *Real Housewives* of anywhere, who would not be caught dead in a flowered apron that wasn't part of a kinky maid's costume. During the intervening years, the real-life Lucys and Rickys sat down at the American kitchen table and Lucy laid down the new rules. At this point Lucy was working, perhaps as a headhunter or a publicist or a Hollywood agent. Ricky meanwhile was still nurturing his "creative pursuits." Lucy was bringing home at least as much money as Ricky, and some years more. Lucy was a woman reborn, hiring and firing, getting promotions, then coming home to put little Ricky to bed. Big Ricky was helping out, too, picking up from day care every once in a while or making a playground run on a Saturday morning so Lucy could go to a spin class. And by now he'd learned to roast a chicken. Wasn't that something? But Lucy, newly attuned to the cadences of her own satisfaction, wanted still more.

By now, going "back to the way we were" was no longer an option. In 1970 women in the United States contributed 2 to 6 percent of the family income. Now the average American wife contributes 42.2 percent. More than a third of mothers, in the United States and the UK, are the family's main breadwinner, either because they are single or because they make more money than their husbands. This latter category of breadwinner wives, also known as "alpha wives," are a particular shock to the usual marriage regime, given that they were once considered as bizarre and exotic as a portly man in a frilly apron. Within one generation, demographers expect them to be the majority of American families, with families in Europe and some Latin American and Asian countries not far behind. In fact, argues Heather

Boushey of the Center for American Progress, the whole question raised in the *I Love Lucy* episode and rehashed in some form today, about whether mothers should work, is moot, "because they just do. This idealized family—he works, she stays home—hardly exists anymore."

In the confines of intimate relationships, women's growing economic power has done extraordinary things. For the 70 percent of Americans without a college degree, the rise of the breadwinner wife is associated with the destruction of marriage. Women are choosing to stay single rather than marry men who can't step up and provide. The divorce rate has stayed as high as it was in the seventies, and every year fewer people get married before having children. In Washington, DC, for example, an astonishing 63.8 percent of mothers act as their family's main breadwinner, largely because the city has so many poor single mothers.

But for the elites, the result is exactly the opposite. Since the seventies, the college educated have become far more likely than anyone else to rate their marriages "happy" or "very happy" and less than half as likely to get divorced; out-of-wedlock births are virtually unheard of among them. Marriage has become yet another class privilege in America, the gated community of human relationships, the "private playground of those already blessed with abundance," in the words of sociologist Brad Wilcox, the head of the University of Virginia's National Marriage Project.

What was the trick? Smashing the old model, which was largely built on the assumption of male economic dominance. In Lucy's time, a woman had no choice but to marry up; how else could she get ahead? Sylvia Plath described these privileged husband-hunters memorably in *The Bell Jar* as "hanging around in New York waiting to get married to some career man or another" and looking "awfully

bored." In fact, she writes, "girls like that make me sick." Now that
women can have their own careers, they can banish the waiting and
boredom and that air of dependence that makes a freethinking
woman sick. They don't *need* a man to get ahead, so they can find one
they really want to be with instead. And isn't that a purer form of
love, anyway?

When I got engaged in the late 1990s, I had a vague concept in
mind of an egalitarian marriage. I'd seen my husband work out some
family finances for his parents one afternoon in a highly competent
way, and remember feeling relieved that I'd be able to offload that
particular task. I'd seen him playing with friends' kids; he seemed to
enjoy it. We were both journalists with about equally successful
careers, and I assumed it would stay that way.

This in itself was a radical enough vision. My mother had worked
sporadically when I was a kid and started her career only after I had
left for college. My father, like most fathers I knew, worked steadily
every day. But I assumed my husband and I would both work, both
raise children, and on into a happy retirement. I am not an especially
precise planner, but if you'd have pressed me for an exact ratio, I
would have given the same one most women of my generation had in
mind: fifty-fifty, with its soothing intimations of yin-yang harmony
and feminist equity.

The new model of elite marriage renders even that simple equation obsolete. The prevailing arrangement now is a constantly shifting equation—sixty-forty or eighty-twenty or ninety-ten. I call it
the seesaw marriage, where any side of that ratio can be filled by
either partner at any given time. A husband can work to support his
wife through school and then she can take over and be the hotshot
lawyer. A wife can start out ahead and then decide to cut back and
take care of the children. These new bourgeois marriages work,

argues marriage historian Stephanie Coontz, because they have "much less rigid gender roles." Anyone can play the role of breadwinner for any period.

In the fifteen years I've been married, I've started to encounter more families where the wife is at least for some period the main breadwinner. Some couples seem to ease into it naturally—the wife is a born workaholic and the husband delights in, say, coaching the sports teams or picking the kids up after school. One woman at our preschool can't stop bragging about her stay-at-home husband—although, I can't help it, I am still startled by the sight of him hanging around the school making handprint T-shirts for the teachers. Some dynamics are not so pleasant—one woman I know, whose husband works part-time as an airline mechanic, never seems to run out of ways to call him a loser. Another, with an out-of-work lawyer husband, complains about petty things—why does he spend all her money on dress socks if he hasn't had a job interview in over a year, and why does he have to subscribe to every damned sports channel? In a couple of cases I know, the disparity never felt natural, and the couple got divorced.

The emotional landscapes of such families were a mystery to me, which is why last year I conducted an extensive survey of seventy-five hundred people in female-breadwinner couples in the online magazine *Slate*, and followed up with interviews. *Slate* readers are much more educated than the general population, and the majority of people who answered the survey were women. Still, the responses start to get to the bottom of some of the more sensitive questions: Does more money mean more power in the relationship? Do more hours worked mean fewer hours taking care of the children? Do the men feel liberated? Humiliated? Do the women feel proud? Taken advantage of? Does a husband ever separate darks from whites?

In fact, nearly 80 percent of people in my *Slate* survey on bread-winner wives described themselves as happy in their marriages, and rated themselves as having a fairly low chance of divorcing. About a third said the men were self-conscious about making less money, and slightly fewer felt judged by the community. Nearly 90 percent said in the future, it will be more acceptable for women to be the main providers. This may be because as financial providers go, women are relatively benign. A surprisingly small number of respondents said the woman has more power because she makes more money; about two-thirds reported that they share power equally.

One recurring storyline I uncovered in my follow-up interviews was *Lady Chatterley's Lover*, only with a Hollywood ending. Lori, an attorney who makes half a million dollars a year, was tired of dating men who considered her professional competition, and whose "entire mood depended on whether they'd inched one step closer that day to being CEO." So she married a train conductor she met on the dating site Match.com. "I wanted a man who didn't talk about his work all day, who would rather go for a bike ride on the beach," she told me. "My husband knows who he is. He's just comfortable in his own skin."

Still, it was clear from my dozens of interviews that there are tensions under the surface. A power arrangement that's prevailed for most of history does not fade without a ripple. In many cases I heard the same old marriage anxieties, only they showed up in the reverse gender. Andy, a stay-at-home dad in San Jose, had had to cancel several appointments with me because he couldn't get his twins to sleep. Before he stayed home with his kids, he was a carpenter. His wife is a physician, and because she makes so much more money it made more sense for him to stay home. For the most part, Andy is completely content staying home and watching the toddlers, but every once in a while he gets wistful about his old life, and somewhat defensive about his new one, just as many moms do. The feelings flood over him when he passes construction crews while taking the twins on a walk: What would it be like to work with a group of guys up on a roof again? What adventures is his wife having while he's wiping off bibs? When his wife and her doctor friends rib him about staying home, he over-aggressively pulls the manual labor card: "How about I come over and help you put that Ikea furniture together, Mr. Doctor?" It's the old Betty Friedan identity crisis, only in masculine form. These days when his wife suggests that he should go back to work, he feels "terrified." It's been a long time, and he's lost the stomach for the outside world.

On the other side of that equation are women who are resentful about carrying the whole economic load, much the way husbands once were. They exhibit the same range of provider symptoms: pressure, fear of the gold digger, frustration at being trapped in the day-to-day with no outlet for creativity. Michelle, an attorney in Los Alamos, complained to me about being "hunted like a deer by men as a desirable wife because of my wage-earning capability and good job." Beverly, an African-American executive in Washington, DC, fed up with her couch-potato husband, warned that "women should be very careful about marrying freeloading, bloodsucking parasites." Julie, an attorney and reluctant family breadwinner, said, "I'm a little envious of the old days, where women weren't expected to go out and make a living on par with men. I just feel it's unfair that women are in a position where there is a ton of pressure to do both things."

Mostly, though, I discovered that the roles do not just reverse. I did not talk to a single breadwinner wife who has entirely ceded the domestic space. This is true even if the woman is working two jobs. It's true even if the woman makes considerably more money than the man, and it's true even if she has a stay-at-home husband. In over three-quarters of the couples in my survey, either the woman did more child care and housework, or they shared equally. This is modern Plastic Woman at her most voracious, taking up ever more space until she explodes: "I HATE HATE HATE the annual 'what should a stay-at-home mom make??' tripe that comes out around Mother's Day," said Dawn, a software engineer and mother of three who has been the primary breadwinner "forever." "I have to do the same house/child-care work, AND if I lose my job, my whole family is fucked."

Over the last thirty years, women have started to work considerably more hours than they once did, without easing off on child care. In fact, the opposite has happened. In 1965 women reported doing an average of 9.3 hours of paid work a week and 10.2 hours of child care. Now women not only do an average of 23.2 hours of paid work a week, but they do *more* child care—13.9 hours. The hours in a woman's week have not expanded, and mostly women have made up for it by shaving off time in other areas—housework, personal grooming and, tragically, free time, which women claim less of now than they ever did. But mostly what the time-use surveys confirm—for the United States and many other Western countries—is a vision of every woman as a slowly expanding and jealous colonial empire, refusing to cede old territories as she conquers new ones.

Men, meanwhile, are moving into new areas much more slowly than women. Over the same period of time, men have decreased their average work hours per week from 46.4 to 42.6. And their child-care hours have upped from 2.5 to only a modest 7. Despite decades of self-help literature imploring men to explore their nurturing sides, the stay-at-home dad remains a rare phenomenon. Only 2.7 percent of Americans in the latest census count themselves as full-time stay-at-home dads, although that does not count single fathers or part-time dads. In fact, one picks up an overwhelming note of reluctance, resistance, and in some cases revolt against the new regime. One man I spoke to aggressively belittled his wife, forged her name on checks, and wasted her fortune, all over jealousy about her professional success. Another got his revenge in the bedroom. After he lost his job, he confessed to forcing his wife to have more violent sex than she was comfortable with, to make up for his feeling of impotence elsewhere.

In more traditional or more macho cultures, the concept of the alpha wife goes down even harder. In Spain, marriages with foreigners have gone up to about 20 percent of all marriages. High-achieving women in Spain marry progressive men from Belgium or Switzerland, while Spanish men seek out wives from Ecuador or Colombia. In South Korea and Japan, men from rural towns, and more recently even cities, are importing brides from poorer Asian countries with more traditional notions of marriage.

But even in the West it's hard to avoid the latest crisis of macho. The 2010 sitcom season was populated by out-of-work husbands, meek boyfriends, stay-at-home dads, killer career wives, and a couple of men who have to dress up like women in order to get a job. For the first time, a slew of new sitcoms were shot with the premise that women go out to work while men stay home to take care of the house, stock the refrigerator with low-fat yogurt, or pretend to be taking care of the baby while watching a hockey game. "Women are taking over the workforce. Soon they'll have all the money, and the power, and they'll start getting rid of men," laments one character in a new show called *Work It*. "They'll just keep a few of us around as sex slaves."

For the last few years, romantic comedies, sitcoms, and advertising have been producing endless variations on what Jessica Grose at *Slate* dubbed the "omega male," who ranks even below the beta in the wolf pack. This often unemployed, romantically challenged loser can show up as a perpetual adolescent (like Ben Stone in *Knocked Up* and many of director Judd Apatow's other antiheroes), a charmless misanthrope (in Noah Baumbach's *Greenberg*), or a happy couch potato (in a Bud Light commercial). He can be sweet, bitter, nostalgic, or cynical, but he is haunted by the idea that he cannot figure out how to be a man. "We call each other 'man,'" says Ben Stiller's perpetually bitter character in *Greenberg*, "but it's a joke. It's like imitating other people."

In decades past, the cinematic loser had a certain broken nobility (Norm on *Cheers*); he may have been out of a job and disappointing his wife, but ultimately his man cave, with its dim lights and its endless procession of amber mugs, contained as much warmth and heart as the most lovingly dysfunctional family. The women on *Cheers* with any ambitions were presented as denatured and destined for failure, and wound up folded back into the bosom of the bar. But in the new era the rules are reversed: The man cave is what has to get sacrificed. Ben Stone lives with his three yo-yo friends running a porn site while collecting some sort of disability payment. He is a lovable degenerate, and his girlfriend is shrill and obsessed with success. Still, Ben loses in the end, and in the final montage we have shots of him as a modern, happy playground dad. So it goes in the new era of on-screen marriage. The men are almost always more endearing than their significant others, but that does not get them very far anymore. In the epic battle of the sexes, they now have to wave the white flag and cross over to the woman's world if they want any hope of a good life. To win, they have to submit.

Of all the days in the year, one might think, Super Bowl Sunday should be the one most dedicated to the cinematic celebration of macho. The men in Super Bowl ads should be throwing balls and racing motorcycles and doing whatever it is men imagine they could do all day if only women were not around to restrain them. Instead, in a 2010 ad that has come to best represent the modern state of gender relations for me, four men stare into the camera, unsmiling, not moving except for tiny blinks and sways. They look like they've been tranquilized, like they can barely hold themselves up against the breeze. Their lips do not move, but a voice-over explains their predicament—how they've been beaten silent by the demands of tedious employers and enviro-fascists and their women. Especially the women. "I will put the seat down, I will separate the recycling, I will carry your lip balm." This last one—lip balm—is expressed with the mildest spit of emotion, the only hint of the suppressed rage against the dominatrix. Then the commercial abruptly cuts to the fantasy, a Dodge Charger vrooming toward the camera, punctuated by bold all caps: MAN'S LAST STAND. But the motto is unconvincing. After that display of muteness and passivity, you can only imagine a woman—one with shiny lips—steering the beast.

DAVID GODSALL describes himself as "adapting pretty well to the new world order." The twenty-nine-year-old Vancouverite is not like one of those blue-collar guys who are just "humiliated and fucked in this new economy" because they can't retool and go to college and find a new profession. He has a master's degree and a job, as an editor at a Vancouver city magazine. He has an apartment he shares with his steady girlfriend, a kitchen full of nice appliances, a car in the garage, a bullmastiff. But this steady accumulation of life's comforts has only uncovered for him how uncomfortable he actually feels.

At the moment, his girlfriend, Clare, makes more money than he does. Not very much more—something on the order of $15,000—plus she has significant student loans to pay off, and he has a modest family inheritance. And he's well aware that in the future, when they have children, the seesaw may very well tip in the other direction. But the difference is enough to unsettle him. "As a generation of educated urban men who never knew a world where our female peers didn't outperform us in almost every meaningful category, we're in the middle of a long, uncertain process of negotiating a new maleness," he wrote me. "Money is inextricably part of that process, even for those of us who really like that our partners are successful."

David couldn't care less about concepts like "head of the family" or "patriarchal authority." He finds the word "breadwinner" funny and thinks the idea of a single "provider" is very "my baby takes the morning train." Clare is a passionate second-wave feminist who earnestly counts the number of female executives in every office, and David is all for that. He gets that the powerful white dude in a suit, à la Jack Donaghy on *30 Rock* or the boss on *The Office*, only exists as a person behind layers of irony and self-parody. And yet he can't seem to allow himself to cross over to the other side, where gender roles are interchangeable and it makes no difference who wears the pants. When he passes the happy dad at the playground at midday, he shudders. "Yeah, he haunts me," David confesses. "It doesn't matter how Brooklyn-progressive we (urban, educated men born after 1980) are, we still think he's pitifully emasculated. I'm progressive and enlightened, and on an ideological political level I believe in that guy. I want that guy to exist. I just don't want to *be* that guy."

David's unease with the changing roles of marriage leaves him stuck in this dead space, where the only momentum comes from the aggressively malignant mutations of his own ambivalence. Some of his friends are in the process of buying their girlfriends rings, but he can't yet bring himself to do it, although he knows that the clock is ticking and one day soon he will relent. The money, you see, has come to symbolize something, some far-off, free-fall, emasculated future he can't bear to contemplate. When they have kids, will she suggest that he cut back his hours or work four days a week? When they need a bigger car, will she pay for it? He is reminded of these fears several nights a week in what he considers the recurring ritual of public humiliation: The waiter puts the bill on the table and slides it closer to him. His girlfriend reaches for her wallet. It makes sense that she should pay and yet she senses some horror in him, and so they just stare at each other, and it's a "slow drip of torture every time."

With the money David's grandparents left him, he and Clare recently went house hunting. They found a nice little airy loft they both liked and moved pretty quickly into purchase mode. But in each conversation they got "bogged down in the specifics." Who would get the loan? How would they split the down payment? The mortgage? How would the equity accrue? At one point David tried to maneuver so the house would be entirely under his name, even though that would mean significantly worse terms for their loan. His girlfriend began to feel that he was going to extensive lengths not to be entangled. They talked and fought for months. They lost the loft, and now they have to try again.

The men of David's generation have been primed by TV shows and movies, or maybe their mothers, to accept that a doctor or law-yer or novelist or even the president can be male or female and it doesn't make that much of a difference; it's all interchangeable. If they pay attention to such things, they would know that this era of female independence has done wonders for the men, that for the educated classes, it leads to better, more stable, wealthier, and hap-pier marriages. Today a married man with a college degree is likely to be healthier and have a lot more money to enjoy in retirement, thanks to his wife. He is also relieved to have a wife he can talk to about work or politics or anything else that interests him.

They should be able to tune in to the fact that the clock is running out slowly, that it's not necessarily them but more likely their sons or grandsons who will be routinely working for women. In the upper levels of society, in the creative and professional classes, women are still a few steps from being in charge. Men still hold many of the top jobs and work more hours than women. Go to a beach in the Hamptons on any summer Friday and you will still find the surf full of moms waiting for their husbands to maybe or maybe not arrive from their jobs in the city—proof that there are still pockets up in the thinner air where men rule the public domain while women rule the snacks and the sunscreen.

Anyway, these young college-educated urbanites are not like the working-class men of the South, who openly mourn the old chivalrous ways and grieve for what the new economy has robbed from them. For these guys, traditional manly ideals exist, if at all, as a fashion statement encountered in Brooklyn boutiques that stock nothing but hunting jackets and flasks and old copies of *Playboy*, kitsch recycled in an ironic-nostalgic mode the same way old Stalin-era buttons wash up in Moscow dance clubs. These men took a feminist theory class or two in college, maybe read Judith Butler and Kate Millett. They know that for a twenty-first-century man, yearning to make yourself a fixture in the ruling class is no longer all that cool. If they are looking back at the past, it's only between quotation marks.

Theoretically this attitude should make the transition to the new world order easier. Men with means should be slowly adjusting to a new, more androgynous world at the top, where a range of options are open to them and they can relinquish some of the burdens of being in charge. But among the rising generation of almost-marrieds or recently-marrieds, ease is not the signal one picks up. Instead what you read in the culture is a mighty struggle where the men, although they have nothing material or concrete to complain about, seem to be haunted by the specter of a coming gender apocalypse.

Finally I asked David: Why? Why does he care so much about things he theoretically doesn't care about? Why does he care so much that he would lose a house over it?

"It's certainly not resentment."

"And it's not really confusion."

"I don't think I could categorize my feelings about my situation as either positive or negative."

Then an answer occurs to him: "It's because our team is losing. All the things we need to be good at to thrive in the world we imagine existing ten or twenty or even fifty years from now are things that my female friends and competitors are better at than me. Than us. And I am loath to tell that to someone who is going to put it in print, but it's true."

BETWEEN 1935 AND 1936 sociologist Mirra Komarovsky interviewed fifty-nine families where the man had been the sole provider for his family, but then had lost his job and had been out of work at least a year. She published the results in her classic 1940 Depression-era study *The Unemployed Man and His Family.* The work is a window into the simple contract between married couples of that era. Different men she interviewed had fared better or worse in diminished circumstances, but what struck me most, reading the book nearly eighty years later, was the universal acceptance of the idea that "provider" was the yardstick by which all men should be measured. No ambivalence, no layers of Jack Donaghy irony; a man was as good as his paycheck and his position. The marriage equation was simple, as Komarovsky explains. The husband provides for the wife, and she honors and obeys him. "What a woman wanted in a husband was a good steady worker who would support the family," explains one Mrs. Johnson. If A is no longer true, then neither, naturally, is B. As one wife tells the interviewer, when asked how she felt about her husband's unemployment, "Certainly I lost my love for him." The slightly kinder wife says, "I still love him but he doesn't seem as 'big' a man."

The men, in turn, accept this diminishment as their fate, referring to themselves as "fallen idols" and explaining dispassionately that their kids no longer say "Hi, Dad" when they come in the door. "They used to come and hug me and now I seldom hear a pleasant word from them," one says. The particular stories are heartbreaking, but the equation is soothingly simple, with its promise of easy reversibility. Everything would be all right, the couple agreed, if her husband "could find something to do." She could pay the grocer, give the children their allowance, and turn on the heat. Peace, along with the timeless contract between man and woman, and the blind faith in the goodness of patriarchal authority, would be restored. Was there an alternative? Could Mrs. Johnson perhaps find a job instead? suggested the interviewer. No, they both agreed. That would be "terrible."

Barely a decade after the publication of Komarovsky's book, the simple contract began to break down. What had been blindly accepted as man's singular destiny since the caveman days—to provide for his family—suddenly seemed like a choice, and a choice many men were rebelling against. In retrospect we can pin the blame not so much on the gender revolution of the 1960s but on the 1950s, where the notion of breadwinner was so brutally enforced as the only middle-class norm that it began to feel like a noose. Authorities relied on the weight of science and psychology to hammer the point home: Men who failed to accept the breadwinner role were "deviant," "unnatural," and "immature," as Barbara Ehrenreich outlines in her 1987 book *The Hearts of Men*. Psychologists laid out clear developmental stages much the way Jean Piaget had done for babies: A man had to select a mate, find a vocation, establish a suitable home. Men who failed to meet these stages on time (meaning before age twenty-three) suffered from diseases such as "psychic immaturity," or "aspiring to 'perpetual adolescence'"—the kinds of conditions Ben Stone would recognize well. This irresponsible man, Ehrenreich writes, even "blurred into the shadowy figure of the homosexual," so much so that psychiatrist Lionel Ovesey created a new category of "pseudohomosexual," meaning a man who was not gay but nevertheless failed to conform to the standards of masculinity.

Peter Tarnopol, Philip Roth's alter ego in *My Life as a Man*, summarizes the prevailing ethos of the fifties perfectly:

> No wonder then that a young college-educated bourgeois male of my generation who scoffed at the idea of marriage for himself, who would just as soon eat out of cans or in cafeterias, sweep his own floor, make his own bed, and come and go with no binding legal attachments, finding female friendship and sexual adventure where and when he could and for no longer than he liked, laid himself open to the charge of "immaturity," if not "latent" or blatant "homosexuality." Or he was just plain "selfish." Or he was "frightened of responsibility." Or he could not "commit himself" (nice institutional phrase, that) to "a permanent relationship."

As you can surmise from the bitterness in Tarnopol's voice, the establishment had turned the screws too tightly. Almost simultaneously the first rumblings of the male revolt began. The best sellers of the mid-1950s—William Whyte's *The Organization Man* and David Riesman's *The Lonely Crowd*—warned men that they had become puppets of large corporations, mechanized versions of real men. Riesman especially lamented the creation of the emasculated, other-directed new man of the American workplace, who was forced to suppress concrete skills in favor of qualities such as perpetual alertness to signals from others and sensitivity to his colleagues. (And how prescient he was! These are now known as "people skills," and they are highly valued in the twenty-first-century workplace.)

How precisely to escape this trap was not at all clear. Midway through Richard Yates's 1961 novel *Revolutionary Road*, April Wheeler comes up with the perfect way to get out of the desperate suburban prison. Her husband will quit his post at Knox Business Machines, "the dullest job you can imagine." They will move to Paris, and she will work as a government secretary while he roams the city and reignites his old creative bohemian self.

> "Don't you see what I'm saying? It's . . . it's your very *essence* that's being stifled here. It's what you *are* that's being denied and denied and denied in this kind of life. . . .
>
> "Don't you know? You're the most valuable and wonderful thing in the world. You're a man."

But the world was not yet ready for this new definition of man, set free from his family duties. April finds herself pregnant, and the plan is drowned by the chorus of men alarmed by such a gender upheaval. His neighbor: "What kind of half-assed idea is this about her supporting him? I mean what kind of man is going to be able to take a thing like that?" His colleague (to Frank): "I don't see you languishing indefinitely at sidewalk cafés while your good frau commutes to the embassy or whatever." His neighbor again, imagining the lovely April Wheeler "grown thick and stumpy from her decade of breadwinning."

The peaceful solution to upper-class breadwinner angst did not present itself in the sixties and seventies, either. Instead marriage became the casualty of the all-out, sexually charged gender wars of the era. The new magazine *Playboy* urged men to reclaim the domestic space for themselves—put on some mood music, mix up a highball, and invite a woman over as a one-night guest, not a permanent resident. For women, meanwhile, marriage and all its accoutrements became the enemy, the barrier to fulfillment and progress. The worst thing one could be was a housewife, enslaved to a master husband. "Prostitutes don't sell their bodies, they rent their bodies," feminist activist Flo Kennedy wrote in *Color Me Flo*, a quote that got reprinted in *Ms.* magazine. "Housewives sell their bodies when they get married." In a 1971 forum captured in the documentary *Town Bloody Hall*, Germaine Greer and her feminist acolytes mocked a culture that believed a woman should "get an orgasm from a shiny floor." The forum ended with three women falling all over one another and making out onstage. This might have been an act designed to annoy and titillate Norman Mailer, who was also onstage, or it might have been a genuine gay rights moment. Either way, the message was that conventional bourgeois marriage was for the dogs.

America's divorce rate began going up in the late 1960s and then took a steep climb during the seventies and early eighties, as virtually every state adopted no-fault divorce laws. The rate peaked at 5.3 divorces per thousand people in 1981. This was the era in which I grew up, and the uncouplings and recouplings were part of the music of my childhood. My best friend lived a couple of blocks away in the tallest building in my middle-class neighborhood in Queens. The building had a pool where the neighborhood divorcées came to meet. One summer Brandi's mother was a dowdy mom with frizzy hair, and the next summer she was a bombshell with black hair and a bikini, who had changed her name to Raven. Robert's father showed up one summer with shiny nails, no wife, and a new sports car. The following summer he showed up with Raven. I had no feel for the deeper traumas. My own parents were the same age as my classmates' divorcing parents, but they were Israeli immigrants, so operated in more of a fifties mode. For me, all the marital turmoil was rolled into the glamour of being American; I may have even been jealous.

Then, when the fervor died down, what got left in its wake was what sociologists call the "divorce divide." Divorce, like so many other phenomena in American life these days, got refracted through the prism of widening income inequality. Divorce rates began to plummet for the college educated while they stayed high for everyone else. Yates's April Wheeler had it exactly right. For the ambitious class, the key was opening up the possibility for the woman to support the family. In fact, the most thorough overview of studies found that when a wife works, a marriage is more stable. Couples where the woman works are vastly less likely to divorce, probably because of less financial stress. If she had lived now, April Wheeler would have ended up like a Washington friend of mine: She would be the US ambassador to the Organization for Economic Co-Operation and Development (OECD) in Paris while her husband worked remotely and took some time to write, and then when they returned to the United States she could take her time finding her next gig while he went back to his big firm.

This is how the new seesaw marriage operates. Couples are not chasing justice and fairness as measured by some external yardstick of gender equality. What they are after is individual self-fulfillment, and each partner can have a shot at achieving it at different points in the marriage. The arrangement got established in an era where the creative class moves more fluidly through jobs and no one expects to stay in the same job forever. It thrives in a culture that privileges self-expression over duty. It's progressive in its instinctive gender blindness and rejection of obligatory work, and utterly conservative in its comfort with traditional marriage. This continued devotion to finding your thrills within the confines of the old two-ring Biblical union is what puts it miles away from Germaine Greer and the hot lesbians onstage at town hall; in fact, so smug are the bohemian bourgeoisie in their current form of marriage that any deviation from the script— divorce, single motherhood, some other "uncommon arrangement"— earns you playground pity and a scarlet letter, as critic Katie Roiphe has often written.

And what of the college-class men in this new era of marital bliss? Have they finally escaped the breadwinner noose? A smart man knows that a wife is no longer a financial drain. Quite the opposite— a wife is a man's ticket to comfort. On the verge of retirement, the average married couple has accumulated assets worth about $410,000, compared with $167,000 for the never-married and $154,000 for the divorced. One study showed that the assets of couples who stayed together increased twice as fast as those who had divorced over a five-year period.

Copious studies prove that marriage benefits the man much more than the woman, and not just in the old generic winking sense that it "domesticates" him. Excellent studies, from dozens of countries, show that married men are happier, healthier, and live longer than their single counterparts. (Also, contrary to the bachelor myth, they report more sexual satisfaction.) Different studies show married men are less likely to develop heart or lung disease, cancer, high blood pressure, diabetes, or serious depression. A recent study conducted by the Canadian Medical Association showed that married male heart attack victims arrive at the hospital, on average, half an hour before single men. (For women there is no difference.) Statisticians Bernard Cohen and I-Sing Lee, who compiled a catalog of relative mortality risks, concluded that "being unmarried is one of the greatest risks that people voluntarily subject themselves to."

Of course it will come as news to no one that women are the diligent caretakers who prod their husbands to go to the doctor and get to the hospital quickly. And perhaps this has always been true. But what's notable is the total reversal in the scientific establishment's focus. Studies about the "normal" male holding the reins are no longer in vogue. These days the establishment is being marshaled to confirm our new cultural notion that men have become the frail dependents in need of a protector. That men need marriage more than women do. In fact, they need it to survive.

There are many prophets of new manhood who would welcome this new dependence as progress. Only by being more flexible in domestic roles can men break free of the armor society binds them in. The most stalwart and well-known such prophet of the men's movement is Warren Farrell, author of *The Liberated Man*, and more recently the best-selling *The Myth of Male Power*. For decades Farrell has been advocating what he calls a "gender transition movement," where sons would have the same options as daughters—they should be free to choose a job they like or work part-time or not at all, and that should be all right with society.

Recently I saw Farrell at a forum in Washington. He is heading a working group to start the White House Council on Boys and Men to bring attention to the suffering of the forcibly machoed. Farrell is still bearded and gentle, with a practiced, nonthreatening voice and a low-key Venice Beach demeanor. At the forum he was lamenting that we teach our men to be "disposable" when we send them out to battle and cheer them at football games even though we know they might get injured.

Farrell often tells the story of how he was in such a hurry to get through his studies and assume his breadwinning role that he failed some of his PhD exams. This experience taught him that men need to be liberated from their constricted sense of manhood. Some aspects of his visions have already come to pass: The younger generation of men does in fact aim for some job satisfaction and decent balance in their lives. Our expectation of fatherhood has changed dramatically since the seventies. There may not be all that many stay-at-home dads, but a father who is never home for family dinner or bedtime is out of tune with the times.

Still, men have not yet fully embraced the message. There are many engaged fathers these days, but no men marching in the streets to demand paternity leave or flexible schedules. Instead, what we have are individual men, isolated in their own new domestic experiments, showing David Godsall and the rest of the world what marriage will look like in the not too distant future, when more women than men are paying most of the bills.

STEVEN AND SARAH ANDREWS moved into this Northside Pittsburgh neighborhood even before the cops had chased away the dealers who colonized the stoops. The beautiful old row houses are a steal, and the neighborhood, known as the Mexican War Streets, holds hidden treasures. Sarah gave me a tour one summer morning on her way to work. Although she was seven and a half months pregnant, she walked and talked so fast, I could barely keep up. She pointed out, across the street, one neighbor's visionary garden crowded with lush plants and flamingoes and a cityscape on his wall made of tiny figurines; down one alley is an asylum house festooned with the Chinese poetry of a grateful refugee; then the famous Mattress Factory one block away. The Andrewses are surrounded by eccentricity and renegade behavior, but that is not, in the long run, what attracts them. In this urban drama the Andrewses play the gentrifiers, and what they want is a settled and safe life for themselves, their twenty-month-old son, Xavier, and the baby to come.

Sarah leaves most mornings just before eight, about an hour before Steven and Xavier make their way downstairs to have breakfast (which many mornings Sarah leaves for them on the kitchen counter). A sociologist taking a brief history of their relationship might mistake them for "marriage naturalists," meaning the old style of couple that just stumble into marriage and life without all that much thinking and planning. They met in high school outside Columbus, on the set of a production of *Ordinary People*; they spent the downtime backstage playing cards. In fact, however, Steven and Sarah, who are thirty-seven and thirty-two, are consummate "marriage planners," the current reigning model among the professional class.

Since their fortuitous early meeting, they've planned everything: the exact timing of each pregnancy, how long Sarah will work at what job, how much money she will make. They haggle over the minute details and individual demands like two executives in a negotiation. They actually possess a piece of paper called the "Master Plan," in which each partner lays out his and her duties and responsibilities, year to year. At the moment Sarah's role is to "feed the family" and "make big money," which means that after graduating from law school she took a job at a law firm working eighty hours a week. In return she got to have a kid a year before Steven wanted to. Now he goes to law school at night, and during the days he takes care of Xavier and acts as "mediocre house dude." Steven likes this phrase. He repeats it often, like a job title—almost as often as he repeats that Sarah is a "superstar."

"I told her no way I can be like my mom, or like she would be," he told me. "I'm just the mediocre house dude." This is what the contract requires of him: He keeps the kid "reasonably happy and mostly fed and the house mildly clean." He might be able to pick up things around the house occasionally, but no laundry, and no cooking meals. Steven could pass for a Brooklyn hipster with his band T-shirts, lack of a clean shave, and black Keds. (Yes, Xavier, whom they call X, has a matching pair, although most of the time he seems to prefer to be naked.) But Steven is also good with his hands, not because he adopted some retro working-class "shop class as soul craft" ethos, but because his dad was an actual shop teacher and taught him how to fix and build. Steven's most notable quality is that he knows his own limits, which makes him a lot less defensive than some other guys might be in this situation. "Women seem to be able to multitask better than men," he says. "If X is busy for ten minutes, Sarah will go do the dishes and start the laundry. I don't transition like that. A toddler *kills* my productivity. I don't multitask."

I spent a couple of summer afternoons hanging out with Steven and Xavier and a friend visiting from Italy. As often happens in the presence of toddlers, time passed in a haphazard way. Xavier moved some branches from one side of the garden to the other. Steven tried to pull some weeds, but it was too hot so he gave up. Unlike most moms I know, Steven did not try to organize the time into tidy quadrants. There was no snacktime, no music hour, no walks to the park, no time-outs or "use your words." Xavier had a rash and Steven acknowledged that "it must burn," so he filled up a bucket of cold water, told him he was a "tough guy," and suggested he hop into the bucket. (I never would have thought of that.) When Xavier's cloth diaper got dirty, Steven sprayed it and left it in the sink. (In the contract his duties here stop at "smearage containment," but Sarah, who insisted on cloth diapers, has to launder them.) A few hours in, it was time for lunch, or maybe a nap. Once Sarah tried to show Steven a website where he could meet other house dudes in the neighborhood. "Why would I do that?" he told her. "I'm not gonna make friends just because some guy has a kid his age. I'm not into that." The great majority of days, Steven and Xavier don't leave the house.

Steven most definitely does not think of himself as conducting some new experiment in modern marriage or gender roles. If he read Warren Farrell's *The Myth of Male Power*, he would laugh. When we were hanging out on the back deck one evening, Sarah, who has a master's in theater history, tried to convince him that he was an example of "post-feminist masculinity." His response: "I'm gonna call bullshit on that right now." To Steven, who has a BS in electrical engineering, their arrangement seems as logical as a simple equation. In 2001 Steven was at a career dead end. He was working as a wireless engineer consulting with companies on where to place new towers, and then the market tanked. As a couple they needed to "diversify." Sarah was thinking of getting her PhD in theater history, which seemed to him "an expensive way to end up as a barista." They bred fancy cats for a while. Then Steven suggested she take the LSAT. She did so well that the school offered her a free ride. "I didn't even know you could get a scholarship for law school," he says.

After that things fell into place. It became clear that Sarah was a "great writer" and a "great talker" who could articulate nuanced ideas in a precise manner, says Steven. She aced law school and net-worked her way into great jobs. "Hey, if you want to win, you put your best batter on the plate," he says. "I knew I wanted to marry someone who was smart, educated, self-motivated, and a hard worker. I got a massively talented wife who in certain areas bested me." While she was in law school, Steven decided his goal was to have his wife earn $50,000 a year, but she was offered more than three times that. When I asked Steven if that made him feel bad or less of a man because she was feeding the family, he genuinely did not seem to grasp the logic behind my question: "I could have my wife stay at home and spend my money, or I could have my wife out and making some big money. Hmmm."

So where does that leave Steven? In theory this setup is tempo-rary, and Steven, now in his third year of law school, is just a few years behind his wife (although Sarah writes his outlines, sifts through his materials, and tells him what he absolutely has to read). After law school he wants to be a plaintiff's attorney taking on corporations, because he likes the fight. "I have time to figure myself out. I don't have to rush. Sarah's got a good job, so I can go after jobs that pay less. I can do more of what I want. I don't care if I make money. I don't have to, because my wife is the one feeding the family." If he graduates on time, he'll be thirty-eight.

Just before six, Sarah walked in from work, sat down to take off her sneakers, and then got right back up again. It's hard to describe what happened next without using cliché weather metaphors like "whirlwind" or "storm of activity." Within minutes Xavier was up in his high chair, his butt now lathered in cream, eating blueberries. Strawberries appeared on the table to be cut for a pie, along with flour and butter. Where was the gelatin? Chopped meat came next, along with corn and some other vegetables, and a cold beer got to my hand. Procuring the beer was Steven's job, but the rest of the time he sat on the stool and watched Sarah work. She made pie dough and set out a bowl of dried peas to distract Xavier. ("Use your words.") The chopped meat got formed into burgers. "Steven, in a couple of minutes I'll ask you to take these to the grill." She set the table, bathed the baby, laid out the burgers, put together the pie. Did I mention she was seven and a half months pregnant? It seemed as if the rest of us had until that point only been lazily squatting in this house, and now the space reverted to its rightful owner who was whipping it back into shape.

Spending a few days with Steven and Sarah made me realize something about my own marriage. My hunch when I got engaged was correct: Over the years my husband and I have in fact split domestic life pretty equally. We both work, we both cook, we both take care of the children. Because of this I assumed that I had shed most of my attachment to traditional gender roles. But now I realize that I am much more deliberate and reactive than I thought. I would never not work, because that decision is loaded with feminist betrayal. I would never let my husband sit back and drink a beer while I was busy in the kitchen. And my husband would never stay home, because it would never occur to him. What I realized in Pittsburgh was that even our intimate relationships unfold in a cultural moment, and my moment was still not far enough removed from old feminist rage to divest these tiny domestic decisions of that kind of meaning.

Steven and Sarah make decisions on a much cleaner slate. They behave almost like corporate partners at a work retreat, taking stock of trends and proceeding from there. Sarah works because she has the "more ready skill set" to succeed as a lawyer, and Steven stays home because in this modern economy "testosterone has been marginalized." Steven feels entitled to check out on evenings and weekends, and this makes Sarah "tired and sometimes angry." But it also means X gets the best of all possible worlds because, as Sarah read in a study, a kid with a stay-at-home dad gets more total parenting hours because he gains the father's time and retains almost all of the mother's, and ends up with higher test scores. Make sense?

Steven and Sarah were both raised with the usual jumble of gender expectations. They both come from conservative Midwestern families with factory roots. Sarah considered herself evangelical in her young life, and at what she calls her "Jesus camp" she was taught that the Bible ordained a man to be the head of the household and the woman to be submissive. In graduate school she rebelled and wrote her thesis on something about the body and corset restrictions, she can't remember exactly what. And that's the point—these feminist constructs are distant memories. On her shelf I saw a book with "Womb" in the title, but it was hidden behind a notebook of recipes. The closest thing I saw to a feminist text was a *Working Mother's Guide to Life* sitting in the bathroom, well thumbed through and marked up, with advice on, say, how to pump breast milk at a high-powered job.

Some days Sarah comes home from work and there is poop on the walls that Steven has not bothered to clean, and then she feels like nothing has changed since time immemorial. On those days Sarah realizes one truth about their situation: Steven stays home during the day, but in fact she is in charge of both realms. By deciding to work full-time she has not actually ceded the domestic space, but only doubled her load, although neither of them ever articulates that. This is one of the many ways in which the transition to a new era is not yet complete, in which couples with breadwinner wives hang on to old ways and habits that make the current setup unworkable. The women take on new roles with gusto, while the men take them on only reluctantly.

In fact, there is a reigning notion in the Andrews house that Steven is ultimately the one in charge, that if anything ever went wrong, Steven would stand between his family and disaster. The dynamic, as Sarah describes it, seems something like *Charlie's Angels*, where Steven is Charlie and Sarah is doing his bidding. "I'm like the planner, and she executes," Steven says. "Follow-through isn't my strength." Sarah puts it this way: "I almost get the sense of him sitting back and indulgently watching me tinker around in my universe and taking this or that over and him thinking, 'Isn't this cool? Isn't she being so competent over there?'"

This may be a fiction they both perpetuate because women have not yet become accustomed to owning the power even when it is so obviously theirs. It may in fact be a new variation on "provider," where men preserve the protector aspect of being the breadwinner even when they are not earning the money. Or it may be because the provider role did not just pass on to women, but passed into obsolescence. When men earned the money, women claimed alternate sources of power—sovereignty over the house or the school community or the couple's social life—so it seems only fair to preserve that system now. Power is diffuse. Maybe that's a satisfying enough explanation to save men from obsolescence and give them space to invent an entirely new way of being a happy, harmonious family in the age of female power. Or maybe not.

One early evening, just after Sarah came home from work and we were all talking, Xavier took off his diaper and peed in the hallway for maybe the third time that day, which prompted this observation from Steven about the future: "All boys do is pee on things. Nothing good comes from being a man. Women bring good things to the world. I live longer if I have a wife. I have a better, healthier life." He picked up the discarded diaper and dropped it in the sink, forgetting to spray. "I wanted a little Anne of Green Gables. Someone creative and good. I would love it if the next one is a little girl. Like my wife. A superstar."

THE NEW
AMERICAN
MATRIARCHY

THE MIDDLE CLASS GETS
A SEX CHANGE

Alexander City, Alabama—In the first days after the mill closed, Pastor Gerald Hallmark of the First Baptist Church was able to keep the prayer requests specific: *Joe Moore got a pink slip today. Let's pray that he finds new employment.* Or, *The Wallers have been called off to Atlanta. Let's pray they find a new church home.* But before long, the numbers got to be overwhelming. In a town of fifteen thousand, Russell Corporation, makers of premium athletic wear, employed seven thousand people, and over the last eight years nearly all of them have lost their jobs. Keeping up with the details of the disaster was like "trying to wrap your hands around a tornado," Hallmark said, so after a while, he just lumped the victims under one all-encompassing prayer. "We pray over those who have been released from employment," he would say at the Wednesday night service. "May God open another door for you."

The ones who left town the fastest to find new jobs were the plant managers who were also the "town doers," as the pastor calls them—the deacons and Sunday school teachers and Little League coaches and Rotary Club chairs. Once upon a time, the patriarchy was not an abstract idea to fight over, but the central organizing principle of a respectable middle-class existence. In Alexander City, the patriarchy that made middle-class existence possible began with the Russell family, after whom many town institutions and main roads were named (Benjamin Russell High School, Russell Medical Center, Russell Road). In a tier just beneath them were the friends and relatives who served as the plant managers and also as the civic leaders. The only woman of note was an honorary matriarch named Big Mama, who lived on a mini-plantation with a rose trellis and pools and a house for each of her sons.

This patriarchy supported the kind of middle-class striving that is romanticized in pop country songs and political speeches. Like many thriving small towns, Alexander City provided a blueprint for the American dream that looked nothing like success in New York City or San Francisco. Here, a man with a degree in textiles or engineering could make $70,000 or even $100,000, enough to afford a second house on the lake and his own boat. Here, a man could drive a Lexus SUV and still imagine himself to be the kind of American cowboy reflected in the Toby Keith song blasting on the radio: "Wearing my six-shooter, riding my pony on a cattle drive." He could take his family on a vacation to Disneyland and come home to a church where, if he needed it, he would be prayed for by name. His kids meanwhile could enjoy shows by dance troupes imported by Big Mama, who loved to say, "New York City didn't have nothing on us!"

But then, just before the start of the aughts, Russell got sucked into the tidal wave that was drowning American manufacturing.

The company got sold to Berkshire Hathaway and moved many of the plants to Mexico and Honduras, where uniform shirts could be made for $1 apiece. The American headquarters relocated to Atlanta because the new class of international executives and marketing aces (not to mention the new CEO's wife) "did not relish the idea of living in the small town of Alexander City," as the company history reads. The busiest office in Alexander City became the "placement service," which gave advice to the newly fired. The town itself, meanwhile, went from being the unlikely home of a Fortune 500 company and proud maker of uniforms for every football and baseball star who ever made a commercial, to the latest victim of the end of the manufacturing age. "It's like someone just turned the spigot off and we couldn't figure out how to turn it back on," said Mary Shockley, who works at Russell Medical Center. What dried up was a path to the middle class and all the familiar landmarks that went along with it.

I visited Alexander City in the aftermath, when the town was still trying to make sense of what had happened. The town was in the same situation as any number of American suburbs near Las Vegas or Houston or Fort Lauderdale, where the recession and the housing crisis had ripped the roots out of the middle class. But here the effect was concentrated and stark, and you could see more clearly what had been lost, and also what was rising up in its place. In the last decade or so, the broad middle swath of America has become unrecognizable, with a rapid decline in marriage and a rapid increase in divorce and single motherhood. The men destined to be breadwinners have lost their way, causing a sudden upending of the rules for sex, marriage, politics, religion, and the future aspirations of young people in places like Benjamin Russell High School. Even in the kind of rules that had always seemed unchangeable, like how two teenagers fall in love.

Sociologists have mostly described this change in the negative, as the hole where something familiar used to be: the sinking of the traditional middle class, the end of the stable white working class, the broken backbone of America, the void between the rich and the poor. But this description fails to take into account that the changes are affecting men and women very differently. In fact, the most distinctive change is probably the emergence of an American matriarchy, where the younger men especially are unmoored, and closer than at any other time in history to being obsolete—at least by most traditional measures of social utility. And the women are left picking up the pieces.

I met Charles Gettys at the Wednesday night supper at First Baptist. For twenty-three years, Charles had risen up the ranks at the plant, becoming a manager in the dyeing and finishing department and later head of national sales for fabrics. Thanks to all those sweatshirts and uniforms, he'd sent three kids to college and built a beautiful house on the lake. Now all those words—"dyeing," "finishing," "textile training"—seemed part of an ancient world, like speaking Shakespearean English, saying "thou" or "thee" out loud at the family dinner table, he mused, and he thought to himself: "Here I am, out in the world, trying to be a typewriter salesman." What rose over the ashes is what Gettys's wife, Sarah Beth, calls the "new norm," something people here only talk about if you push them, because it so disturbs the Southerners' sense of themselves and the natural order.

"For years I was the major breadwinner, and this has flipped the family around," Charles said. "Now she is the major breadwinner." Charles and Sarah Beth, both in their fifties, make a point to attend the Wednesday night supper every week, although Sarah Beth is exceedingly busy with her work and volunteering. Sarah Beth started out as a nurse and over the years has moved up in the ranks, and she is now an executive at Russell Medical Center, the award-winning local hospital. "Probably no one has had their wife move up the ladder as far as I've moved down," he says. Sarah Beth spends her days in an office sandwiched between the CEO and the CFO of the hospital. She has a secretary and endless series of meetings. Her job sets the rhythms of the household, pays the mortgage and basic household expenses. In her free time she is the ultimate town doer, teaching Sunday school and leading various civic groups. She has only so much patience for Charles's brooding. "Build a bridge and get over it," she tells him. "Don't just sit and whine and carry on."

Everywhere I went, couples were adjusting to the new domestic reality: the woman paying the mortgage, the woman driving to work every day, the woman leaving instructions on how to do the laundry. The townspeople referred to the ex-Russell men as three types: the "transients," who drove as far as an hour to Montgomery for work and never made it home for dinner; the "domestics," who idled at the house during the day hopefully, looking for work; and the "gophers," who drove their wives to and from work, spending the hours in between hunting or fishing. "You're gonna laugh at this," Charles told me, "but it was harder on the men than the women. It seems like their skills were more, what's the word, transferable?" The women from the mill got jobs working at the local doctors' or attorneys' offices, or in retail, or they went back to school to become nurses or teachers. This came home to Charles one day when he called the unemployment office in Montgomery to ask when his benefits were due to run out. The voice on the phone sounded familiar to him, and after a few minutes he realized it was a woman who had worked with him at Russell. She transferred him to her supervisor, who turned out to be another woman who had worked with him. "I was born in the South, where the men take care of their women," he said. "Suddenly, it's us who are relying on the women. Suddenly, we got the women in control." This year, Alexander City had its first female mayor.

The tornadoes of spring 2011 had mostly bypassed Alexander City and yet the place felt posttraumatic, as if a different kind of tornado had ripped out some deep roots and left people unsure how to rebuild or move forward. Wherever I went in town I met couples like the Gettyses, where the husband was stuck in place and the wife was moving ahead, yet no one would quite acknowledge the new reality. "What's the expression? Smoke and mirrors," said Rob Pridgen, a young friend of the Gettyses. "The wives are making more money and paying the bills, but the Southern man has to pretend he's the one holding it all together."

Rob learned that his job would be phased out a couple of months after he started dating Connie, and as a result, for a year he would not ask her to marry him. They were both in their forties and each had already been married, and Rob knew right away he wanted to marry her, but without a job he could not bring himself to ask. Connie was a teacher making a steady salary, and Rob was struggling week to week, trying to start a network-consulting business. The whole situation was getting awkward, with neither of them having any idea what to call each other or what to tell people at church.

"He is absolutely the guy who says 'I provide for my family. I'm the man of the house,'" said Connie.

"You're saying that as if I'm the dictator. It's not the whole sit-in-the-kitchen-with-your-apron thing. But the way I was brought up, it's a man's responsibility to take care of his family," he says, then turns to me. "I don't want to make the queen analogy, but my job is to make her the queen."

"Honey, you know I would teach anyway."

"But the point is, you shouldn't have to."

"It bothers him a lot," Connie says to me.

"I pretty much internalize it. It's like, if I can't take care of her, then I'm not a man."

At this point, Connie's nineteen-year-old daughter, Abby, pipes in with her own new-generation perspective on this Southern code of chivalry, which sounds like so much Shakespearean nonsense to her, given how the boys she knew actually behaved. "That's so cute," she says to Rob, "it's gross."

SINCE 2000, the manufacturing economy has lost almost six million jobs, nearly a third of its total workforce, and has taken in few young workers. The housing bubble masked this new reality for a while, creating work in construction and related industries. But then that market crashed as well. During the same period, meanwhile, health, education, and services have added about the same number of jobs. But those sectors continue to be heavily dominated by women, while the men concentrate themselves more than ever in the industries—construction, transportation, and utilities—that are fading away.

In the last decade, across eastern Alabama, the old mills have been snuffed out one after another—socks, tires, pulp, factories, poultry—leaving the economy in shambles. In Tallapoosa County, which contains Alexander City, the unemployment rate at the time I did my reporting was nearly 13.3 percent—pretty standard for the region during the height of the recession.

"Even twenty years ago there were jobs available for the class of men with limited education and skills. These were pretty good jobs that could get you into the middle class," says Joe Sumners, who runs the Economic & Community Development Institute at Auburn University. "But now those jobs are disappearing. If they want to work they have to be retrained, and that's hard on a lot of people." In 1967, 97 percent of American men with only a high school diploma were working; in 2010, just 76 percent were. That same pattern shows up not just in the United States but in almost all rich nations as they've put the industrial age behind them. "Forty years ago, thirty years ago, if you were one of the fairly constant fraction of boys who wasn't ready to learn in high school, there were ways for you to enter the mainstream economy," says Henry Farber, an economist at Princeton. "When you woke up, there were jobs. There were good industrial jobs, so you could have a good industrial, blue-collar career. Now those jobs are gone."

Lately economists have begun to focus on this lack of wage opportunities for men as "the single most destructive social force of our era," says Michael Greenstone, an MIT economist and former chief economist on the White House Council of Economic Advisers for President Barack Obama. *New York Times* columnist David Brooks memorably defined this problem as "the missing fifth," referring to the percentage of men—most of them without a college diploma—who are not getting up and going to work. In 1950, roughly one in twenty men of prime working age was not working; today that ratio is about one in five, the highest ever recorded. When asked by *The New York Times* what keeps him up at night, Larry Summers, Obama's chief economic adviser, zeroed in on the same phenomenon. "I worry for the medium and long term about where the jobs are going to come from for those with fewer skills. One in five men between twenty-five and fifty-four is not working, and a reasonable projection is that it will still be one in six after the economy recovers. . . . That has potentially vast social consequences."

The change is especially noticeable in a small town like Alexander City, but it's happening all over the country, from the Pacific Northwest to the Northeast, in big old industrial cities, suburbs, and rural communities alike. The men in the urban centers of the Rust Belt have been decimated by the decline of the American auto industry and the disappearance of unionized plants. The new suburbs of Nevada and Florida have been shelled out by the collapse of the housing industry. In the Spike TV show *Coal*, the miners of McDowell County, West Virginia, are romanticized as the last real men of America, holdouts from a time when America revered "hardworking men" who are "patriotic" as the producers often say. But this brand of macho exists only within the narrow span of the cameras. In *The Big Sort*, author Bill Bishop reveals the real McDowell County as part of a region rife with "civic dysfunction," where many of the former miners have succumbed to OxyContin addiction, marriage rates are plummeting, and one out of every three children is born to one of the area's many single mothers, who by default are left to stitch things together by working at Walmart or in service jobs around town.

In all these places, in fact, the women are stepping into the traditional "provider" role. MIT economist David Autor calls it the "last-one-holding-the-bag" theory. "When men start to flame out, women by necessity have to become self-sufficient, to take care of the kids. They don't marry the men, who are just another mouth to feed." It used to be that in working-class America, men earned significantly more than women. Now in that segment of the population, the gap between men and women is shrinking faster than in any other, according to June Carbone, an author of *Red Families v. Blue Families*. The women go to the local community colleges at far higher rates than men, to study nursing, cosmetology, or administrative skills. Very often they work at the local Walmart, often the sole source of steady jobs in town. If they have to, they pick up extra work babysitting, waitressing, or cleaning houses. In Alexander City, Leandra Denney's husband got the call telling him he'd been fired from Russell at eight in the morning on January 2, 2009, and "it just broke him," she recalled. Over the following year he became an OxyContin addict and a scary, unreliable husband, who might at any time pull a gun on her and her two children, and who stopped contributing anything to the household. How did she make ends meet for that year? "I cleaned houses," she says. "I'm the kind of person, if I have to clean a toilet, I just put the Mr. Bubble in and make it work."

This script has played out once before in American culture. Starting in the 1970s, black men began leaving factory jobs; by 1987 only 20 percent of black men worked in manufacturing. The men who lived in the inner cities had a hard time making the switch to service jobs or getting the education needed to move into other sectors. Over time, nuclear families fell apart, drug addiction shot up, and social institutions began to disintegrate, as William Julius Wilson chronicles in his 1996 book *When Work Disappears*. As a result, in the intervening two decades, the society has turned into a virtual matriarchy. In poorer communities women are raising children alone while one third of the men are in jail. In fact, one recent study found that African-American boys whose fathers are in jail have higher graduation rates than those whose fathers are around, suggesting that fathers have become a negative influence. African-American men and women have the greatest gender gap in college graduation rates, and *Ebony* magazine often laments how difficult it is for a black woman to find a suitable man.

In 2010 I visited Kansas City to follow one of the court-sponsored men's support groups that have sprung up throughout the Rust Belt and in other places where the postindustrial economy has turned traditional family roles upside down. Some groups help men cope with unemployment, and others help them reconnect with their alienated families. Many of the men I spoke with had worked as electricians or builders; one had been a successful real-estate agent. Now those jobs are gone, too. Darren Henderson was making $33 an hour laying sheet metal until the real-estate crisis hit and he lost his job. Then he lost his duplex—"there's my little piece of the American dream"—then his car. And then he fell behind on his child-support payments. "They make it like I'm just sitting around," he said, "but I'm not." As proof of his efforts, he took out a new commercial driver's permit and a bartending license, and then threw them down on the ground like jokers for all the use they'd been. His daughter's mother had a $50,000-a-year job and was getting her master's degree in social work. He'd just signed up for food stamps, which is just about the only social welfare program a man can easily access. Recently she'd seen him waiting at the bus stop. "Looked me in the eye," he recalled, "and just drove on by."

Mustafaa El-Scari, a teacher and social worker, leads some of these groups in Kansas City. El-Scari has studied the sociology of men and boys set adrift, and he considers it his special gift to get them to open up and reflect on their new condition. The day I visited one of his classes, earlier this year, he was facing a particularly resistant crowd.

None of the thirty or so men sitting in a classroom at a downtown Kansas City school had come for voluntary adult enrichment. Having failed to pay their child support, they were given the choice by a judge to go to jail or attend a weekly class on fathering, which to them seemed the better deal. That week's lesson, from a workbook called *Quenching the Father Thirst*, was supposed to involve writing a letter to a hypothetical estranged fourteen-year-old daughter named

Crystal, whose father had left when she was a baby. But El-Scari had his own idea about how to get through to this barely awake, skeptical crew, and letters to Crystal had nothing to do with it.

Like some of them, he explained, he grew up watching Bill Cosby living behind his metaphorical "white picket fence"—one man, one woman, and a bunch of happy kids. "Well, that check bounced a long time ago," he says. "Let's see," he continues, reading from a worksheet. What are the four kinds of paternal authority? Moral, emotional, social, and physical. "But you ain't none of those in that house. All you are is a paycheck, and now you ain't even that. And if you try to exercise your authority, she'll call 911. How does that make you feel? You're supposed to be the authority, and she says, 'Get out of the house, bitch.' She's calling you 'bitch'!"

The men are black and white, their ages ranging from about twenty to forty. A couple look like they might have spent a night or two on the streets, but the rest look like they work, or used to. Now they have put down their sodas, and El-Scari has their attention, so he gets a little more philosophical. "Who's doing what?" he asks them. "What is our role? Everyone's telling us we're supposed to be the head of a nuclear family, so you feel like you got robbed. It's toxic, and poisonous, and it's setting us up for failure." He writes on the board: $85,000. "This is her salary." Then: $12,000. "This is your salary. Who's the damn man? Who's the man now?" A murmur rises. "That's right. She's the man."

FOR THE RISING GENERATION, these upended gender dynamics have made marriage seem a lot less appealing. This is the first time that the cohort of Americans ages thirty to forty-four has more college-educated women than college-educated men. An increasing number of those women—unable to find men with a similar income and education—are forgoing marriage altogether. In 1970, 84 percent of women ages thirty to forty-four were married. In 2007, 60 percent were. The same year, among American women without a high school diploma, 43 percent were married. And yet, for all the handwringing over the lonely spinster, the real loser in society—the only one to have made hardly any financial gains since the 1970s—is the single man, whether poor or rich.

The divorce statistics alone tell an incredible new story. In the 1970s, a divorced woman could expect to watch her income plummet by at least a quarter, while very few divorced men experienced a similar decline. This change in circumstances drove the plot line of many a pulp novel of the era, the wife struggling to hold it together as a part-time piano teacher and babysitter. Now, the percentage of men and women who see their incomes drop by a quarter is about the same. On the other end, the number of divorced women who see their income rise substantially has nearly doubled. In fact, a greater percentage of women than men see their income rise by at least 25 percent, giving a whole new perspective on who was whose ball and chain.

The changes have reached into unlikely places, scrambling the cultural map of America. Alabama is among the most socially conservative states in the country. The state has voted Republican in every presidential election since 1964 except two, both times for native sons of the South—George Wallace and Jimmy Carter—and has one of the highest proportions of citizens who identify as evangelical Christians. Yet despite a steady increase in population, the percentage of households with married couples has declined from 57 percent in 1990 to 48 percent today. In 2008 the Census Bureau began publishing divorce rates, meaning the percentage of people in the state who got divorced in the last year. In each year since, Alabama has made the top of the list. In fact, the entire list has run counter to cultural stereotype, with Oklahoma, Kentucky, and Alabama at the top and New York, California, and Massachusetts close to the bottom. Last year, among the areas with the highest divorce rates in the nation were two small towns in Wayne County, Indiana.

The sociologist Kathryn Edin spent five years talking with mothers in the inner suburbs of Philadelphia. Many of these neighborhoods, she found, had turned into matriarchies, with women making all the decisions and dictating what the men should and should not do. "I think something feminists have missed," Edin told me, "is how much power women have" when they're not bound by marriage. The women, she explained, "make every important decision"—whether to have a baby, how to raise it, where to live. "It's definitely 'my way or the highway,'" she said. "Thirty years ago, cultural norms were such that the fathers might have said, 'Great, catch me if you can.' Now they are desperate to father, but they are pessimistic about whether they can meet her expectations. So they have the babies at nineteen or twenty, but they just don't have the jobs to support them." The women don't want them as husbands, and they have no steady income to provide. So what do they have?

"Nothing," Edin says. "They have nothing. The men were just annihilated in the recession of the nineties, and things never got better. Now it's just awful."

The situation today is not, as Edin likes to say, a "feminist nirvana." After staying steady for a while, the portion of American children born to unmarried parents jumped to 40 percent in the past decade. A child born to an unmarried mother, once a stigma, is now the "new normal," *The New York Times* reported in a 2012 front page story, as more than half of births to American women under thirty occurred outside marriage. Many of these single mothers are struggling financially; the most successful are working and going to school and hustling to feed the children, and then falling asleep in the elevator of the community college. Still, they are in charge. "The family changes over the past four decades have been bad for men and bad for kids, but it's not clear they are bad for women," says sociologist Brad Wilcox.

Over the years, researchers have proposed different theories to explain the erosion of marriage in the lower classes: the rise of welfare, the disappearance of work for men, or in the eyes of conservative critics such as Charles Murray, plain old moral decay. But Edin thinks the most compelling theory is that marriage has disappeared because women are now more economically independent and thus able to set the terms for marriage—and usually they set them too high for the men around them to reach. "I want that white-picket-fence dream," one woman told Edin, and the men she knew just didn't measure up, so she had become her own one-woman mother/ father/nurturer/provider. Or as Edin's cowriter, the sociologist Maria Kefalas, puts it, "everyone watches *Oprah*"—or whatever the current *Oprah* equivalent is. "Everyone wants a big wedding, a soul mate, a best friend." But among the men they know, they can't find one.

Some small proof for this theory that women don't marry because they're on top can be found in a recent study of Florida Lottery winners, called "Lucky in Life, Unlucky in Love?: The Effect of Random Income Shocks on Marriage and Divorce," published in the *Journal of Human Resources* in 2011. Researchers discovered that women who recently won the lottery were significantly less likely to marry, whereas for men it made no difference. Women who had won relatively large prizes ($25,000–$50,000) in the Florida Lottery were 41 to 48 percent less likely to marry than women who won less than $1,000, suggesting that money does in fact affect women's decisions.

It's far from definitive, but the results do confirm a certain picture. The whole country's future could look much as the present does for many lower-class African-Americans: The mothers pull themselves up, but the men don't follow. First-generation college-educated white women may join their black counterparts in a new kind of middle class, where marriage is increasingly rare.

These changes are not merely spreading around the fringes; they are fundamentally altering the core of American middle-class life, as Wilcox and his colleagues chronicle in a groundbreaking report called "When Marriage Disappears: The Retreat from Marriage in Middle America." Wilcox's work concentrates on what he calls the "moderately educated middle," meaning the 58 percent of Americans who do not have a college degree but are not high school dropouts, either, and might have some higher education. This is the class that used to strive upward and model itself on the upper classes. Now, in this vast swath of Middle America, "marriage, that iconic middle-class institution, is foundering," writes Wilcox, and at an "astonishingly fast pace."

By nearly every important social measure, Middle America is starting to look like high-school-dropout America. By the late 1990s, 37 percent of moderately educated women were divorcing or separating within ten years of their first marriage, almost the same rate as among women who didn't finish high school and more than three times that of college graduates. Middle America also caught up in rates of infidelity and number of sexual partners. By the late 2000s, nonmarital childbirths accounted for 44 percent of children born to moderately educated mothers and 6 percent of children born to highly educated mothers. Teenagers in Middle America are now less likely to say they would be embarrassed if they got pregnant, and less likely to have a strong desire to attend college.

The middle class still aspires to a happy soul-mate marriage, but increasingly their life experience is not matching up. From the 1970s to the 2000s, the percent of spouses who reported they were "very happy" in their marriages dropped among moderately educated Americans from 68 to 57 percent. Marriage, writes Wilcox, "is in danger of becoming a luxury good attainable only to those with the material and cultural means to grab hold of it." As Kefalas puts it, "Stable marriage has become a class privilege in America, just like good school and access to health care and healthy foods."

WHEN I VISITED Alexander City, the kids at the high school were high on a song by Jason Michael Carroll called "Where I'm From." In it, the singer, dressed in jeans and boots, meets up with an Armani-clad businessman in first class. The businessman asks him "Son, where do you call home?" In pop country music, this is a cue to describe the American dream, the front pew of the church, the court-house clock, a place:

> *Where a man's word means everything*
> *Where moms and dads were high school flames*

But that place, where a "man's word means everything," no longer exists. In 2000, Maria Kefalas began doing fieldwork in a small rural town in Iowa. At that time she was still hearing about shotgun wed-dings, and ministers still refused to marry couples who had been living together. It was a town of classic "marriage naturalists," who assumed without thinking much about it that life proceeded in a cer-tain order: you got married, you had some babies, and at various points along the way you worked until you retired. If by some accident the pregnancy came before the marriage, you pretended like it hadn't, and did your best to keep up appearances.

In 2007, with the recession in full swing, she returned to the town and found the landscape completely changed. She met kids in their teens who were having babies first, no marriage on the horizon and what's more, they seemed unembarrassed about it. "They were more like the kids in North Philly," she recalls. Over the course of the decade, they had essentially copied the professional classes and switched to "marriage planners," who no longer assume marriage will just happen but consider it a distant goal to be earned at some distant point in the future after much waiting and planning. Only in their case, the future never really arrives. "I became increasingly convinced that as this twentieth-century industrial economy is breaking apart, marriage naturalists are disappearing. This whole cultural narrative—you get a job, you marry your sweetheart, you buy a house, you educate your children, you go to church—has been torn to shreds. Without the economic foundation, the script can't support itself. And this is Iowa—the idyllic heart of white America!" A cultural chasm—which did not exist forty years ago and which was still relatively small twenty years ago—has developed between the traditional middle class and the top quarter or third of society.

The First Baptist Church in Alexander City is a thriving community, with packed pews every Wednesday and Sunday and events nearly every day of the week. But as with most evangelical churches, the changes in gender relations have forced a rethinking of a basic philosophy. As R. Albert Mohler Jr., president of the Southern Baptist Theological Seminary, recently asked, "What does it mean for large sectors of our society to become virtual matriarchies? How do we prepare the church to deal with such a world while maintaining Biblical models of manhood and womanhood?" Christians, he warned, "had better know that matters far more important than economics are at stake. These trends represent nothing less than a collapse of male responsibility, leadership, and expectations. The real issue here is not the end of men, but the disappearance of manhood."

One day Pastor Hallmark from First Baptist saw a guy who used to be a plant manager selling shirts at J. C. Penney. The guy tried to avoid him, but Hallmark did his best to make him feel comfortable, by walking up and asking him how the new job was working out. Since then, Hallmark has had to make slight adjustments in the philosophy he's been preaching for nearly thirty years. Instead of reminding the men that the Bible instructs them to be the head of the household, he tells them, "Your manhood shows in your reaction to hard times."

Here and there, you can see the women making small adjustments themselves. Sarah Beth Gettys's Sunday school class contains a group of ambitious senior girls headed to Auburn, one of whom says her biggest earthly temptation is likely to be "pursuing too many higher degrees," and another her friends in the group call "future president." Gettys still understands that even dynamic women cannot be called to the pulpit, and she still teaches them that a man is head of the household, but these days, she asks the girls to reflect on what being "submissive" means and sneaks in lessons about how to negotiate better salaries and move up the corporate ladder.

For Connie Pridgen, the younger woman I met at church, her personal revelation came in a Bible study group. They were mulling over a passage in Proverbs that's sometimes read at church for Mother's Day. The passage describes the "wife of noble character," who works with the wool and flax, brings the food from afar, who "gets up while it is still dark," buys the field, plants a vineyard, turns a profit, and "her lamp does not go out at night." Her husband, meanwhile, "is respected at the city gate, where he takes his seat among the elders of the land."

Connie reads the passage aloud to me, Rob, and Abby one spring Saturday while we are sitting around on the living room couch of the small lake house they rent. What has been dawning on her these last few months becomes obvious to all of us as she speaks. The wife is doing absolutely everything. And the husband?

"Sounds like he's sitting around with his buddies shootin' the breeze, talkin' about the ball game and eatin' potato chips," says Rob, always one for a dose of bracing honesty.

Abby says the husband sounds "sketchy." In fact, she says he sounds like the "sketchy" guys who hang around the Ruby Tuesday bar where she works on weekends and where half her fellow waitresses seem to be pregnant with the babies of said sketchy guys, "who may or may not be there the next day."

Connie and Rob have both been through divorce, and she's the one with the steady job. But to her, these upheavals still feel like bumps in the road. She grew up in the old order, and she knows the value of love and marriage. For Abby's generation, however, raised in the wake of the economic turmoil and family breakdown, there is no more road.

CONNIE'S JUNIOR ENGLISH CLASS at Benjamin Russell High School files in after lunch, setting half-drained Sprites and Dr. Peppers at the edges of their desks, wiping potato chip salt off their fingers before opening the appointed text for the day. Today the class is finally finishing reading *Romeo and Juliet*, and most of the kids are delighted—far too delighted, as far as Connie is concerned—to be done with it. In years past her students had been entranced by the play, absorbed by the romance between the teens. "They were oooh so sappy," she recalls. "'Oooh, he loves her so much, he would die for her!'"—so much so that she had to include a warning about teen suicide. Connie has the proof of their infatuation in the romantic paintings and line drawings made by former students that now hang above the board in her classroom. One shows Romeo serenading Juliet from the balcony, another shows him draped forlornly over her tomb-bed, and a third shows Juliet winged like an angel rising to heaven.

This year she saved the play for the springtime, "when the sap rises and the high schoolers make goo-goo eyes at each other," she says. But her students are unmoved. Not just unmoved: disgusted, mostly by Romeo's "whiney lameness," as they constantly tell her. Act 5, Scene 3: Romeo has already discovered Juliet's body and is now returning to her tomb. He is distraught, mad with grief. He has just killed Paris, and it's becoming clear that, so deep is his grief, he is determined to end his own life and make this a twin grave. Connie plays a recording she found on the web. "I will stay with thee and never from this palace of dim night depart again." Romeo crawls into the tomb. He kisses Juliet, takes the poison, kisses her again. "Here's to my love! O true apothecary! Thy drugs are quick. Thus with a kiss I die." On the tape, there is an audible sound of gulping as he swallows.

Someone throws her book across the room. This is Tanner Harris, a strawberry blonde who has failed to disguise her disgust over the last few weeks. "This is just the stupidest stuff," she says. "I just think it's pointless. And ridiculous."

Connie has been teaching long enough to manage all opinions, even those verging on disrespect, so she teases out the conversation. "Well, isn't it possible that when you're in love, you don't necessarily act rationally?" she asks.

"I think that's just him," says Tanner. "In my opinion, he's just a little sissy boy and he's not normal. Any other guy would just go get him another girl. He wouldn't just kill himself over some girl. What's the big deal? *Find another one.*"

"Well, does anyone think it's romantic?" Connie asks, and elicits a resounding chorus of *"Nooooo."*

"He's just lame," someone offers. "Yeah, and crazy."

After a while Connie opens the discussion further, referring them back to journal entries the kids are writing about the play in relation to their own lives. "Okay, show of hands, how many of you plan to get married?" About fifteen out of the twenty-five raise their hands, and many more boys than girls. "How many of you think you'll get married before you're twenty-five?" About six of them raise their hands. "After thirty?" Four raise their hands, all girls. One of them is Gabby Humber, a tall blonde with dark roots in jeans and a heart choker, who looks like she would be the first to be snatched up.

"Well, I get tired of people very, very easily," she says, by way of explanation. "Marriage is not for me."

"But how will you support yourself?" someone asks.

"I will go to college and I will support *myself,*" she hisses. "I don't need a man to support me."

Connie has her own theories about why her students have suddenly soured on romance. In the years since Russell left, town life has lost its comforting routine of meet, marry, go to school, work at Russell, and somewhere in there have a few babies. For those left behind, life has turned a little more unpredictable and brittle, and these young people along with it. The percentage of students at the high school receiving free lunch rose to 50 percent. More parents are stressed, or divorced, all of which has led them to believe that "marriage is disposable," she says.

I asked Lou Ann Wagoner, the school superintendent, what had changed the most in the last few years, and she mentioned two things. For the first time, the white girls have taken to fighting. She says in the last two years, the atmosphere has gotten "almost *Jerry Springer*" with girls threatening to beat one another up—much more than boys do. She also mentioned the "rash of pregnancies" this year— twelve in the high school and a few more in the middle school, "even though we teach abstinence and everything." Connie has noticed, too, that it's not just the poorer African-American girls getting pregnant in high school anymore. Once they were the girls who were "more matriarchal, I guess you'd say, but now everyone is headed that way."

In the week I visited, the hallway downstairs was festooned for school elections, with sparkly signs reading ROSIE FOR VP, LINDSEY FOR SECRETARY, ANNA LEE FOR PRESIDENT, PAIGE FOR SECRETARY, MARIE GRACE FOR TREASURER, KAYDEE FOR REPRESENTATIVE—and not a boy among them. Wagoner's main goal is to prepare her graduates for college; these days the college talk starts in third grade, where they bring in successful graduates to tell their stories. But she can't seem to get through to the boys. "They still think, 'I don't need an education. I'll just work at Russell.' Like it's still here! We can't seem to break that mentality." The city pays for any child who wants to continue their education for two extra years at the community college. Wagoner was startled to discover that 65 percent of the students who take advantage of the program are women, and that the men tend to drop out after a year. "That number just jumped out at me," Wagoner told me. "I'm not sure where the males go or what happens to them. I think they're just not as motivated."

*   *   *

A FEW YEARS AGO, Shannon was one of the girls who drew those sappy pictures for Connie's class. She did it in colored pencil, making cheeks for Juliet with a color she remembers was called "rose red" and a gown she now admits was maybe a little too low cut. Juliet is lying on what looks like a soft bed, and she is smiling in her sleep. Romeo, who looks a little like Johnny Depp, stares at her with more adoration than despair. At the time she found a color copier in town and xeroxed the drawing to make a valentine card for her boyfriend, Troy. These days, if she is handing Troy a paper, it's more likely to be a napkin to wipe his greasy hands after he's been trying to fix the car again, or to wipe their son Brandon's nose. The way Shannon sees it, she has "two babies at home, and I can't decide which of them is more work."

At eleven A.M. on a Wednesday morning, Shannon sees the cigarette smoke under the bedroom door, which means Troy is awake. Brandon, who is now three, has been up for four hours already and is starting to "tornado the house." The three of them share a trailer just off County Road, about a mile from where the town's block of federally subsidized units are hidden. At night, when Brandon's asleep, the trailer feels just big enough, but when he's crammed into one room and it's too hot to go outside and she has to keep him quiet, the place is torture. "Tee-tee, Tee-tee!" he says, because he recognizes the smoke, too. Occasionally he calls Troy "Daddy," but Shannon has tried to put an end to that, because she says he can't be a daddy until he acts like one from "Monday to Sunday, and not just when he feels like it."

Troy is "better than SpongeBob" at making Brandon laugh, and he's good at calming Shannon down when it looks like she's about to give someone a left hook at work. But he's not so good at bringing home a paycheck. In the last month he's worked exactly four days, helping a friend build a patio for a family in Auburn. Otherwise, he's just spending their money on cigarettes and gas. A year ago he landed a job doing maintenance at Walmart, but he quit because, he says, his boss was a bitch who made him "spit and polish the doorknobs like she was some sergeant." Troy cracks the door open so Brandon can come in and jump on him.

Troy is an emotional guy and always spilling his feelings—"like I'm half gay or something," he jokes. He has both "Shannon" and "Brandon" tattooed on his right arm—his version of "till death do us part." He always tells people he's "married," but by this he means that he is, for the moment, tied down to one lady, since he always follows that up with "married—in here" and points to his heart. The two of them have talked a lot about what a great party their wedding would be, and Shannon even went once to pick out a dress—a low-cut, lacy thing not unlike the one she drew for Juliet. But somehow a wedding never happens.

Shannon works a part-time shift at the Walmart so she can go to school and study nursing at the local community college in the late afternoon and evenings. To make the rest of the income they need, she works as an exotic dancer in Birmingham, where she can some-times bring home $250 a night. Troy is not crazy about it because "she's in there with doctors and lawyers who are making more money than me. Who are making *a lot* more money than me." But even he can do the math: Right after Brandon was born, there was a spell when neither of them was working and he had to borrow $10 at a time from his mom, Shannon's sister, and his two best friends to get through the week. For six months they were on welfare—"first one in my family," he says. But $250 times three adds up to a box of diapers and groceries, with money to spare for a few Happy Meals and beer. The only downside is that Shannon is always too busy to do the grocery shopping, which means he has to decipher her handwriting on the shopping list, with no one to ask for help because at the supermarket he sees only "aisles and aisles of dudes."

Most nights when Shannon is dancing he can distract himself by watching a game or having some beers with his buddies in town, but some nights the thoughts go spinning in his head. Troy's favorite expression is "ain't a man," which he uses in several contradictory ways. Sometimes it's a kind of boast—"Ain't a man who wouldn't want my lady, even if he's gay," he will say, and enumerate all the ways in which Shannon is "smokin' hot." Sometimes, though, the expression betrays his own humiliation: "Ain't a man who would take that from his wife," he says, recalling the time when, for three nights straight, Shannon came home at four in the morning, with no explanation. "Ain't a man would do that" refers to night three, when he waited up for Shannon to come home and then choked her until she passed out. "It was my darkest hour," he says. To make it up to her, he bought her a choker with a really big silver heart to cover the bruise.

Troy likes to say they have a "*Jerry Springer* relationship," by which he means they fight a lot, almost always about the same two subjects: sex and work. Troy complains that when they first met they were "doing it three times a day, and now it's like, 'I got a headache, my foot hurts, Brandon was up all night, I had a fight with my mom,'" he says. "I mean, come on, all the ducks have got to be lined up perfectly for it to happen. But it's not like a NASA launch or anything. I mean, we're just having sex!" Shannon complains that Troy never brings home a paycheck. But what really drives her crazy is when he brings home another piece of paper instead, a clipping from the newspaper mentioning this or that little operation opening up in one of the old Russell plant buildings. "Get over it," she yells, because she knows he is living in his father's memory of the great days of Russell, when they made jerseys for Bo Jackson or "The Refrigerator" Perry. "Troy. Seriously. Get over it." She says it the way you would say it to someone still feeling a phantom limb.

Shannon is especially impatient with this line of wishful thinking at the moment because she is pregnant, although she hasn't even told her mom yet and she's not showing. She is sure it's a girl; she wrote that in her journal, along with a name (Eliza) and a future she has spelled out in handwriting not all that changed from high school, where on the day Eliza herself graduates from Benjamin Russell High School, she finds out that she got into college—Auburn University, to be exact—and Eliza's father (who in the story goes by the name Thomas, not Troy, for some reason) is the last one in the house to see the acceptance letter because he's late coming home from work.

A KID GROWING UP in Alexander City, especially the kind of kid who wants nothing to do with hot, noisy plants and textiles and who wants another kind of life he or she might have seen on TV, dreams of going to Auburn, about a forty-five-minute drive southeast on 280. This is the way it's always been, even before Russell closed, because in the limited geography of a teenager's mind, Auburn is the closest place with a real movie theater and a mall. It has the university with a football team and kids from all over the world and a Gap on the main street off campus, and the way the kids talk about it makes it sound practically as exotic and glamorous as New York. All the top students at Benjamin Russell High School head there after gradua-tion. Connie's daughter, Abby, had enrolled in community college to save money and planned to transfer there in a year.

Across eastern Alabama, Auburn is considered the one city that got it right, that avoided the pitfalls of the rest of the region, a place that carefully engineered its future so it would survive in the modern economy. All the surrounding counties have had unemployment rates in the double digits during the recession, and one had spiked as high as 19.3 percent. But Lee County, which contains Auburn and its sister city, Opelika, has weathered the recession and now has a modest unemployment rate of 8.1 percent, close to the national average.

What makes Auburn different? Part of the answer is obvious: The city has a thriving university, which has anchored its economy for more than a hundred and fifty years. But the full answer is surprising—as surprising to the leaders of Auburn as it was to me, because it so thoroughly disrupts this Southern city's sense of itself. Auburn has become the region's one economic powerhouse by turning itself into a town dominated by women.

In 2010, market researcher James Chung stumbled on a data set that seemed to illuminate a whole new future America. He looked at two thousand metropolitan regions in the United States, covering 91 percent of the population. In 1,997 of them, the young women had a median income higher than the young men. This held true in big cities and smaller ones, richer and poorer. Chung's findings made the cover of *Time* magazine, with Chung becoming an oracle for a fast-approaching gender upheaval. "These women haven't just caught up with the guys," he said. "In many cities they're clocking them. We've known for a long time that women are graduating at higher rates than men, and the question was: Did that translate into greater economic power? Now we have our answer. This generation of women has adapted to the fundamental restructuring of the economy better than their male peers."

In spring of 2011, I called Chung again and asked him if any of the regions stood out as having a particularly large disparity. "Yes," he said. "Someplace called Auburn-Opelika." Auburn-Opawhat? Yup, it turns out that the median income of young, single, childless women there is estimated at 129 percent of the median income of similar men, and has reached 140 percent some years. This fact was hard to wrap my mind around. After all these years, we have located our feminist paradise in a small college town in the deep South, a place where the ratio of churches to people is still about one to twelve, and where the football team still makes the front of the local paper three days out of seven.

What does the modern-day Herland look like? It's a town with much of the old Southern charm and very little of the old racist, sexist legacy. It has enough stately mansions lining the main streets to signal prosperity, and enough untamed wildness not to tip over into suburban. A herd of cattle graze near the latest research park. The town was on *U.S. News & World Report*'s 2009 list of top ten places in the United States to live. The week I visited there were ribbon cuttings scheduled for a knitting store, a fitness center, a Weight Watchers, a women's clothing boutique, a place called Paris Bakery Garden, and a Publix ("where shopping is a pleasure"), a grocery chain that bills itself as a regional competitor to Whole Foods. The local Chevy dealership tried to tempt people to a weekend sale with the promise of freshly baked chocolate chip cookies. (What man would fall for that?) More important, Auburn was a perfect reflection of the modern, feminized economy: a combination of university, service, and government jobs, with a small share in manufacturing.

The typical Auburn woman is someone like Meghan McGowen, who works in the city's female-dominated economic development department. McGowen was a leader in her sorority in college and took a tour of schools to decide on business school. She chose Auburn because she could walk to campus, and there was no crime. When she graduated she had offers from the top two accounting firms to work in Los Angeles, where she is from. But she turned them down to work here, because it's a "better place to live." She makes less money, but her standard of living is higher and the schools are amazing. Her three best girlfriends are a consultant, a lawyer, and an engineer, and they have all worked out deals where they can work remotely. They love this place, but they will never be homegrown Southern belles; they could be from anywhere; they are part of the army of upwardly mobile women in search of a good job and a better life, wherever they happen to find it.

Does any place still belong to the men? The manufacturing plants at least? I paid a visit to Briggs & Stratton, a plant that produces generators and small engines for lawn mowers and snowblowers. The factory is only a few miles away from where *Norma Rae* was filmed, the movie that won Sally Field her memorable Academy Award for her portrayal of a union organizer in a textile factory. It's not far from the workplace of Lilly Ledbetter, for whom an equal pay law is named. But the view from the ground gave an impression of a world Norma Rae could only have dreamed of.

I expected to find the last bastion of male dominance, where men with their sleeves rolled up barked orders over the loud machines. Instead I learned that the rules of the new women's world held true even on the factory floor. Once rising up through the ranks meant getting in good with the plant manager. But managers are no longer called simply "managers" here; they are, in the lingo of the new feminized workplace, "team facilitators" and "coaches." "I want them to think of themselves more as a mentor, where their job is to motivate the people on their team," explains Cisco King, who is the plant's human resources manager.

A few years ago King contracted with the local community college to hold classes at the plant from three to five P.M., right after the shift. Instructors come in to teach electrical power or electrical applications or some other aspect of plant operations. "The people who do well here are the ones who are motivated to take advantage of these educational opportunities," he explained. "They don't just ask me about classes when there happens to be a position open," he went on. "They take the classes whenever they are offered. This shows me they want to position themselves to move ahead of the pack." Those people tend to be mostly women. Women like Monica Hodge, mother of two, who took a class on electrical applications because, as she explains, "I want to rise up one day." Recently, the employee population tipped to 55 percent women, King told me.

AUBURN'S SUCCESS SUGGESTS something hopeful but also disorienting. For the towns around it that are still struggling, Auburn offers a model of future success that requires not looking backward and yearning for the old manufacturing age to come back, but instead embracing what has already begun to happen, turning themselves over fully to the new feminized economy.

And what about the men? How do they fit in to that kind of economy? In the last year or so manufacturing jobs around the country have bounced back and the men have been rushing to fill them. But this will only make up for a small percentage of the recently unemployed. Local community colleges have started to get very creative about how they prepare men for the new economy. In Opelika, the college is using 3-D simulation technology that feels like living inside a video game in order to keep the interest of the young men. The sign over the simulation lab does not say "use your hands" but "expand your mind." Other colleges have begun to specialize in green technology or other fields of the future. And some at Opelika have started to run close studies on ways to make men feel less out of place in school and to set up a support system for them.

Success in the future will also involve some easing off on the old codes of manliness, which won't come naturally to men in the South. But even in Alabama I could see that if only out of sheer necessity men were beginning to settle into new roles—picking up kids from school while their wives were at work—and enjoying it, even if they were not quite ready to admit it. Rob Pridgen spent long afternoons teaching his son how to ride a motorbike, and you could tell it was some solace.

Shannon, for one, has tried at least to tackle the first step: banish denial that the world is just going to revert to the way it was. One day Shannon does not wait for Troy's smoke signal but marches into the bedroom at ten A.M. and pulls him out of bed. "Come on," she yells, "move it," and lights the first cigarette of the day for him, to speed up the process. Downstairs, she puts Brandon in the backseat of the car, gets in the passenger seat, and without telling Troy exactly where they are going, directs him to the old plant. They have driven by the place hundreds of times but never stopped to really look and listen. At first Troy stops at every stop sign along the circular roads connecting the various buildings, but then he realizes no one is here, and so he zooms through the stop signs like he's playing Need for Speed, his favorite arcade game.

From inside, the place looks like an abandoned village, with solid brick buildings connected by a small winding road. Plants these days are generic white boxes that could just as easily hold a Walmart as a Kia plant, but this factory has the feeling of a pioneer village from an earlier century. Right near the entrance to the complex is the Russell Afternoon Center for Creative Learning, which features a big painting of a circle of children holding hands, the universal symbol of peace and hope for the future. Brandon wants to stop at the playground, but the slides are covered in rust and the swings have long been pulled off.

Shannon makes Troy pull onto a patch of gravel overlooking a wide field, and they get out of the car. There are giant furnaces and generators around, but they are all idle. The loudest noise is the birds, some of whom have made nests among the signs and discarded shovels. Troy lights a cigarette and doesn't say a word for a while. In the field is a truck trailer sunk into the earth. On its side is an enormous painting of a football player in full uniform running with the ball tucked in his hands, next to the words RUSSELL. THE EXPERIENCE SHOWS. The player is seconds from a touchdown, with no one on his tail. But over the years the tires have rooted themselves in the mud, and the picture has faded into a dull lavender, like an old snapshot from a small town boy's high school glory years. Troy notices the picture at the same time Brandon does. It's depressing, really, this big trailer stuck in the dirt, this mockery of imminent victory. But Troy doesn't register that emotion. In a quick movement he adopts the stance of the player, yells *"Hike!"* in a loud voice that makes Shannon jump, throws his pack of cigarettes at her, and then tackles her onto the grass, where both of them fall, for the moment, laughing.

PHARM GIRLS

HOW WOMEN REMADE
THE ECONOMY

Hannah Cooper's house contains only one visible clue that Billy, her boyfriend of eleven years, lives here, too: a quartet of walleyes, once wild spawn of a Wisconsin lake and now mounted over the dining room table with their mouths shellacked into a permanent gape. ("I said okay, we can put them up, but only on one wall.") Otherwise, Billy's things are hidden away in rooms where Hannah is pretty sure visitors won't see them. His beer posters and fishing equipment are laid out on the pool table in an unheated room off the garage. His hunting jackets and guns are in the basement, sharing space with several pairs of snowboarding boots ("Boy toys," she says coolly). At the foot of the basement stairs sit two dozen or so buckets of paint in standard colors—white, basic white, eggshell—which he needs for his day job as a housepainter, and special rollers idle over the basement sink.

The rest of the house is a testimony to Hannah's persistent attempts to swim upstream, away from her roots. A plush red sectional couch dominates the living room—she saved up the $3,000 it cost after seeing it in an interior design magazine because it looked to her "like New York." Most days after school she sits on it and studies for her pharmacy school exams, playing the Classical Masterpieces music channel on the TV. "I read somewhere that classical music activates parts of your brain you don't really use." When Billy comes home she retreats to her study, which she asked him to paint a particular shade of sage. There, Hannah has built a fortress of self-improvement: neat stacks of her school textbooks and scientific papers and books from the library she wants to read (*The Story of Edgar Sawtelle*) and books she thinks she ought to have read (Jane Austen, George Orwell) and books for future projects (about gardening and organic food). Above her desk in a gilded frame hangs her acceptance letter to pharmacy school, a reminder of the singular achievement that changed her life. Near it hangs her life motto, printed in a romantic font on a small piece of paper: "I Believe that our background and circumstances may have influenced who we are but we are responsible for whom we become."

I met Hannah in the winter of 2011 when I visited the University of Wisconsin pharmacy school in Madison, one of the nation's top ten pharmacy schools, with a freshman class that is 62 percent women. Pharmacy is one of the many middle-class professions that have lately come to be dominated by women, and I wanted to see what this new generation of hungry female professionals was like. Hannah stood out at the pharmacotherapy lab I sat in on, where all the instructors and a majority of the students were women. The instructor was verbally testing the students on various chemotherapy drugs, and Hannah, with less arrogance than a sense of duty, immediately pointed out a mistake on one of the already approved answers—a mistake, the instructor pointed out, which would have led to a fatal dosage.

Like many of the women I met in the course of researching this book, Hannah did not see herself as a feminist trailblazer or a woman at the forefront of anything. She just saw herself as someone who noticed a bridge one day and crossed over it. More than anything, women like Hannah remind me of immigrants like my parents: They seem propelled by a demonic, mysterious force to keep moving forward even though they are nervous about what is ahead, and by moving forward together they permanently transformed the country. Hannah seemed determined and unstoppable and tried not to think too much about what would happen as all the women she knew kept swimming upstream and the men got caught in the eddies; when the men became the equivalent of the family left behind in the Old Country, beloved maybe, but inert and frustratingly stuck in the past.

Hannah now wears her hair in a wavy red bob. Her old eyebrow piercing is barely visible and her lower back tattoo is well hidden under the "business attire" the school requires the students to wear under their lab coats. But even without the lab coat, Hannah is barely recognizable to her old friends. One evening when I came back to visit, we ate dinner at the Caddy Shack, a bar Hannah's mother owns in a nearby town. The bartender is an old schoolmate of Billy's, and it took him a minute to figure out she was Billy's girlfriend and to remember that she was in pharmacy school. "I know a girl who went there," he offered. "And now she's making in the six figures." Hannah just smiled, clearly not wanting to discuss money in a crowded bar. "Me, I prefer the homegrown kind of medication," he added. "Ginger brandy."

Hannah and Billy met in high school and partied their way through their twenties, smoking pot, going to raves, working minimum-wage jobs. Since then, both have mellowed, but in different directions. Billy learned how to paint houses from an ex-girlfriend's father

over a decade ago, and he is still doing that, although much less frequently now that jobs are drying up. After work, or if there is no
work, he fishes with his buddies. *"Every single day,"* says Hannah.
"He just doesn't want anything more." If his life is a straight line
with dips representing spells of unemployment over the last couple
of years, Hannah's is a steady climb up. Hannah is calm and reserved
and something of a homebody, but she has an internal drive that's
exhausting.

It started to take off for her one day when she was working as a
technician at a pharmacy company, hourly work that requires minimal training and is basically a fancy title for "packer." Hannah was
shelving the drugs when an older woman who was a pharmacist came
in to ask her a question.

"Where's the Trileptal?" the woman asked.

"Oh, it's under the oxcarbazepines," Hannah answered, using the
generic term for the type of drug. "And she just turned around and
looked at me, astonished."

"You should go to pharmacy school," the woman said.

"Why, just because I memorized all the generics?" But pretty
soon that hesitation turned into: "I need to get back to school. *I just
have to.*" She got her college degree and then got accepted to the
University of Wisconsin. In her last set of exams, she got all A's and
made the dean's list.

This winter she chose to skip the pharmacy students' annual
charity ball rather than take Billy because "he'd be completely out of
place. People are so much more educated, and he would feel like he
couldn't fit in. I would be embarrassed for him. I know who he is,
and I love him for it. But he'd be uncomfortable." Why does she stay
with him? "Because we crack each other up," she says. Her mom
worries that she does it for the same reason she takes out those

eight-hundred-page novels about India from the library: because she is attracted to suffering.

IN 2009, for the first time in American history, the balance of the workforce tipped toward women, who continue to hover around 50 percent. About 80 percent of women aged twenty-five to fifty-four years old work for pay, and an even higher percentage of female college graduates do. According to the Bureau of Labor Statistics, as of 2011, women hold 51.4 percent of managerial and professional jobs— up from 26.1 percent in 1980. They make up 61.3 percent of all accountants and hold about half of all banking and insurance jobs. About a third of America's physicians are now women, as are 45 percent of associates in law firms—and both those percentages are rising fast as women come to dominate law and medical schools. In the UK, women are poised to outnumber their male counterparts by 2017, prompting a national debate about whether medicine is becoming "overfeminized." In France, women make up 58 percent of doctors under age thirty-five, and in Spain, it's 64 percent.

At some point in the last forty years, the job market became largely indifferent to size and strength, and from then on, in many pockets of the workforce, men no longer held the cards. Technology began to work against men, making certain brawn jobs obsolete and making what economists call "people skills" ever more valuable. The coveted and lasting professions were the ones that required a boutique skill or a nurturing touch—things a robot could not easily do. Traditionally feminine attributes, like empathy, patience, and communal problem-solving, began to replace the top-down autocratic model of leadership and success. For the first time in history, the global economy is becoming a place where women are finding more success than men.

Upper-class women leave home and enter the workforce, filling the ever-growing ranks of the creative class—publicity assistant, wine critic, trail mix creator, sustainability consultant, screenwriter. And that, in turn, creates an industry of jobs based on the things those women used to do for free—child care, food preparation, elder care. The booming health-care industry provides jobs all along that chain, from gastroenterologist to home health aide. Right in the middle falls pharmacist.

Of the many surprising professions that women have started to dominate over the last forty or so years—accounting, financial management, optometry, dermatology, medical genetics, forensic pathology, law, veterinary practice, among hundreds of others—pharmacy stands out as a unique example. Women made up about 8 percent of pharmacists in 1960, and they make up almost 60 percent today. In the earliest days pharmacists had the aura of shamans; they were men of great stature, magicians deft at mixing potions far too dangerous for women to touch. Think of Monsieur Homais, the pompous apothecary in Gustave Flaubert's 1857 novel *Madame Bovary* who, in the final sentence of the novel, wins the Legion of Honor, and think of what happens when Emma Bovary breaks into his lab and steals some arsenic. Now in Hannah's class it's mostly women who handle bags of bright red concoctions labeled "hazardous" and women who win all the prizes. Well over 60 percent of pharmacy graduates are women, and male pharmacists are retiring at a faster rate than women. This has caused a pharmacy magazine to ask in a recent editorial the obvious question: "Is Pharmacy Becoming a Woman's Profession?"

Historically that phrase—"woman's profession"—would be a big wet blanket to any respectable trade. Wages would drop, men would flee, and all the prestige would drain out of the job. This is what happened over the years to the job of secretary, for example, or teacher.

Columbia University labor historian Alice Kessler-Harris has dubbed this the typewriter paradox: Women master a machine or a set of skills that opens up job opportunities for them, and then that job becomes immediately devalued. Harvard economist Claudia Goldin uses a different term for the entry of women into a trade: pollution. The flooding of women into a trade landed like the gentle falling of acid rain, or nuclear waste. Men feared it, and when they saw it coming they did anything they could to put up a protective shield. If that failed, they put on their gas masks and fled to a different office. In 1937, just as pictures of women in white lab coats started popping up in pharmacy magazines, the editor of the *American Journal of Pharmaceutical Education* wrote a satirical op-ed referring to President Roosevelt's "girl control" measures and the "Committee on the Study of Menace of Women to Pharmacy."

But these days the story ends differently. Pharmacy, as a profession subservient to doctors, was always nervous about prestige. So its leaders made sure to stay one step ahead of the game. They did everything they could to make sure they could not be easily replaced by pill-dispensing robots or factory workers in India. They began to call themselves "health professionals," who were at the "forefront of patient care." They instituted a mandatory six-year professional degree, which included training in advising patients and managing complicated medicine regimens. Hannah and all her classmates take a "communications" class where they are graded on their ability to show empathy and get through even to ornery patients. "We get graded on people skills," Hannah says about her upcoming residency, and then "the drug knowledge is important, too."

As a profession, pharmacy put itself on the right side of history. It sidestepped a future in manual labor and moved itself into the more feminine-friendly service and information economy, where higher degrees are always required and technology does not make your job obsolete; instead it frees you to shake hands and smile. Pharmacy followed the script for success in the modern economy. And in that script, the flood of women into the profession is no longer a sign of pollution, but the assurance of a bright, happy future.

Pharmacy—the woman's profession—now has an average salary of somewhere around $110,000, a secure future, and the promise of a reasonably balanced life. In job lists it often appears on the "best" side of the ledger with statistician, accountant, paralegal—all jobs considered clean, safe, and growing, and all jobs where women are thriving. On the opposite side are roofer, welder, lumberjack, sheet metal worker, and roustabout, all jobs dominated by men. It may be happening slowly and unevenly, but it's unmistakably happening: In the long view, the modern economy is becoming a place where women are making the rules and men are playing catch-up.

The girls come to pharmacy school for the same reason girls went to clerical schools in the 1920s and 1930s: They want a respectable profession where they won't get their hands dirty. ("I love science, but I faint at the sight of blood," one of Hannah's classmates told me.) They want some financial independence and a better life than their mothers had. At the University of Wisconsin, 35 percent of the students are the first ones to graduate college in their families. But unlike the dewy secretaries, they are not immediately disappointed upon graduation. Una Golden, the heroine of Sinclair Lewis's *The Job*, the first in his trilogy about the new woman and office life, is delighted by secretary school but at the office finds only "loveless routine," and young men who are "very slangy and pipe smelly" and press her to do endless tedious tasks.

But pharmacy school—like the many professional schools women are flooding—is no empty promise. A group of three roommates I'd met had all gotten one another jobs at the Walgreens, and spent fifteen minutes listing what they loved about it: the computer that scanned the medication instantly and gave you an "amazingly fast visual" of the drugs; their boss, a forty-year-old woman with two kids who works four days a week; the racks of neatly organized little white bottles "as clean as Justin Bieber's teeth." The day the third got her job offer—purely on the recommendation of her friends, and without an interview—they started what they secretly call the "109 Club," named for the salary they expect to earn within a few years. The plan is that every October ninth they will meet at a certain bar on State Street, no matter what else is going on—exams, kids, emergencies, football games. And the husbands? "They'll fall into line," one said.

Early one morning I watched the three roommates leave their apartment for school dressed in ruffled blouses and three-inch heels under their lab coats. They were the cultural heiresses of Mary Tyler Moore and Murphy Brown and all the single career ladies in silk blouses who had made their way in a man's world, rolling their eyes at their gruff, white-haired bosses, hoping that they're "gonna make it after all!" as the theme music said. But several decades later they are no longer tentatively feeling their way through new terrain. Instead they are ruling a global economy turned upside down, where the women work the hardest and there is a casual assumption that they will get all the best jobs after graduation, where the men are somewhat pitied and misunderstood and in need of special assistance— where late one night, one of the roommates shared her fantasy future in which, in a perfect reversal of the happy housewife, "as soon as he hears me come in from work, he rushes to greet me with flowers and a freshly baked cookie!"

Economic upheaval like this seeps into the culture. It can warp dreams and aspirations and make young people believe that even their intimate lives will take place on fantastically strange new terrain. That morning, as the roommates were putting on makeup, someone's computer was playing "Hey, Soul Sister," a favorite song around campus because the girls tease the boys for coming to pharmacy school to get their MR degree and find a good woman to take care of them. In fact, in the time I spent with the students I came across several songs the women here sang in reverse—"I ain't saying he's a gold digger," and "boys just wanna have fun," while the girls just wanna fill out fifteen different job applications and fret about mortgages they don't even have yet.

Jeanine Mount is the associate dean for academic affairs and only the second woman tenured at the school. She comes from a different generation and sacrificed a lot for her position. Her husband has a job in Silver Spring, Maryland; they've lived in different states and commuted for the twenty years of their marriage. These days she marvels at what she calls the "fluidity" of the female students, and "their amazingly wide constellation of choices."

"All my top academic students, my really top performers, have heavily been women," she says. "I don't know why. They are not inherently more intelligent than the men. Maybe they bring a different kind of focus to their work." The men, meanwhile, she calls a "lost generation." They come because their fathers were pharmacists, or maybe they're searching for a second career. But they don't have the same "hunger."

Recently she helped interview applicants to head the diversity program. She asked one applicant what diversity means, and the question elicited a standard response that alluded to gender and disability and sexual orientation. So she asked a follow-up: "If you look at pharmacy right now, isn't the most underrepresented group men?"

The applicant was unconvinced, and explained that men had been in a privileged position all their lives—a sure sign for Mount that the applicant had been locked in academic ideology too long and was missing the obvious facts on the ground.

"I thought, 'This person just doesn't get it,'" she said. "He just doesn't get how bad it's gotten." Recently she printed out photos of the various student groups—school government, campus fraternities, national service organizations—for a newsletter she had to write. It was the first time she noticed that the entire leadership of nearly every group was made up of women. "I can think of one young man in leadership," she said, and named him. "But come to think of it, he's a little androgynous. And his fiancée has a really strong personality. In fact, a lot of guys here are in that situation. . . ."

A COUPLE OF YEARS AGO Hannah's boyfriend, Billy, started to notice he didn't always have painting jobs lined up a month in advance, but this year was "the worst I've seen in eleven years," he says. Sometimes his boss will send out two guys on a painting job meant for one so they can split the pay. A few months of this year Billy has had to apply for unemployment. Hannah suspects that the boys are happier during those months because they can set out for the lake earlier. His fishing buddies—an electrician and two plumbers—are also underworked this year. But everyone knows that they are happy only so long as the checks last. Unemployment pays less than half of what Billy usually makes, but more important, it runs out after two years. Hannah's father, who is also an electrician, is reaching the deadline, and you can see it. His usual garrulousness has sharpened into a manic pitch, and he's talking about schemes that Hannah knows will never happen. Recently he was rejected for a shift job in a local

factory that makes plastic tarps for truck beds—a job she remembers
him scoffing at when she was a kid.

Of the thirty professions projected to add the most jobs over the
next decade, women dominate twenty, including nursing, accounting, home health assistance, child care, and food preparation. (They
dominate twelve of the fifteen projected to add the absolute most jobs.)
Many of the new jobs in the working class, says Heather Boushey of
the Center for American Progress, "replace the things that women
used to do in the home for free." Some of the jobs are not especially
high-paying, but the steady accumulation of these jobs adds up to an
economy that, for the working class, has become more amenable to
women than to men. When we look back on this period, argues Jamie
Ladge, a business professor at Northeastern University, we will see it
as a "turning point for women in the workforce."

The list of working-class jobs predicted to grow is heavy on nurturing professions, in which women, ironically, seem to benefit from
old stereotypes and habits. Theoretically, there is no reason men
should not be qualified. But they have proved remarkably unable to
adapt. Over the course of the past century, feminism has pushed
women to do things once considered against their nature—first
enter the workforce as singles, then continue to work while married,
then work even with small children at home. Many professions have
gone the way of the pharmacist, starting out as the province of men
and now filled mostly with women. Yet I'm not aware of any that
have gone the opposite way. Nursing schools have tried hard to
recruit men in the past few years, with minimal success. Teaching
schools, eager to recruit male role models, are having a similarly
hard time. The habits of Cardboard Man die hard. The range of
acceptable masculine roles has changed comparatively little, and has
perhaps even narrowed as men, operating under the outdated pollu-

tion rules, still shy away from some careers as women begin to dominate them.

Most economists agree that wages for a full-time male worker have stagnated. In 2009, men brought home $48,000 on average, roughly the same as they did in 1969 after adjusting for inflation. In fact, as a recent report written by former White House economist Michael Greenstone discovered, the truth is even more dismal. Calling it stagnation fails to take into account the fact that fewer men are working full-time now or making any salary at all, and many more are incarcerated. If you add in those factors, the median income for men ages twenty-five to sixty-four has not only stagnated, but fallen sharply by almost $13,000 since 1969—a reduction of 28 percent.

The most obvious pattern in the economy over the last forty years is the polarization into low-skill and high-skill jobs, with the middle class getting squeezed out. But this polarization has affected men and women very differently, as MIT economist David Autor shows in a 2010 report. Men and women both dropped out of the middle class, but women moved dramatically into high-skills professions, while men drifted in both directions. Two of the causes Autor names for the gender disparity are fairly easy to grasp and familiar: "automation of routine work" and "the international integration of labor markets." But the last is more perplexing: The demand for college-educated labor—what he calls "literate, numerate, and analytically capable workers"—has been rising for decades. "The economy has been standing at the top of the highest mountain, using its biggest loudspeaker, shouting, 'Get a college degree! If you get a degree we will give you a shitload of money,'" says Greenstone. "It's been doing that for twenty-five years. And yet men are failing to get the message." Why are men failing to get the message? It's a "deeper mystery," Autor writes.

It's a mystery that Hannah's mom, Dian, thinks she has figured out. She's hired plenty of guys behind the bar who won't go to college. She married one (Hannah's father) and now she lives with another. "Lazy," she calls them. "They don't like to think too hard." This experience has made her intent on pointing out to Hannah the practical problems with this upside-down life her daughter is getting herself into. "How's he gonna hold up his half of the mortgage if you're making, what, three times as much money as him?" she asks Hannah one afternoon. But Hannah is sticking to her vision. She wants a house by Lake Wisconsin with a path lined by ferns and hostas. She'll pay the mortgage, he can cover utilities. Already she keeps a whiteboard where she writes down every week who is responsible for what bill and everything Billy owes her. "He has no opinion at all. He wants me to tell him what to do."

But as women have known for a long time, that kind of domestic hierarchy starts to grate after a while, even on the most gentle of spouses. One night Hannah was watching a documentary about Cleopatra on the HISTORY channel. When she got up to check on a homework assignment, Billy changed it to Comedy Central to watch *Tosh.0*, a lad comedy show where Tosh does hilarious recaps of bad movies out on DVD, or uses giant swords to slice things open— his lunch sandwich, a coffeemaker, a watercooler. Billy is compact in size and also in his speech; he never uses words when silence is acceptable. And at the end of a long day, whether spent working or fishing, he likes what he likes.

"Oh, that's real educational," she said when she came back from her study.

"Why would you need to know about Cleopatra?" he snapped back.

"He gets defensive, like I'm insinuating he's stupid. I know he's not stupid. He's just not as educated as I am," she told me later. "But sometimes I feel like because I spend all these years going to school, I should be shown a certain amount of respect. I did all this, so he should respect it."

A CENTURY AGO pill-making required considerable physical labor and detailed handiwork. A pharmacist and his apprentice would have to haul fifty-pound bags of compounds, grind noxious substances in a giant mortar and pestle, and then carefully roll each pill using just the right pressure. The shaman factor for pharmacists came from mixing ingredients at the front counter, dazzling patients with a miniature magic show that ended with a personally tailored spell in the form of a pill. Magazines from that era are filled with letters from groupies, writing in for the "scientific secrets" of various potions and even the secret formula for various sodas—the other mainstay of the local pharmacy.

Then at the start of the twentieth century, just as Remington typewriters were infiltrating the market, pharmacists began to covet a piece of machinery manufactured by the Arthur Colton Company in Detroit, Michigan. Every year the moss green–covered catalogs arrived, boasting the latest offerings: Automatic Pill Making Machine No. 2 Complete, an amazing Willy Wonka contraption with twelve rotary wheels turning in all different directions, or a pill-coating machine loaded with tubes and dipping plates, or the company's gem, the rotary tablet machine that resembles a modern-day she-bot, with four elegant legs and rotary wheels for eyes and two funnels upraised like proud pom-poms. The machine, the catalog promised, is "practically noisless [*sic*], and pours out a continuous stream of tablets at the rate of 325 per minute."

The machines promised considerable ease for pharmacists, but like all machines, they also stole some of the mystique. As novelist Sherwood Anderson would write in his bizarre 1931 tract, *Perhaps Women*, "The machines make me feel too small. . . . My manhood can not stand up against them yet. They do things too well. They do too much." Men in the profession became nervous about the specter of women pharmacists, although at the time there were relatively few. In the pharmacy magazines, male writers insisted that women could still not carry heavy bags of equipment over to the machines, and that they could never answer the night bell—a traditional duty of pharmacists' apprentices, who would sleep in the shop. Rumors began to recirculate about Civil War–era wives who had used rat poison mixed with butter to poison their disabled husbands—proof that women could not be trusted with chemicals. The magazine *Pharmaceutical Era* began running a series of fables in which one recurring character was a lady drug addict who kept coming into the shop begging for refills.

Here and there a few writers defended the profession as suitable for women, drawing on the mythology of Florence Nightingale as a saving angel and mother saint with an uncanny gift for organization. An 1893 article discussing the prospect of the "new woman druggist" argued that prescriptions should not be filled by machines but rather by a "fresh complexioned young girl with delicate touch, glad eyes and gold braids of hair [that] has prepared them, and gives them to you with a bright glance, and a modest smile and a something about her manner which means that she is a business woman as well." Around the same time, the *Druggists' Bulletin* (1887) ran this love-struck and utterly condescending poem to the "girl pharmacist," advertising her as the perfect wife:

Like sparkles of morning sunbeams,
All sweet with the flowers they kiss,
Comes the gentle evangel of brightness,
The "Registered" girl Pharmacist . . .
Make room all you bachelor chemists,
Make room for this queen on your list
And crown her with all the attributes,
A "Registered" girl Pharmacist.

But in the Louisville College of Pharmacy for Women, started in 1883 because the regular college would not admit women, the first commencement speaker opened the graduates' eyes to a less romantic reality: "You have chosen to align yourselves with man. You have become his competitor for bread, his rival in work. Look for no other treatment than he gives his fellows." Feminists began to take it up as a cause: "We [will not accept] the weakling cry of individuals affrighted for the safety of their own unstable positions who entreat that woman be kept out of the professions of pharmacy lest she cheapen it," wrote Emma Gary Wallace. "No! A thousand times. No!"

In the twenties, "girls" started to flood white-collar jobs. Just as they do today, they graduated high schools at higher rates than boys, and then went on to clerical schools. The aim was to get hired in white-collar jobs, which were described in the same terms Hannah and her friends describe pharmacy work: "clean, pleasant, respectable." A woman could bring shame on her family by working in a factory; the enterprise had an air of danger and desperation. But as a secretary in one of the burgeoning new mechanized offices of America, she could brag about her career.

Before that era, secretaries had been of the Dickensian variety:

gentlemen in black frocks and green shades who added columns of numbers in their heads. They were not functionaries but guardians of their firms' treasured secrets, and apprentices to the boss. They could hope to rise quickly and even one day succeed him. Pamphlets for the new career woman at the time reminded her hopefully that "clerk" derives from the word "cleric."

But once the secretary became female, she had no such hallowed role. In the rapidly expanding economy, she was a stenographer at the insurance firm or a PBX operator at the oil company or a switchboard operator at the bank. But she would never rise beyond that. In a 1939 survey of firms in five states, companies reported that certain jobs were set aside exclusively for women and certain jobs for men, who "would be dissatisfied" if they had "no chance for advancement," as one firm wrote, explaining why men could not be stenographers. Jobs, economist Claudia Goldin explains, essentially acquired "secondary sex characteristics." And even for college girls, says Goldin, a job interview centered on one question: Can you type?

A 1939 report on what was known as the "toilet industry," comprising drugs, medicines, toilet waters, and creams, gives an account of the gender breakdown. In the grand new pharmacy manufacturing operations, men did the "highly skilled" and specialized work, processing and mixing raw materials, supervising the "intricate machinery," checking the identity, purity, and strength of each chemical mixture. Women, meanwhile, did what was called "finishing operations": filling containers and labeling. The average salary for men was $27.60; for women, ten dollars less.

The culture was starting to accept the slow entry of women into the profession, but it still exacted a high cost. From 1934 to 1942, the magazine *Drug Topics* ran a weekly cartoon about a pharmacist named Betty Brown. Betty, although charming and attractive, served as a warning to girls who rose above their station. She is first hired by pharmacist Bob Steele as a "fancy goods sales lady" to boost his sales. Eventually she confesses that she is in fact a trained pharmacist herself, and then buys the store from him. After that bit of hubris, she turns into a Dick Tracy heroine who wins the small battles but never the game of life. She triumphs over counterfeiters, hoodlums, and thieves. ("I'll fill her so full of holes she'll look like a fishnet," says one.) But her personal life falls apart. One love interest dies of a heart attack, and she loses another to her plain-looking cousin after she gives the cousin a makeover. "Love is like some prescriptions," she concludes. "If it doesn't cure you, all you get is a bad taste."

After a brief wartime boost, the rise of the girl pharmacist, and the girl professional as a whole, came to an ominous halt as the men returned from war and the women moved back into the kitchen. Pharmacies were in the heyday of the mom-and-pop era. This was before the era of fast-food chains, and the local pharmacy almost always doubled as a soda fountain and lunch counter. People came mostly to eat and hang out, and only occasionally to get medicine. If they worked at all, women were relegated to roles that looked a lot like wife: cooking, serving, helping their husband behind the counter. A new tradition was established among the state pharmacy associations of holding an annual beauty contest to decide on the next Miss Pharmacy, who would grace the covers of the trade magazines: "There's a beauty in Birmingham!" reads the caption under the photo of the comely Margaret Jacks, a fresh-faced teen with natural curls.

In the sixties the rigid domestic facade starts to crack. Suddenly in the photos the girls are wearing the white lab coats normally reserved for men. They are not yet pharmacists, though; they are "cosmeticians," usually engaged in intense conversation with customers about a new glue for press-on nails or home permanents or color charts designed to "scientifically determine a woman's lipstick shade." They stand in front of counter displays described as having "intriguing modern designs" with hundreds of white lipstick tubes tucked into holes like so many bottles of pills. They "beam" one another through intercoms that "relieve them of the embarrassment of not having immediate answers to their patrons' queries." But those white lab coats and the faux scientific authority must have given the women a taste for the real thing. Before long, *Miss* and other women's magazines were running ads claiming that "thousands of pharmacy students in the next ten years will be women!" and inviting YOU to join the herd.

Soon civil rights would make it unacceptable to keep women out of certain colleges, or to reserve certain jobs for unmarried women, or for men. In the seventies women began to flood colleges and professional schools, training to be doctors, lawyers, and businesswomen. With objective measures and explicit credentials, women could easily make the case that they were just as qualified as their male counterparts; after all, they had the exact same knowledge and degrees. By the 1980s women were graduating from college at about the same rate as men; for pharmacy school the tipping point was 1985.

If machines dealt the first blow to work as the exclusive realm of men, office life dealt the second. "Where would a sense of maleness come from for the worker who sat at a desk all day?" historian Elliott Gorn wrote. "Where was virility to be found in increasingly faceless bureaucracies?" Joel Garreau picks up on this phenomenon in his 1991 book, *Edge City*, which explores the rise of suburbs as home to giant swaths of office space along with the usual houses and malls. Companies began moving out of the city in search not only of lower rent but also of the "best educated, most conscientious, most stable workers." They found their brightest prospects among "under-employed females living in middle-class communities on the fringes of the old urban areas." As Garreau chronicles the rise of suburban office parks, he places special emphasis on 1978, the peak year for women entering the workforce. When brawn was off the list of job requirements, women often measured up better than men. They were smart, dutiful, and, as long as employers could make the jobs more convenient for them, more reliable.

Pharmacy, too, was becoming more like office work, with all the same consequences. The mom-and-pops were disappearing and being quickly replaced by national chain stores, which split the old business model. Fast-food chains took over their old lunch-counter business, and a new distinct entity we now know as the pharmacy took over prescriptions, cosmetics, and toiletries. By the 1970s, Walgreens had more than six hundred stores around the country and employed fifteen hundred pharmacists. The image of the pharmacist was no longer an entrepreneur and community leader dishing up fizzy concoctions and cures. A pharmacist was increasingly a salaried employee, and more and more often a woman. As one William S. Apple said at a 1971 gathering of a pharmaceutical group, "Once pharmacy shed the Victorian view that you had to 'own a store' in order to practice the profession," it would unleash "a wave of woman-power into our profession."

The new setup was more practical for women. Owning and running a store was a monumental undertaking that virtually guaranteed working nights and weekends. But a salaried employee could dip in and out of work at various phases of life and work more flexibly. The workforce was headed in this more agile direction anyway. Workplaces were moving away from a priesthood model with a patriarch at the top who demanded lifetime loyalty. Instead workers were becoming more like free agents who could move between jobs with impunity. Women were just ahead of the curve.

But there was another reason why women were critical to the profession: The death of the corner store may have liberated the practice of pharmacy from Victorianism, but it saddled the profession with a new identity crisis, common to many professions. "Robots can count tablets more accurately and at less expense than humans, technicians can compound medications in pharmacies and huge, automated factories can do likewise. Persons without professional education at University are able to sell drugs and to serve as cashiers," explained a manifesto by a leading pharmacist scholar, Albert Wertheimer.

Yet in the near future, there will be a need for a person who understands the overall health-care delivery system, who can serve as a health educator, gatekeeper, referral agent, problem solver and coordinator. . . . The pharmacist of the future will offer the missing hand-holding function now disappearing . . . a person who is able to work on incentives, understanding the principles underlying the health belief model, and who is an empathetic, caring professional.

"Problem solver," "coordinator," "hand-holding," "empathetic, caring professional." This new definition made it clear that in order to survive, the profession would have to feminize. The profession began to refer to itself as "social pharmacy" or "clinical pharmacy." Schools began moving from a four-year bachelor program to a six-year professional degree called a "Pharm D," as women were becoming the majority of graduates from pharmacy school, and their numbers have climbed steadily ever since.

This philosophy happened to dovetail with precisely what was prized in the new economy. Lately economists have tried to measure what are known as "soft skills" or "people skills" and their impact on labor market success. In a 2005 international study called "People People," Bruce Weinberg, Lex Borghans, and Bas ter Weel did a complex analysis of how attributes such as the ability to work with people or patience and motivation became assets in the job market. The team separated jobs where interpersonal skills are important (nurses and salespeople, for example) from jobs where they are less important (machine operators and truck drivers). What they found was that starting in the 1970s, the growing demand for soft-skills jobs corresponds exactly with the rise in women's wages.

Companies no longer wanted to present themselves as faceless arbiters of authority; in an increasingly democratic, multicultural age they wanted to be seen as approachable and consumer responsive. In choosing a logo or an ad campaign, a company did not want to project just the old checklist of attributes: strong and dominant in the market. Now they also wanted to be innovative, dynamic, caring, says advertising expert David Redhill. As time went on, the imperative only got stronger. Now, in the era of self-expression and social media, stone-faced patriarchy is the kiss of death.

The irony is noted: Just as suburban developments are named after the things they destroyed, so it went with the large and ever dominant multinational corporations, who strove to convey the warmth of the mom-and-pop stores they had put out of business. Recent Target ads that ran on city buses showed a series of broadly smiling women of various ethnicities with the tagline, ASK ME ANY-THING ABOUT ANYTHING: TARGET PHARMACISTS ARE YOUR FRIENDLY RESOURCE FOR ALL QUESTIONS FROM ASPIRIN TO ZINC. SWING BY FOR AN IN-STORE CONSULTATION (OR JUST TO SAY HI). Would anyone stop by a Target pharmacy "just to say hi"?

But with pharmacists the transition was not entirely disingenu-ous. In the mom-and-pop era there weren't all that many drugs to distribute. But now there are thousands, and errors in mixing them could be dangerous. As doctors and drug manufacturers came to represent the face of cruel and indifferent corporate medicine, the pharmacist could step in and present herself as the first responder with a friendly face, a modern-day version of a small-town doctor, who knew her pills but also your children's names.

Over time the feminization of pharmacy, and office work, acquired a life of its own. Women took over human resource departments and hired more women. Once they reached critical mass they began to normalize certain workplace demands—working four days a week, say, or leaving early. The more women worked, the more economic power they had, multiplying the effect even further. Soon marketing experts began warning companies that if they had no women in their executive ranks they would never be able to understand the con-sumer of the future and they would be doomed.

In the "People People" study, Weinberg paints a picture of this new innovative workplace as a haven for teamwork and reciprocal altruism. The modern era's new workers, whom he refers to as "car-ing agents," go far beyond giving and receiving instructions; they display a talent for successfully interpreting feelings and ideas. For many men, this new innovative workplace sounds like their girlfriends' book group, or maybe hell.

The 1999 movie *Office Space* was maybe the first to capture how alien and dispiriting this new feminized office park can be for men, and how resistant they are to adapting. Disgusted by their jobs and their boss, Peter and his two friends embezzle money and start sleep-ing through their alarm clocks. At the movie's end, a male coworker burns down the office park, and Peter abandons desk work for a job

in construction. Earlier eras of male anxiety were driven by prema-
ture fears and delusions about the specter of female takeover. But
this time the men had actual, data-driven reasons to worry. Women
were actually coming to dominate the workforce, which threw the
whole corresponding set of male roles into turmoil. A 2002 study of
the pharmacy workforce described the emasculation in more dispas-
sionate terms: "Wage rates for female pharmacists have grown to a
point where it is more beneficial, from a financial standpoint, for a
family to have the female work full-time and the male work part-
time. Gender role reversal may be more common in families where
one spouse is a pharmacist."

What does "gender role reversal" look like for the next generation? After the morning rush of classes I had lunch with a group of
women to talk about their lives. Most grew up in traditional working-
class families around Wisconsin, yet their conceptions of their future
home life were, as the dean of student affairs had described them,
shockingly fluid. They did not assume that they would quit working
once they had children, or even work part-time. They did not even
assume that they would be the main caretaker at all. Being the traditional "mother" was a gender-neutral role that anyone could fulfill.
"You can either stay home or give that role to your spouse, whoever
wants it," said Laura Burt, one of the younger students I spoke with.

Their expected salaries still made them giddy, except when their
greater earning power seemed like a burden. One girl showed me an
IM she'd just sent to her friend, who'd inquired about her dating life.
"They're either intimidated by you (and your salary)," she wrote, "or
they can't afford you." Five of the women had long-term boyfriends
or husbands, who worked, respectively, as a cop, logger, head of a
construction crew, electrician, and caterer. Katie Scarpace, a pretty,
freckled girl whose boyfriend was the police officer, told me, "He

jokes that he'll retire when he's thirty and I start working. He calls me his sugar mama."

Sarah VandenHeuvel is a charismatic character with long dark hair and pointy-toe heels under her lab coat. She had just gotten married the summer before and described her husband, Andrew, to me as "not what anyone would picture as an alpha male." Later in the day, Andrew stopped by to pick her up. He had the air of a Judd Apatow sidekick, tall and lanky with shaggy hair, only he didn't seem to resent the overbearing wife. He liked living in a small town, but when Sarah announced she was moving to Madison, he'd said, "I'll go with you." Now he works as an IT guy at the help desk of a large company, a job he describes as "grunt work" but likes. His philosophy of work? "Get a good job, go to work, do the best you can, and don't overdo it." I asked how he saw his career unfolding, and he said, "Me? I mean, I would still like to work in the future, I think. But with IT I hope I can do freelance work and work at home. It depends what kind of job I get. I think if my job pulls in only the same amount of money we'd have to use to pay for day care, then it wouldn't be worth it. My mom was always there, and that would be nice, to have a parent at home. . . . My friends joke, 'Oh, you'll have to stay home and take care of the kids while Sarah makes all the money,' and I'm like, 'Uh. Yeah. That's the plan.'"

In the first semester of pharmacy school, one of Sarah's professors read her workplace statistics showing that, historically, women pharmacists are more likely to work part-time and, on the whole, work fewer hours than men. "I felt so irritated," she says. "Here I saw women excelling and taking all the leadership roles, and they were talking about it in that same old way, as if women would come in, have babies, and then ruin the profession." In fact, full-time women pharmacists do work, on average, 2.4 hours fewer than men, and more women work part-time.

But Sarah is absolutely right. The old scolding approach to women working fewer hours a week does not make sense anymore. The numbers her professor cited are merely evidence of a profession agile enough to bend to the needs of its best-trained professionals, and prepared for a future where both men and women might be interested in more flexible work at different points in their careers.

WHAT WILL IT TAKE to succeed in the economy of the future? Education will remain essential; the premium a college degree will set on income is likely to remain at an all-time high. Technology will continue to affect jobs—and increasingly high-skills jobs—in unpredictable ways. (Law firms, for example, now use computers to scan documents for discovery, replacing a key source of low-level legal work.) But the sure bets for the future are still jobs that cannot be done by a computer or someone overseas. They are the jobs that require human contact, interpersonal skills, and creativity, and these are all areas where women excel.

Flexibility will increasingly become a magnet for talent. Consider the medical profession, which women are starting to dominate. Goldin has done a close breakdown of medical professions to see why women choose certain ones. It turns out the choice of pediatrics over brain surgery, for example, has less to do with love of children or disgust at slicing open brains than control over time. Gastroenterology is a perfect example. For years this specialty had among the lowest percentage of women. Just 5 percent of gastroenterologists ages fifty-five to sixty-four are women, but among the younger doctors—under thirty-five—it's 30 percent. What happened? Have women developed a sudden love of rectal exams? The answer is controlled, regular hours. The expanded use of routine and scheduled colonoscopies has made it easier for women choosing the field to know they will be able to live manageable lives.

Veterinarians are another example. The profession has lately been effectively taken over by women. Is this because women love animals more than men do? Not really. A vet used to live a life much like that of a corner pharmacist—an entrepreneur with unpredictable hours and night duties. Now, regional vet hospitals have taken over those duties, making ordinary vet work more like salaried office work. Women succeed in jobs where they pay a low "career cost," as Goldin calls it, meaning a penalty for taking time off or otherwise deviating from the standard career path. But this doesn't mean women are compromising their careers. Women are taking advantage of new technologies and innovative workplace restructuring. Their rise is associated, in other words, with the forward-looking workplace of the future.

What were once considered exclusively women's concerns are now becoming the habits of the rising workforce. Surveys of Generation Y reveal them to have almost exactly the same workplace expectations and desires as a forty-year-old working mother: They want flexibility, the option to work remotely, to dip in and out of full-time, and to find their work meaningful, according to a 2009 article in the *Harvard Business Review*. "Why would I want to spend twelve hours a day at an office?" asked one young business major, who was male. "I want a life." And companies eager to attract and retain talented workers and managers are responding. The consulting firm Deloitte, for instance, started what's now considered the model program, called Mass Career Customization, which allows employees to adjust their hours depending on their life stage. The program, Deloitte explains, solves "a complex issue—one that can no longer be classified as a women's issue." Women have written the blueprint for the workplace of the future. The only question left is, will the men really adapt?

At around eight thirty in the evening—twelve hours after he left—Billy gets home from a day of fishing. Hannah and I have been sitting on the couch, talking about her upcoming year of residency and whether she wants to work at an independently owned pharmacy or a chain, when he walks out of the kitchen and shows us his prize catch, a thirty-one-inch northern pike. "Are you dripping?" Hannah asks. "He dripped."

Billy is tired and does not feel like cutting up the fish right now, but Hannah says he has to because it would be "wasteful" not to, and anyway if he leaves it in his truck bed overnight it might stink. Downstairs in the basement, on one of the tables by the sink, Billy gets to work. He has a bucket for the bones and blood and two knives, one to cut through bones and the other for flesh. He's not quite sure how to go at it, though, because he's never caught a northern pike before. "Don't you have a book for that?" Hannah asks, but he ignores her and keeps hacking.

Hannah wants to get away from the whole operation ("It stinks"), but I am curious, since I don't get to see a fish-gutting every day. We watch as he slices open the body cavity to reveal various parts that she guesses could be liver or spleen. "I should get my bio textbook," Hannah offers, and recalls that in school, they used to dissect fish to learn about the central nervous system. She winces when Billy mispronounces "vertebrae" as "vertebrate." "I should go get my biology textbook to see what all this stuff is," she offers again. The fish guts are dominated by tiny yellowish eggs. "They look like grits," he says. "They look like quinoa," she says at the exact same moment.

Earlier that day, Hannah's mother, Dian, had volunteered to me what she called her "defining moment," or the moment she cracked in her marriage. She had been working at the Caddy Shack chopping up vegetables for coleslaw and potato salad. Her husband at the time—Hannah's father—came into the bar. He was going up north on a hunting and fishing trip and he needed some paper plates. Dian asked him if he could get her a bucket of ice from the ice chest, and he answered, "I didn't come here to do your work. I came here to do mine." This was when she was working twelve-hour days, barely seeing her daughter. This was after he had failed to keep up steady work and had used up Hannah's college fund for his truck-pulling hobby. "Something in me snapped," Dian recalled. She had a knife in her hand—chop chop chop—and her thoughts spat out in that staccato rhythm: "Work like a man. Think like a man. Act like a man."

The next week she walked out on her husband and on Hannah, who was a young teenager at the time. She had an affair. She made the bar a great success, and over the years, Hannah forgave her, even admired her. She became "much more than just a bar owner," Hannah says. She funds a few of the local sports teams. She runs the town's annual Fourth of July parade. She's like the unofficial town mayor, and part of its mythology. A gold shoe hangs in the bar from the time a strange and regal woman, blind drunk and curiously dressed up, walked out of a white limousine into the bar. White limousines were as rare around here as palm trees, and a white limousine housing a woman in a long dress seemed like a mirage. They called the woman Cinderella because she was too far gone to give her name. Dian sat with her at the bar and gave her some concoction she had brewed in the back. She stayed with Cinderella until she was coherent. As a thank-you, the woman left her golden shoe, now a reminder of the time Dian played the role of someone like Monsieur Homais, the town leader and mythical healer.

When Billy comes up from the basement, he puts on Comedy Central to see if Tosh is on. He is, but it's an episode they've already seen. Hannah agrees that it's kind of funny. He switches channels, and lands on *Jackass 3D*. Hannah rolls her eyes because, she says, those jackasses do the same exact thing, year after year. "What's wrong with that?" says Billy.

DEGREES
OF DIFFERENCE

THE EDUCATION GAP

In 2009, Gail Heriot, a professor from the University of California, San Diego, came across a chart about college admissions labeled "Girls Need Not Apply." The chart, which had originally appeared in *U.S. News & World Report*, revealed not the old familiar forms of discrimination—women excluded from Ivy League eating clubs or secret societies—but a new variety women had not really encountered before. The chart revealed how much more readily several well-known private colleges all over the country, including Vassar and the University of Richmond, accepted men than women. From the chart it looked as if a vastly greater percentage of female than male applicants was being turned away from these schools, meaning that it was much harder for the average woman to get in than it was for the average man. The implication was that bright female applicants might be turned away in favor of *less qualified* men. In other words, if Heriot was reading the chart correctly,

American private colleges had quietly begun to practice affirmative action . . . for men.

The quotes that follow in the accompanying story seemed to confirm Heriot's suspicion. Men should be given some extra allowance because they "have perspectives to offer that a woman doesn't have," one student suggested. A college counselor advised that they should "emphasize their maleness." If they happened to have a gender-ambiguous name like Alex or Madison, they should not hesitate to send in a picture or brag about sports in order to "catch an admission officer's eye."

Different perspectives to offer. A distinct admissions advantage. Send in a picture. These are the kinds of euphemisms admissions officers have historically offered up to minorities and women. How could it be that affirmative action, an institution set up to break white men's exclusive hold on power, was now the crutch they needed to get by? And at the University of Richmond, no less? And how had it come to pass that women now found themselves in the same spot as the angry white males of the 1990s, frustrated at getting shut out despite their qualifications?

At the time she saw the article, Heriot was a member of the U.S. Commission on Civil Rights, and the apparent gender gap in admissions seemed to her like an appropriate phenomenon for the group to look into. There might be some perfectly innocuous explanation for the discrepancies. Maybe some colleges were getting unusually large numbers of female applicants, or unusually strong male applicants. For years, however, researchers had suspected that private colleges were giving men special treatment. After all, state schools, which by law are not allowed to consider gender in making admissions decisions, were now edging toward 60 percent female. How could it be that so many private colleges kept their classes even?

No one could know for sure what was going on, because private colleges kept their admissions policies a secret. But a systematic analysis that gathered information about SAT scores and GPAs and other relevant credentials, and then compared those to admission rates, would help get to the truth. Heriot wrote up a proposal for the commission's approval, suggesting it might be an "open secret" among private colleges that they let in men over more highly qualified women, and her proposal was accepted.

For private universities, sex discrimination in admissions is perfectly legal; unlike public universities they are not bound by Title IX. But Heriot thought this issue was serious enough that it might be covered by a more general statute against discrimination. And because she seems inclined against affirmative action anyway, she wanted to force the education establishment into a confession so that they could begin to figure out why men weren't succeeding, rather than to continue just shuffling them among institutions.

The commissioners picked nineteen colleges randomly with the aim of covering the basic categories—big, small, religiously affiliated, selective, less selective, and historically African-American. They restricted themselves to the mid-Atlantic states, where they figured they had more clearly defined subpoena power. Over the course of a year, the commissioners collected data from most of the schools, although all were reluctant to provide it, Heriot told me. The most elite schools in the bunch, Johns Hopkins University and Georgetown University, agreed to participate only on condition that they crunch the data on their own, using the group's research protocols.

During that year, I checked in on the commissioners' work periodically. If they were to discover a pattern, I figured it would represent a pretty bracing conceptual shift: Here, in the institution considered the single most important engine of class mobility over the course of the century, men were being treated as the official underdogs. And in the nation's esteemed private universities, which had until recently been the training grounds for the future male elite.

Around April 2011 I checked for the latest update only to discover that news about the commission's work had petered out. I tracked down Heriot to find out what had happened, and I happened to get her at a moment when she was annoyed enough to talk. "It is suspicious, isn't it," was the first thing she said. Apparently, a month earlier, without warning, the commissioners had voted to shut down the investigation. The public reason they gave was "inadequate" data—a very thin reason, Heriot pointed out, because the mound of raw data they had just begun to analyze would have been vastly more revealing than anything else that existed. And already Heriot had seen enough of the data to suspect that "there was evidence of purposeful discrimination, meaning that when admissions officers are making decisions they are taking into account who is male and who is female."

Politics appeared to be behind the abrupt shutdown of the investigation, although not in the way you might reflexively imagine. Between the investigation's start and abrupt end, two of the commissioners who had been appointed during the Bush administration were replaced by two Obama appointees, tipping the group Democratic. Wouldn't progressive Democrats interested in civil rights jump at the chance to prove that a bunch of entitled private institutions were practicing wholesale discrimination against hardworking young women? But acknowledging the larger dynamic that would give rise to such discrimination was a whole other kind of threat. It meant letting go of our attachment to the idea that in certain elite sectors of society, young women were still struggling. It meant admitting that in these realms it was in fact men who needed the help.

This reversal of the power dynamic on American college campuses was staring everyone in the face, but it was too unsettling to the commissioners on the left and probably to those on the right as well. (What Republican would want to acknowledge such vulnerability in men?) But the commissioners were only doing what the rest of the nation has done when faced with these college gender statistics, which is to pretend that they are not meaningful or extraordinary. In fact, women's dominance on college campuses is possibly the strangest and most profound change of the century, even more so because it is unfolding in a similar way pretty much all over the world.

To see the future—of the workforce, the economy, and the culture—you need to spend some time at America's colleges and professional schools, where a quiet revolution is underway. More than ever, college is the gateway to economic success, a necessary precondition for moving into the upper-middle class—and increasingly even into the middle class. It's this broad, striving middle class that defines our society. And it's largely because women dominate colleges that they are taking over the middle class.

Women earn almost 60 percent of all bachelor's degrees—the minimum requirement, in most cases, for an affluent life. Between 1970 and 2008, the percentage of white men ages twenty-five to thirty-four getting college degrees rose only modestly, from 20 percent in 1970 to 26 percent in 2008. Among white women in the same age range, the rate tripled, from 12 to 34 percent. This means that every year tens of thousands more women than men graduate from college. In engineering and science, which taken together are the most common fields of study, women are beginning to crowd out men. Among college graduates sixty-five and over, women make up only 23 percent of those with degrees in science and engineering; among those twenty-five to thirty-nine years old, 45.9 percent are women. "One would think that if men were acting in a rational way, they would be getting the education they need to get along out there," says Tom Mortenson, a senior scholar at the Pell Institute for the Study of Opportunity in Higher Education. "But they are just failing to adapt."

The pattern is moving up into advanced degrees as well. Women now earn 60 percent of master's degrees, about half of all law and medical degrees, and about 44 percent of all business degrees. In 2009, for the first time women earned more PhDs than men, and the rate was starting to accelerate even in male-dominated fields such as math and computer science.

The education gap is widening not just in the United States, but all over the world. Each year the Organization for Economic Cooperation and Development publishes data on college graduation rates in thirty-four industrial democracies. In twenty-seven of those countries, women have more college degrees than men. Norway has the largest difference, at about 18 percent. Australia and most of the European countries hover at about 10 percent. In all of these countries, a college degree is just as important as it is in the United States for getting ahead.

The same is true in less prosperous countries as well, according to a UNESCO report. In Latin America, the Caribbean, Central Asia, and the Arab States—nearly everywhere except Africa—women outnumber men in college. In some surprising countries—Bahrain, Qatar, and Guyana, for example—women make up nearly 70 percent of college graduates. And in several countries women outnumber men in the sciences as well as in the humanities. In Saudi Arabia, for example, women's schooling at all levels was strictly controlled by the Department of Religious Guidance until 2002, when it was moved into the Ministry of Education. By 2006, a host of women's colleges and foreign universities open to Saudi women were established. Now women in Saudi Arabia make up more than half of undergraduates and PhDs.

A college degree is of course not a woman's ticket straight to the top. But the sudden existence of so many well-educated, well-qualified women itching to enter the workforce puts tremendous pressure on the ruling classes. In Asian countries, women who have gone through years of grueling exams and earned top spots at local and foreign universities are no longer content to aim for middle management. In Brazil, 80 percent of college-educated women say they aspire to "top jobs," and nearly 60 percent describe themselves as "very ambitious"— a far higher percentage than in the United States. Nearly a third of Brazilian women now make more money than their husbands.

In Islamic countries, this new cadre of educated women finds so few opportunities after earning degrees that they channel their frustration into protest. Middle East experts suspect that such women have helped to fuel the Arab Spring. In many conservative countries women are delaying marriage, because they are no longer content to shelve their degrees and revert to the old, traditional roles. Among economists, a consensus is forming that unless these developing economies begin to take advantage of the talents and training of all their citizens, their progress will stall.

IN THE MERITOCRATIC United States, college has always been linked to upward mobility and open horizons. Beginning around the 1920s, as many women as men went to college, although most of the women went to teachers colleges, as the economists Claudia Goldin,

Lawrence F. Katz, and Ilyana Kuziemko point out in a 2006 article "The Homecoming of American College Women." In the 1930s, men began pouring into colleges to hide out from the Great Depression. The pattern continued through the next couple of decades, with men gravitating to college in order to take advantage of the G.I. Bill, and later to escape the Vietnam War. By the early 1960s, three men took home a degree for every two women who did so.

College became the place where the men and women of the American elite, and increasingly of the middle class, began to define their roles. Men would stock the rising managerial and professional class, while educated women would uphold American values at home. As Adlai Stevenson told a Smith graduating class of 1955, a housewife's task was to keep a man "truly purposeful, to keep him whole." If the Cold War was a showdown of minds, then "we will defeat totalitarian, authoritarian ideas only by better ideas." An educated wife could accomplish nothing in the workplace that could compare to being a full-time propaganda machine for her childern.

The story of what happened in the 1960s and 1970s is pretty familiar, but what's remarkable is how quickly women took advantage of opening opportunities and adjusted their self-image. Reliable birth control allowed women to better plan their futures; feminism opened up the labor market and gave them a reason to try harder; and increased rates of divorce made it necessary for women to think about supporting themselves. Girls had always done better than boys in high school, but now that they could see a real working future ahead of them they raced ahead. Girls had always taken more language arts courses, but now they began to take more math and science courses. In 1957 the average boy took one semester of physics and the average girl took 0.3 semesters, but within several years boys and girls reached near-parity, and girls continue to outpace boys in foreign languages. On standardized tests, girls began to widen their lead in reading and narrow the gap by which they lagged behind boys in math. They took more college-prep courses and more AP exams. High school boys, meanwhile, began to spend fewer hours doing homework, and to manifest more discipline problems and learning disabilities.

Within a few years women expanded their views about their own futures. Between 1968 and the late 1970s, the fraction of women who reported in the national Longitudinal Survey of Young Women that they expected to work by age thirty-five rose from around 30 percent to almost 80 percent. By 1973, only 17 percent of female college freshmen agreed with the statement posed by another survey: "The activities of married women are best confined to the home and family." Women from elite backgrounds were first through the college gates, but very quickly women of all classes and races followed. By 1982, the old gender gap had vanished and women and men were graduating from college in equal numbers.

In a logical world, graduation rates should have come to rest at this happy equilibrium. But to the surprise of many economists, the gender gap began to reverse itself. The labor market was still paying a premium for a college degree, but women were responding more strongly to that incentive, while men were stalling. Now, according to the Census Bureau, about 30 million American men and 30 million American women have college degrees. But the balance is elusive, because the men are on average much older. Young people live in a world in which the educational elite is as lopsidedly female as it once was male. And this imbalance affects every important area of life. Many women now have the choice of marrying down, delaying marriage, or not getting married at all. Men meanwhile start out in life internalizing the idea that women are more successful than they are, and that when it comes to the knowledge, drive, and discipline necessary to succeed, women are the naturals with whom men have to strain to keep up.

IN 2010, I visited a few schools around Kansas City to get a feel for these new gender dynamics of higher education. I started at the downtown campus of Metropolitan Community College. Metropolitan is the kind of place where people go to learn practical job skills and keep current with the changing economy, and as in most community colleges these days, men were conspicuously absent. One afternoon, in the basement cafeteria of a nearly windowless brick building, several women were trying to keep their eyes on their biology textbooks and ignore the text messages from their babysitters. Another crew was outside the ladies' room, braiding one another's hair. And when I got in the elevator I saw the image that has stuck with me, that epitomizes the contradictions of the new striving middle-class matriarchy—a woman, still in her medical-assistant scrubs, fell asleep between the first and fourth floors, so tired was she from studying, working, and taking care of her kids by herself.

When Bernard Franklin took over as campus president in 2005, he looked around and told his staff early on that their new priority was to "recruit more boys." He set up mentoring programs and men-only study groups and student associations. He made a special effort to bond with male students, who liked to call him "Suit." "It upset some of my feminists," he recalls. Yet, a few years later, the tidal wave of women continues to wash through the school—they now make up about 70 percent of its students. They come to train to be nurses and teachers—African-American women, usually a few years older than traditional college students, and lately, working-class white women from the suburbs seeking a cheap way to earn a credential. As for the men? Well, little has changed. "I recall one guy who was really smart," one of the school's counselors told me. "But he was reading at a sixth-grade level and felt embarrassed in front of the women. He had to hide his books from his friends, who would tease him when he studied. Then came the excuses. 'It's spring, gotta play ball.' 'It's winter, too cold.' He didn't make it."

It makes some economic sense that women attend community colleges—and in fact, all colleges—in greater numbers than men. Women ages twenty-five to thirty-four with only a high school diploma currently have a median income of around $25,000, while men in the same position earn around $32,000. But it makes sense only up to a point. The well-paid lifetime union job has been disappearing for at least thirty years. Kansas City, for example, has shifted from steel manufacturing to pharmaceuticals and information technologies. "The economy isn't as friendly to men as it once was," says Jacqueline King of the American Council on Education. "You would think men and women would go to these colleges at the same rate. But they don't."

In 2005, King's group conducted a survey of lower-income adults in college. Men, it turned out, had a harder time committing to school, even when they desperately needed to retool. They tended to start out behind academically, and many felt intimidated by the schoolwork. They reported feeling isolated and were much worse at seeking out fellow students, study groups, or counselors to help them adjust. Mothers going back to school described themselves as good role models for their children. Fathers worried that they were abrogating their responsibilities as breadwinner.

Cameron Creal is one of Franklin's handful of male stars. He's studying to be a teacher, which Franklin especially appreciates because he can reach out to the next generation of boys. His high school friends all started out saying they could go to college, but few of them followed through. "They see the commercials and think it's easy to get a degree," Cameron told me. "But then they get there and they're just not prepared for the work." Instead they got jobs in call centers doing customer service or janitorial jobs where "there's not much room to progress."

Cameron, now twenty-two, was the class clown in high school and when he graduated was also intimidated by the idea of getting a higher degree. He spent the first two years out of school working at a Taco Bell. But he was also living with his sister, who showed him that even the near impossible could be done. A single mother, she gets her three kids to school by seven, goes to the community college until three, and then works her night job at the IRS from six in the evening until three in the morning. "Like lots of these girls," he says, pointing to another woman falling asleep on the bench in the lobby, "her day is *full*, and she's *hustling*."

The student gender gap started to feel like a crisis to some people in higher education circles in the mid-2000s, when it began showing up not just in community and liberal arts colleges but in the flagship public universities—the UCs and the SUNYs and the UNCs. Like many of those schools, the University of Missouri at Kansas City, a full research university with more than 14,000 students, is now tipping toward 60 percent women, a level that many admissions officers worry can permanently shift the atmosphere and reputation of a school. In February 2010, I visited with Ashley Burress, UMKC's student body president. (The other three student government officers that year were also women.) Burress, a cute, short, African-American twenty-four-year-old grad student who was getting a doctor of pharmacy degree, had many of the same complaints I heard from other young women. Guys high-five one another when they get a C, while girls beat themselves up over a B-minus. Guys play video games in their dorm rooms while girls crowd the library. Girls get their degrees with no drama, while guys seem always in danger of drifting away. "In 2012, I will be Dr. Burress," she said. "Will I have to deal with guys who don't even have a bachelor's degree? I would like to date, but I'm putting myself in a really small pool."

UMKC is a working- and middle-class school—the kind of place where traditional sex roles might not be anathema. Yet as I talked to students, I realized how much the basic expectations for men and women had shifted. Many of the women's mothers had established careers later in life, sometimes after a divorce, and they had urged their daughters to move more quickly to establish their own careers. Victoria, Michelle, and Erin are sorority sisters. Victoria's mom is a part-time bartender at a hotel. Victoria is a biology major and wants to be a surgeon; soon she'll apply to a bunch of medical schools. She doesn't want kids for a while, because she knows she'll "be at the hospital, like, one hundred hours a week," and when she does have kids, well, she'll "be the hotshot surgeon, and he"—a nameless he—"will be at home playing with the kiddies."

Michelle, a self-described "perfectionist," also has her life mapped out. She's a psychology major and wants to be a family therapist. After college, she will apply to grad school and look for internships. She is well aware of the career-counseling resources on campus. And her fiancé? "He's changed majors, like, sixteen times. Last week he wanted to be a dentist. This week it's environmental science." Erin says, "Did he switch again this week? When you guys have kids, he'll definitely stay home. Seriously, what does he want to do?" Michelle sighs. "It depends on the day of the week. Remember last year? It was bio. It really is a joke. But it's not. It's funny, but it's not."

Among traditional college students from the highest-income families, who can afford to go to private schools such as Vassar or University of Richmond, the gender gap seems to disappear. Incoming classes are often more evenly balanced between men and women. But elite private schools live by their own rules, and are legally free to consider gender in admissions. In 2005, a study by the economists Sandy Baum and Eban Goodstein found that among selective liberal arts schools, being male raises the chance of college acceptance by 6.5 to 9 percentage points. In other words, they are keeping some women out to keep their schools from becoming "too female," as Heriot once put it.

Jennifer Delahunty Britz, the dean of admissions and financial aid at Kenyon College, in Ohio, let out this secret in a 2006 *New York Times* op-ed. Gender balance, she wrote, is the elephant in the room. And five years later, she told me that the problem hasn't gone away. When it tips toward 60 percent of women, "you'll hear a hint of desperation in the voices of admissions officers." In her op-ed she described a typical dilemma facing her office. A young woman from Kentucky had racked up an unseemly number of accomplishments, although her grades put her in the middle of the pool. They hesitated, something they would never do if she had been a man. "Because young men are rarer," she wrote, "they're more valued."

But not necessarily more impressive. A typical female applicant to Kenyon, Delahunty said, manages the process herself. She lines up the interviews, sets up a campus visit, requests a meeting with faculty members. But the college has seen more than one male applicant "sit back on the couch, sometimes with their eyes closed, while their mom tells them where to go and what to do. Sometimes we say, 'What a nice essay his mom wrote,'" she said, in that funny-but-not vein.

To avoid crossing the dreaded 60 percent threshold, admissions officers have created a language to explain away the boys' deficits: "Brain hasn't kicked in yet." "Slow to cook." "Hasn't quite peaked." "Holistic picture." At times Delahunty has become so worried about "overeducated females" and "undereducated males" that she jokes she is getting conspiratorial. She once called her sister, a pediatrician, to vet her latest theory: "Maybe these boys are genetically like canaries in a coal mine, absorbing so many toxins and bad things in the environment that their DNA is shifting. Maybe they're like those frogs— they're more vulnerable or something, so they've gotten deformed."

Whatever its origins, the problem of young men falling behind is becoming entrenched. In a 2006 paper, sociologists Claudia Buchmann and Thomas A. DiPrete proposed a fascinating explanation as to why. Both sons and daughters born before the mid-1960s into families where both parents were college educated were likely to finish college as well. Less-educated families of that period, the strivers hoping to get to the middle class, sent mostly sons, following old cultural habits. But over time this pattern has reversed. Now, in families where the fathers have a high school education or less, girls are much more likely than boys to finish college. If the boys do go, they are more likely to drop out. The difference is especially pronounced in families where there is no father.

A mother who went to college seems to have some effect on the daughter's chances of finishing college, but no effect on her sons; they just don't seem to consider her a suitable role model, or to be inspired to follow her example. These dynamics set the stage for a matriarchy laying down roots. Women in the middle class are less likely to get married these days, and if they do marry, more likely to marry someone without a college degree. Thus we look into a future where, generation after generation, mothers serve as role models for aspiring daughters while sons look on, lost. And, reversing centuries of tradition, families are investing in their daughters. The son preference that prevailed for so much of history was not based only on sentimental attachment or habit. Families poured their resources into sons because sons were the most likely to succeed, and perhaps to help support their parents in old age. With women dominating American colleges, the still-striving middle class is putting its best bet on its daughters.

How DID THIS come to pass? What goes on in the earlier years of schooling that discourages more boys from going to college? Throughout the late 1990s and early 2000s, various experts have looked in vain for the magic index or theory that could explain what is going wrong with boys. Many of their theories contradict one another. Christina Hoff Sommers caused a storm in 2000 with her *Atlantic* story "The War Against Boys," which blamed a misguided feminism that treated normal boys as incipient harassers. Many other experts blamed a rigid and overly macho insistence on competition and testing.

The latest trend is to look for answers in brain scans. Boys, writes Michael Gurian, best-selling author of *The Wonder of Boys* and several other books explaining the "male mind," are "graphic thinkers and kinesthetic learners," meaning they like systems and prefer to move around a lot when they learn. In a *Newsweek* story, "The Trouble with Boys," Peg Tyre referred to the "kinetic, disorganized, maddening and sometimes brilliant behaviors that scientists now believe are not learned but hard-wired." But as neuroscientist Lise Eliot has written, brain science has only begun to figure out the fundamentals of neurological gender difference, and all those colorful illustrations of the male mind and the female mind are at this early stage, "frankly, bogus." Neuroscientists know something about the different form and functions of the male and female brains, but not nearly enough to decide on "any meaningful differences between boys' and girls' mental or neural processing as they learn how to speak, read, or memorize their times tables," writes Eliot.

The Nation's Report Card (officially the National Assessment of Educational Progress) is a series of tests that's been given every few years since the late 1960s by the Department of Education, as a kind of check-in on the progress of students in different grades. In the latest assessment, girls scored much higher than boys in reading, but girls have always scored higher in reading. The only significant change over the last decade or so is a dip in twelfth-grade boys' scores. The dip is most acute for boys from poor and minority families but is not exclusive to them. At the end of high school, nearly one in four white sons of college-educated parents scored "below basic" on the reading section of the NAEP, compared to 7 percent of girls. In math, scores of both boys and girls have been steadily improving, but in the last few years girls have been closing the gap.

In any given year the differences are not alarming, and in some years boys in certain grades even do better than girls. But cumulatively the numbers paint a picture of an education system that plays to girls' strengths, and a new generation of girls who are confident and ready to rise to those expectations. Schools have in effect become microcosms of the larger economy. Richard Whitmire, author of *Why Boys Fail*, summarizes the trend this way: "The world has gotten more verbal; boys haven't." In the late 1990s, educators acted on the correct assumption that all jobs now require more sophisticated writing. Cops now need advanced degrees and practice in communication skills; factory workers are expected to be able to fill out elaborate orders. Society expects most workers to have college-level literacy, even if their day-to-day jobs do not really require that.

Schools responded accordingly and began pushing verbal skills earlier in the curriculum. Now a typical pre-kindergartner learns what a first-grader used to learn. The verbal curriculum heats up long before boys are mature enough to handle it. As a result, they start to think of themselves early on as failures in school. Their discouragement builds and, many years down the road, schools face what Whitmire calls the ninth-grade bulge. That year often produces much larger classes than subsequent years, because classes are full of boys waiting it out until they are old enough to drop out altogether. Girls meanwhile amp up their ambition as they progress through school. They are more likely than boys to take college-preparatory classes, including geometry, algebra II, chemistry, biology, and foreign languages, although boys are more likely to take physics. A University of Michigan study found that 67 percent of female high school seniors say they plan to graduate from a four-year college, compared with 55 percent of male students.

Beyond straight verbal skills, boys tend to get tripped up by what researchers call "noncognitive skills," meaning the ability to focus, organize yourself, and stay out of trouble. Boys of every race and background have a much higher incidence of school disciplinary and behavior problems and suspensions, and they spend far fewer hours doing homework. They are much more likely to be in special ed programs or diagnosed with a disability or some form of autism. Teachers consistently rate girls as being less disruptive and putting in more effort than boys in high school. And these days the temptations that can siphon off effort are much greater. Boys and girls both fritter away time on technology, but studies show that boys tend to do it in much longer blocks, spending hours after school playing video games. In fact, a consensus is forming that the qualities most predictive of academic success are the ones that have always made up the good girl stereotype: self-discipline and the ability to delay grat-ification. In other words, the ability to spend two hours doing your homework before you take out the PlayStation.

Of course, it's possible that girls have always had the raw material to make better students, that they've always been more studious, organized, self-disciplined, and eager to please, but, because of lim-ited opportunities, what did it matter? In George Eliot's *The Mill on the Floss*, published in 1860, it's clear that Maggie is much better suited to higher education than her brother Tom. She's more curious and open-minded, and always has a book in her hand (although in that era, Maggie's hunger for learning is interpreted as rebellious, not obedient). But the day Tom comes home from school and Mag-gie offers him two half crowns and a sixpence, he says: "What for? I don't want *your* money, you silly thing. I've got a great deal more money than you, because I'm a boy. I shall always have half sover-eigns and sovereigns for my Christmas boxes, because I shall be a man, and you only have five-shilling pieces, because you're only a girl." Silly though Tom thinks she is, he promises to take care of her always.

Now girls have much more of a sense that their efforts in school will count for something. "Monitoring the Future," a large and long-running national survey of high school students, showed a rising generation of girls brimming with ambition. Nearly half of the girls said it's important to be a leader, up from 19 percent in 1975. Seventy-one percent said they wanted to make a contribution to society. And for all the talk of girls' declining self-esteem in the middle and high school years, in the most recent survey girls of that age rated them-selves happier than ever before. Are they satisfied with "life as a whole"? Again, 71 percent said yes. And 75 percent said they were satisfied with themselves.

* * *

MY SCHOOL-AGE SON AND DAUGHTER are equally good students, but I can see how the system strains him in ways it does not strain her. In the early days, when my daughter was restless or nervous in school she created a series of imaginary finger puppets—the tooth-paste fairy, the penny fairy—and played with them silently under the hem of her dress. A teacher watching her would see nothing other than a girl looking down, sitting still; if called on she would snap back to attention and answer. My son, in the same circumstance, would stand up and talk without being called on, fidget and take off his shoes, or, if he was really restless, poke or shove one of his class-mates until he got a reaction. Whether the school demands unrea-sonable stillness from him is hard to say. I only know that what was expected came much more naturally to her than it did to him.

As they have gotten older, they have continued to do well, but she does it with much less effort and assistance from me. At night before going to bed she makes lists of what she needs to get done on the fol-lowing day or week and sends me e-mail reminders of what I need to buy her for projects. Her weekly to-do list can sometimes be longer than mine: practice piano, clean recorder, write essay in Spanish, frost cupcakes for the bake sale, etc. I realize I am making her sound like a stereotype of the good girl, but that's not a fair way of seeing it, really. Why should she not be rewarded for her diligence and sense of responsibility?

As school gets more complicated, my son, by contrast, gets more easily overwhelmed. He sometimes remembers his projects and sometimes forgets, and as a result I can never just count on him remembering and take them off my list. I recall a few years ago a friend joking with me that in an age where school demands so much more, so much earlier, moms have become their sons' secretaries. I've never forgotten that. Now I do everything in my power to help him develop his own inner secretary—write checklists he can look at himself every morning, put up a calendar where he can note future deadlines—anything to avoid him becoming the boy about whom the college admissions officers say, "What a nice essay his mom wrote."

Recently I gathered together a focus group of my kids' friends to ask them about their experiences in school. Immediately the difference between the boys and the girls became obvious. The boys seemed much more unruly but at the same time highly sensitive to being criticized. They had the sense that school was set up in a way designed to trip them up. "Don't stand this way. Do stand that way," as one second-grader told me. (Or as my son recently captioned a stick figure of his third-grade teacher: "Da-da-da, don't do that! Put that down!") Pretty soon all the talk of school sent the boys' minds wandering over to action heroes, and they started acting out *Raiders of the Lost Ark*. I could see for myself what the teachers were dealing with. Tell a boy what to do and he will start to mastermind his escape. "You have to get in trouble *sometimes*," one boy asserted.

This, I suppose, is the "kinetic," "disorganized," and "sometimes brilliant" behavior that *Newsweek* was referring to. But there are only so many Bill Gateses and Steve Jobses who get to behave that way and still succeed. In the last few years, educators have started to think of ways to marshal that rebellious energy in more productive ways. Australia and the UK are already several years ahead of the United States on this. In Australia, for example, the government has set up a task force to address the boy crisis, and has run several experimental programs that pay special attention to boys. A law-maker in China recently proposed "differentiated" education, after noting that women were outperforming men in college entrance exams and dominating all the top high schools and universities, and men accounted for 80 percent of the fifty million children who are rated "poor students."

Some of these programs do things as simple as introducing reading material that boys might like better—books that involve more adventure or mischief. Some break up academic tasks into smaller chunks to keep boys' attention. Some just add breaks for boys to run outside or skateboard. There is even a new fad for all-boy classrooms, following the logic that the new underdogs need their own specially tailored environment to succeed. Any of these strategies might work in particular neighborhoods or situations.

Many parents I know agonize over a boy-culture that discourages academic or brainy behavior. Just before middle school, parents start to think of their boys as facing a choice of two roads: trouble or success. The responsible ones recognize that they can't change the way the world is heading, but they can put a boy in an environment that doesn't make him feel like a failure, and give him enough tools at least to keep up.

The first step, however, is to stop pretending the problem does not exist. As some Australian educators told Whitmire: "We're over that debate. That was a debate twenty years ago."

A MORE
PERFECT POISON

THE NEW WAVE
OF FEMALE VIOLENCE

In 2007, forty-seven-year-old Larissa Schuster of Clovis, California, was tried for killing her husband, Timothy, by stuffing him in a vat of acid. According to the prosecution, Schuster and a young male accomplice used a stun gun on Timothy, put him to sleep with chloroform, and then stuffed his body, headfirst, into a fifty-five-gallon blue barrel. Afterward, Schuster poured a few jugs of hydrochloric acid into the barrel to disintegrate the body. When police discovered the barrel in a storage unit, they found only the liquefied remains of the lower half of the body, and hardly any identifiable tissue. Forensic pathologists and other experts surmised that the body had been sawed in half, or that his feet had been sawed off in order to fit into the barrel. "She wanted to wipe him out completely," said Bob Solis, a friend of Timothy's, told me. "Make it as if he were never here."

As the California "acid murderer," Schuster joined a long line of infamous lady poisoners who work with lethal chemicals instead of brute force. Poison has long been considered the woman's weapon of choice, although it's not really a choice—women are generally weaker than men and can't overpower them in a physical fight. Still, poison crimes have come to stand for women's supposed lack of raw aggression and will to confront. A poison crime connotes domestic entrapment, the abused wife, or the wife with a lover, too timid to ask for a divorce. The weapon is typically something she bought for less than $5 during her regular round of oppressive errands, at the supermarket or the auto parts store. The favored poison these days is bleach, although many women opt for a more organic approach. Recently a Colorado woman slipped leaves from a foxglove plant into her husband's salad and told him to make sure he ate his greens. Foxglove leaves contain the deadly poison digitalis.

In mythology and literature, poison is associated with witches, midwives, and cooks, and represents an "attempt to assert power by the powerless," writes Joyce Carol Oates in a review of Shirley Jackson's *We Have Always Lived in the Castle*. In that novel the Blackwood sisters are town misfits, suspected by their rural neighbors of casting spells. They are also curiously obsessed with kitchens. Food is a fetish in the novel: home-cured bacon, fresh preserves, cookies, coleslaw, and endless pourings of tea. After poisoning the sugar bowl one day, the queer and childlike sister Merricat announces, "I am going to put death in all their food and watch them die."

Schuster, however, did not fit this model of powerlessness at all. At the time of the murder, she was running her own successful biochemical lab, Central California Research Laboratories. (BAD CHEMISTRY was one headline favored by papers during the case.) Neighbors described her as working from six thirty A.M. until seven thirty P.M. most days, leaving Timothy, who was a nurse, to drive their two children to doctor's appointments, music lessons, and football games

("Mr. Mom," the media called him). During the trial, witnesses described Larissa as "intelligent," "domineering," "exciting," and "ambitious," and Timothy as "meek," "timid," "quiet," and "accommodating." Financial records showed that she made about twice as much money as he did and paid most of the mortgage on their new house. Schuster's attorney, Roger Nuttall, described her to me as the "definite breadwinner" who "ruled the roost." In fact, on the day of the murder, Timothy had just lost his job at Saint Agnes Medical Center; friends called the police to report him missing when he failed to show up for his exit interview.

Their relationship soured when Larissa started traveling around California, meeting with other chemical company executives, and then came home and measured her husband against them, Bob Solis told me. "She decided he was—what's the word—too domesticated?" Timothy liked to garden and hang out with the kids. He was a great bargain shopper and loved to cook—the night of his death he made Solis and his wife his famous vanilla custard ice cream in the churn, a recipe from his mother. Larissa, meanwhile, "was rubbing shoulders with a new class of people, and she thought he wasn't quite up to her stature," said Solis.

Larissa would come home and talk to their friends about what a "chickenshit" her husband was and how he should "grow up to be a man." Over time, she became outrageously abusive. During the trial, prosecutors played voice-mail tapes in which she harangued him about how little money he made and his supposed impotence. "You couldn't even fuck a dog," she yelled into his voice mail. "You impotent gay faggot." Timothy kept a gun under his couch cushion because, his friends testified, he was afraid of his wife.

At one point in the trial, the defense tried to shoehorn Larissa into the familiar lady poisoner trope. Psychiatrist Stephen Estner was called to testify that Larissa was suffering from battered spouse syndrome. "My impression was that Mrs. Schuster was a very direct and assertive person, and Mr. Schuster was a more passive and nurturing personality. And I think they started butting heads over that." In Estner's tortured logic, Tim's passivity and his failings as a husband were making Larissa physically and mentally ill, with symptoms ranging from depression to irregular heart rhythms and hair loss. In a reversal of the usual scenario, she was a battered spouse, Estner posited, because Tim was not *enough* of a man—the first known use of what will perhaps become known as the "end of men" defense. But the jury didn't go for it. Instead they believed the more straightforward motive, which was only novel in a case of spousal murder because it manifested itself in the wife rather than the husband: Larissa killed Timothy because she was afraid that in a divorce proceeding, he would take half of the very lucrative business she had built.

Larissa Schuster stands in a new league of females who are remaking the lady poisoner archetype to fit with the upheaval in our modern domestic arrangements. She holds company with Ann Miller Kontz, a North Carolina chemist with GlaxoSmithKline convicted in 2005 of running arsenic through her husband's IV, and Tianle Li, a New Jersey chemist at Bristol-Myers Squibb who was accused in 2011 of poisoning her estranged husband with thallium, a toxic metal that was banned in the 1970s. Their weapons are not household staples accessible to the average unhappy housewife, but chemicals available only to someone with an advanced professional degree and an impressive job at a biochemical or pharmaceutical company. (One blogger covering the Schuster case offered this advice to fellow men: "If you're thinking of marrying a biochemist, think again.") Their stories are anchored not in female oppression but rather in female success at infiltrating scientific fields that were once largely reserved for men. The old poison trope tapped into fears that women, resentful of being dominated, would use their domestic wiles to passively sneak in death. The new one taps into a fear that as they gain more power, women will use violence and their new specialized skills to get what they want. Singular and exotic though these cases may be, they raise the broader unsettling possibility that, with the turnover in modern gender roles, the escalation from competitiveness to aggression to violence that we are used to in men has started showing up in women as well.

Why would aggression contain itself in women any more than it does in men? In men, we have long assumed that the lines of aggression are fluid. The same drive that leads one man to murder can cultivate in another a killer instinct on Wall Street. The flash of rage that leads to a street fight can also be tapped to make a risky entrepreneurial deal. Often the language we use is the same. Brett Steenbarger, who gives advice on how to succeed on Wall Street, tells traders to act like boxers. If you see your opponent hurt, he writes, "go for the kill." Sometimes the destructive and productive forms of the drive can get mixed up in the same man. By the end of Bret Easton Ellis's *American Psycho*, Patrick Bateman's urges are running in all directions at once. In one scene, he sits in a trendy New York restaurant carrying on a conversation with his Wall Street colleagues about "how to use power effectively" while at the same time scanning the restaurant to see which of its patrons he can murder next.

Bateman is demented, but entirely consistent with the origin myth of male dominance, in which the role played by each gender remains fairly rigid over the course of two hundred thousand years. The way anthropologists explain it, early man shared the same instinct as the elk who butted horns or the beetle who locked his jaws over those of his male competitors and crunched them to death. The bravest and most skilled fighter "would have earned the highest social status, and thus secured the most wives and offspring," as Cambridge psychology professor Simon Baron-Cohen summarized it. In order to ensure the spreading of his seed he had to be brave, take risks, and relish competition. Occasionally men banded together in armies to defeat enemies and win over women from the enemy side. The woman, meanwhile, had to be choosy and cautious. She had to invest in her offspring and thus keep herself safe and avoid risks.

Over the years, evolutionary psychologists have connected the rest of the dots these early patterns suggest. Such evolutionary origins "have important ramifications in the workplace," argues law professor Kingsley Browne in his book *Divided Labours: An Evolutionary View of Women at Work*. Deep in their psyche, men are primed to achieve power and status; women are programmed to hang back.

At the extremes, these assumptions bear out, at least at the moment. When it comes to the expression of rank physical aggression, men vastly outnumber women; global homicide statistics show that men account for about 80 percent of all murders. And women, unlike men, rarely murder strangers. Questionnaires and studies measuring hostile acts show that men remain more likely than women to hit or yell or deliver what they believe to be electric shocks. Neuroscientist Lise Eliot explains the crude logic of this phenomenon in *Pink Brain, Blue Brain*: "You can't face down a fierce opponent if you're distracted by how he might be feeling."

In *The Better Angels of Our Nature: Why Violence Has Declined*, linguist and cognitive scientist Steven Pinker attributes the historical decrease in violence partly to the feminization of culture. It's not merely that men are vastly more likely to play violent games, vote for warlike policies, or commit violent crimes, or that women like to start pacifist organizations, he writes. What's driving the change is a vast feminization of culture of the kind conservatives like to complain about, a swapping of the old manly codes of martial glory for a more feminine emphasis on justice and empathy. "We are all feminists now," he writes, and quotes the declaration of Tsutomu Yamaguchi, a survivor of Hiroshima, that the only people who should run countries are breast-feeding mothers.

As always, Pinker's broad, sweeping truths are hard to argue with, except by thinking of counterexamples. (Was Margaret Thatcher a pacifist? Did Condoleezza Rice oppose the Iraq war? Did wars end after women got the vote? Is there anyone fiercer than an anonymous mommy blogger ranting about women who don't want to breast-feed?) From a mile-high view, Pinker's assertions seem mostly correct; yes, men are generally more violent, and yes, the decline of martial glory is likely connected to less warlike behavior in Western countries. But that perspective obscures all the changes taking place alongside the dramatic behaviors he focuses on—changes in women's violence patterns that can shake up our notions about whether men are in fact the more "naturally" dominant sex.

Anyway, there are simpler and just as convincing historical explanations for male aggression, as philosopher Jesse Prinz points out in his recent influential article in *Psychology Today*, "Why Are Men So Violent?" In hunter-gatherer societies, men depended on women to gather food. But once farming started, men, who had more upper body strength, did most of the work themselves. Men became the sole providers and women became economically dependent on them. This allowed men to eventually take over social and political institutions and keep women under their control. And once they had the power and resources, men had every incentive to fight hard to keep them.

Which version is true we will obviously never know for sure. But we do know that lately, the man-as-elk narrative isn't holding up so well. As researchers parse forms of aggression more subtle than throwing spears and killing people, sex differences become more elusive. More and more women seem to be cribbing "male" behaviors, and also inventing entirely new ways of being violent. As bestselling crime writer Patricia Cornwell recently mused to *The New York Times*, "The more women appropriate power, the more their behavior will mimic that of other powerful people."

AT THE START of the aughts, criminologists began to notice something curious in the crime trends. The great crime wave of the midnineties was finally coming to an end. Rates of all violent crimes were plummeting—that is, violent crime committed by men. In fact, rates of arrests overall for men, especially juveniles, were at an all-time low. But arrests for women were moving in the opposite direction. The share of women arrested for violent crimes rose from 11 percent in 1990 to 18 percent in 2008. The share of women arrested for property crimes rose from 25 percent in 1990 to 35 percent in 2008. Juvenile girls were showing remarkable increases. Between 1992 and 2003, arrests of girls for assault climbed an astonishing 40.9 percent, while for boys arrests climbed only 4.3 percent, according to FBI numbers. Women were by no means catching up to men, but they were fast closing the gap. In 1980, for example, the juvenile male arrest rate for simple assault was more than three times the female rate; by 2008, the male rate was less than twice the female rate.

The increase in arrest rates was showing up in all ages of women. In fact, one of the curious anomalies in the statistics was the spike in violent crime among women over forty. In that age group, arrests for violent crimes were up 307 percent since the 1980s, arrests for property offenses were up 114 percent, and arrests for drug offenses were up 1,040 percent. Typically, younger women can be counted on to commit more violent crimes than women of an age to be their mothers. But in the latest cohort, that trend was reversed, with more middle-aged women getting arrested for violent crime and drug offenses than women under eighteen.

The result was, for better or worse, an explosion of girls and women tied up with the criminal justice system. From 1985 to 2002, girls' juvenile court cases increased by 92 percent, while boys' court cases increased by 29 percent. During about the same period, the detention of girls increased by 98 percent, while the detention of boys rose by only 23 percent. The criminal justice system—and especially the juvenile system—long in the habit of treating girls with a lighter hand and a more forgiving patriarchal protectiveness, was enacting what some criminologists call "vengeful equity." In the eyes of the law, girls were now viewed as having almost the same destructive potential as boys.

Criminologists continue to fight about whether girls have become inherently more violent, or whether the culture has only come to treat them that way. The answer is unknowable, and in a sense it does not matter. As criminologists like to say, violence can be a self-fulfilling prophecy. The more authorities perceive girls as violent, the more they come to see themselves that way, and the cycle continues. Criminologist Melissa Sickmund calls the change over the last two decades "a subtle shift in people's perception of the norm. How the police act and what people read in the paper or see on TV changes our expectation of how girls can behave. And the girls rise"—or maybe sink—"to those expectations."

With crime—and particularly the kind of crime that captures the public imagination—women are moving into new terrain. In the past, female crimes tended to be family affairs—husband stabbings or baby killings, for example. Often they were attached to a sympathetic backstory that could be seen through a feminist lens: a battered wife who attacks her abusive husband (Lorena Bobbitt), a woman with psychotic postpartum depression (Andrea Yates). But perhaps the most notorious lady killer of the last few years was Amy Bishop, the neuroscientist who shot six of her colleagues, killing three of them, at the University of Alabama in Huntsville. Bishop did not fit any of the archetypes of a female killer. In fact, much like Larissa Schuster, she fit a familiar male one: She was a deranged loner committing an unprovoked, premeditated attack. Also like Schuster, her twisted internal logic justified violence as a way to protect her career ambitions. Each era gets the criminals it deserves. The 1930s had the swank Al Capone, the late 1960s had the cultish Charles Manson, and the 1980s had the excesses of Charles Keating. It's possible that the early 2000s will choose for its age-defining criminal the killer career woman. "The uncomfortable fact is that for all her singularity," wrote Sam Tanenhaus in *The New York Times*, "Dr. Bishop also provides an index to the evolved status of women in twenty-first-century America."

On a less lethal scale, women have stepped out to enter, even dominate, the public brawl. Perhaps the most infamous brawler of the last few years is Snooki, the squat little star of the reality show *Jersey Shore*. An episode isn't complete until Snooki throws a drink in someone's face or shoves someone over a table. In the MTV show *Teen Mom*, girl violence is at least as common as cooing over the babies. (Jenelle Evans, one of the stars of *Teen Mom 2*, was arrested after the website TMZ posted a video of her punching and attacking another girl.) A whole corner of YouTube could be devoted to women who go ballistic in fast-food restaurants. In 2010 the blond and comely, but drunk, Melodi Dushane of Toledo, Ohio, was arrested for punching two McDonald's employees and smashing a drive-through window because she couldn't get Chicken McNuggets before ten thirty A.M., which the security cameras captured on video. Another video, from a Denny's in Chicopee, Massachusetts, shows a white woman and a black woman, both dressed for a night on the town, picking up a fight their dates had abandoned. And at a Burger King in Panama City, Florida, a girl in a bikini jumps over the counter to throw jabs at the cashier.

When I asked Sickmund what typified the new style of female violence, she pointed me to a recent video of a group of African-American girls attacking a random middle-aged man at a Washington, DC, Metro stop. The girls walk up to the man one by one and push him, until he is stumbling down a long corridor. "I mean nothing to you!" he yells hysterically, his backpack slipping off his shoulder. But they keep coming at him, braids flying as they take punches. "What's up? What's up?" the girls taunt as some of their friends take pictures. There is no possible argument that the girls are provoked or victimized, or that anyone has the upper hand on them. I suppose there is some larger sociocultural argument to be made about class and race oppression and limited means of expression, but even that is a stretch. It's three thirty on a Friday, school's out, and the cats are toying with a mouse. If there is any relevant ethnography to apply, it's in a 2010 book by Cindy Ness called *Why Girls Fight*, about inner-city violence. Ness is one of the few writers on the topic whose analysis does not exclusively invoke oppression and victimization. Violence for the girls, she argues, is a "source of pleasure, self-esteem, and cultural capital." The girls in her study "enjoy physically dominating others and take pleasure in inflicting pain and emerging victorious." As one girl she interviews puts it, "I know I don't rule the world, but I can feel like I do, make you think I do."

In the summer of 2011 I visited a program near Fort Lauderdale, Florida, called PACE, or Practical Academic Cultural Education, which functions as an alternative to the criminal justice system for girls. Judges refer teenage girls to PACE when they see in them the seeds of delinquency—an emerging pattern of truancy, drug use or dealing, or physical violence. For a few years, the girls go to a PACE center instead of high school, attending counseling sessions as well as classes, and living by semi-restrictive rules. A dress code requires a polo shirt and slacks, and the girls have to sign out whenever they leave the building. PACE lives by the principle that girls in the system need to be treated differently from boys, and they set up what they call a "gender responsive" program. "The girls are generally misunderstood," said director Aggie Pappas. "They've usually suffered some kind of trauma or victimization, and that drives their behavior. We give them a space to express themselves, to find their voice." In a group session, I watched as the girls talked to counselors about what to do when their dads don't trust them and lock them in the house, or their mom goes AWOL. They came from all parts of the area and were about equally divided among white, African American, and Latino. At the time I visited, a group of the girls were doing a moving, if awkward, dance to Pink's perfectly apt girl-power hit of the moment: "Pretty pretty please, don't you ever ever feel, like you're less than fuckin' perfect . . ."

The girls I spoke to seem to have absorbed the basic message of PACE that college is better than jail, and that talking about problems is better than hitting. But even the two model students the PACE staff allowed me to interview maintain a relationship with violence that is at best ambivalent. When they talk about fights they've won, they do it with unmistakable pride. Delores, a seventeen-year-old I spoke to, had Beyoncé's eyes and a curvy figure hidden under a big brown sweatshirt. She also had a sweet, childish voice, which caused her no end of grief in her life, "because people think I'm soft." As a result, Delores was always in a position of having to prove herself. She got into fights with cousins, girlfriends, boyfriends, even the cops. Of her last fight with her cousin Princess, she told me, "To be honest, and maybe it sounds sick and sad to you, but I got joy out of hitting her. It made me feel really good because now nobody thinks I'm scared of her. You know, people think all they have in the world is their respect. That's the only thing worth fighting for." This updated version of the old macho martial code is still very real to them, maybe the most real thing in their lives.

Delores's fifteen-year-old friend Christine was with us, and she was an entirely different type—white, cheerleader-peppy, and quick with the uplifting girlfriend-y phrases ("You can totally go to college!")—but she had no trouble relating to Delores's life philosophy. She, too, had gotten in trouble for fighting with a girl at school. A year later, she still watches a cell phone video of the fight, which someone posted on Facebook, and especially loves to replay the moment when the other girl screams, "Get off me! Get off me!"

"I feel good because she really needed me to get off her!" says Christine. "And then my friends sent me all these messages: 'Oh damn, you got that girl good,' and 'She's never gonna show her face again.' Stuff like that, and maybe it sounds sad, but that made me feel really good, too. I don't think it's just boys or girls. It's everyone. If you lose, people will think you're soft, and if you win, they will show respect."

When I asked if they ever got into fights with boys, they laughed.

"Of course! We're the only ones ever doing the fighting," Christine said, and told me about the time she left a bruise on her boyfriend's face when she threw a twenty-pound weight at him.

WHAT LOOKS LIKE warped logic in one context can look like empowerment in another. A corollary to the recent increases in violence is the remarkable decrease in victimization of women. Women today are far less likely to get murdered, raped, assaulted, or robbed than at any time in recent history. A 2010 White House report on women and girls laid out the latest statistics straightforwardly, to the great irritation of many feminists. The rate of nonfatal violent victimization of women has declined drastically since the 1990s, the report said. In 1993 there were forty-three violent incidents for every thousand women; now there are eighteen. The rate of rape meanwhile declined by 60 percent since 1993, and has stayed steady at the lower rate throughout the decade. The most accurate measure of crime, the Bureau of Justice Statistics' National Crime Victimization Survey, shows that rape and other violence against women have declined sharply over the last thirty-five years, and especially in the last decade. In the last twelve years, girls and young women report plummeting rates of completed rape, assaults, attempts, and threats, and all other violent crimes.

This decrease has happened even while the definition of rape has expanded to include acts that stop short of penetration—oral sex, for example—and circumstances in which the victim was too incapacitated (usually meaning too drunk) to give meaningful consent. The most dramatic declines are in assaults by an acquaintance or family member. "Women have a lot more ability to leave a terrible relationship," says Melissa Sickmund. "They don't have to stay until they get killed." Adds criminologist Mike Males, "Girls have achieved a great deal more power. And that makes them a lot harder to victimize. People don't admit these trends because there is a lot of discomfort, even among liberals, about girls succeeding so well. Girls are getting into the job market at higher rates, doing well financially, while boys are on a destructive decline. A lot of things are going right, and I think this really unhinges some people who are attached to a different story."

A recent British study showed that women were three times more likely to be arrested for domestic violence, and far more likely to use a weapon. Since the United States passed mandatory arrest laws for domestic violence in the late 1990s, arrest rates for women have skyrocketed, and in some states reached 50 percent or more of all arrests. Domestic violence victim advocates are often incensed by this development and say women are being accidentally ensnared in a trap meant for abusive men. But the more nuanced explanation is that, just as with men, the aggression is fluid and exists along a continuum. Women these days are more likely to defend themselves or fight back, and sometimes they may be taking the first punch. One British study found that 40 percent of domestic violence victims were men.

Our attachment to the notion of women as vulnerable runs deeper than politics, of course. It's hard to fathom that women's new circumstance could shift something so fundamental as raw, physical power. In most movies and crime thrillers, women are still victims and the female aggressor is still an exotic anomaly. TV shows like *Snapped* on the Oxygen network, which does biopics of female criminals, still play on this expectation that female violence is a freak occurrence. "These shocking but true stories . . . prove that even the most unlikely suspects can be capable of murder," the opening narration explains. We find it hard to let go of the old story about women, even when women are inflicting the worst kind of harm.

Since 2000, there have been well over a hundred suicide bombings carried out by women, in Russia, the Middle East, India, Sri Lanka, and other countries. When the Black Widows of Chechnya again exploded a bomb in the Russian subway in 2010, news stories described them in terms of a Greek tragedy, as women so burned up and dena- tured by personal loss that they set themselves to Medea-level vio- lence as a form of revenge. One of the bombers was "emotionally distressed after her husband was murdered in what appeared to be a business dispute," attorney Natalya V. Yevlapova told *The New York Times*. These girls, she said, "are just pushed into a corner."

The media always describes the motives of these suicide bombers according to a few female-specific tropes: young and psychologically disturbed, revenge-seeking, or naive and under the sway of charis- matic male influence. The first known female suicide bomber was a sixteen-year-old girl working with a Syrian resistance group who drove a truck into an Israeli convoy in Lebanon in 1985. News reports at first described her as pregnant, and then depressed, but it turns out that she was neither; the descriptions were only so much sentimental overlay.

"Women, we are told, become suicide bombers out of despair, mental illness, religiously mandated subordination to men, frustra- tion with sexual inequality, and a host of other factors related spe- cifically to their gender. Indeed, the only thing everyone can agree on is that there is something fundamentally different motivating men and women to become suicide attackers," writes Lindsey O'Rourke, a doctoral student at the University of Chicago who did an exhaustive study of all the known female suicide bombers. "The only problem: There is precious little evidence of uniquely feminine motivations driving women's attacks." Like men, the women have a range of motivations. They may have lost a family member in an enemy's previous attack, for example, but so have most male suicide bombers. In the broad view, the great majority—95 percent—carry out attacks as part of a military operation against an occupying force.

What motivates them is partly loyalty to a cause and some grievance, in about the same proportion as these factors motivate men. But their greatest motivation is something else entirely, O'Rourke concluded, something the girls at the PACE center might understand: They are remarkably effective. In her dissertation, O'Rourke discovered that the women's attacks were almost twice as lethal as the attacks of men. A female suicide bomber is more likely to be successful, and kills 8.4 victims on average, as opposed to 5.3 killed by the average male suicide bomber. The women have the advantage of surprise, and societal norms often prevent security officers from searching them thoroughly. As British agencies discovered, women in traditional Muslim garb can hide twelve pounds of explosives under a chador.

IN THE MID-1990s, sociologists at Princeton conducted an experiment in the boundaries of female aggression. Two groups of college students, each a mixture of men and women, were given instructions on how to play a specially designed video game. They were told that an unseen opponent would drop bombs on their target for the first three rounds, and then they would be allowed to retaliate. In the first three rounds, an overwhelming number of bombs were dropped in order to provoke the players into feeling angry and frustrated. The researchers then measured how the subjects responded.

When they first came in, one group of subjects was asked to move close to the experimenter and to identify themselves by name. They each received large name tags and answered personal questions in front of the group, providing information about their families, where they came from, and what they liked to do. The interviewer wrote down the answers in large black letters, echoing back the gender of each subject in the process. When this group began playing the game, the experimenter came to check in on them. This group was what the research calls "individuated," meaning actively reminded of who they actually were. The other half of the students were kept in the back of the room and told that they were not required to provide any information. They remained anonymous, and no experimenters stopped to check in on them during the game.

In the individuated group, the men dropped significantly more bombs on their opponents than the women did. In the anonymous group, men and women dropped the same number of bombs. "When the restrictions on aggression inherent in the female gender role were lifted," concluded researchers Jenifer Lightdale and Deborah Prentice, "women behaved as aggressively as men." (Although true to gender stereotype, the women rated themselves as worse at the game than the men did, and reported that they behaved less aggressively than they actually did.)

The study was crude in its very literal and narrow definition of violence—dropping (pretend) bombs. And the results were not necessarily unexpected. Earlier studies, including the famous Stanford Prison Experiment, showed that when people took on deindividuated "roles" they could carry out more violence than they would when unmasked. (Anyone who has watched kids in Darth Vader costumes can attest to that.) But in the context of gender, it took a very crude and straightforward study to raise an important point.

Psychological studies have always shown that men and women have a similar threshold for anger, but that women suppress the anger while men express it. What if women were more free of social constraints? How far would they move along the aggression continuum? (It's worth noting that later studies have replicated the video study's finding in varied forms, including my favorite, the "hot sauce" study, where the subjects were asked to punish someone who had criticized their work by putting extra hot sauce on their crackers. When anonymous, the women larded it on!)

Studies have suggested that if the social acceptance for female aggression expanded, women would move in to fill the space. And this is exactly what seems to have happened. This is one of the areas where the Bem Sex Role Inventory—the key gender role measure administered since the 1970s—comes in handy. On that measure, women have increasingly described themselves in traits that are traditionally considered masculine: ambitious, self-reliant, assertive. Between the 1970s and the late 1990s, men made few changes in their self-reporting, while women "increasingly reported masculine-stereotyped personality traits," writes San Diego State psychology professor Jean Twenge in the *Journal of Personality and Social Psychology*. Men's sense of their own assertiveness has proved fairly rigid, while women's seems to change according to the historical moment. In 2001, Twenge analyzed personality tests dating back to the 1930s to try to quantify how much women internalized cultural norms. It turned out that, true to the nature of Plastic Woman, their self-identity changed in perfect harmony with the times. High school and college women's senses of their own assertiveness and dominance rose from 1931 to 1945, when women were first flooding the workplace. It dipped from 1946 to 1967, a period of great emphasis on domestic roles. It increased again from 1968 to 1993. Women's scores have increased so much in recent years, writes Twenge, that there is virtually no measurable sex difference in assertiveness. Social change gets "internalized," she argues, and shows up as a "personality trait."

A 1999 analysis of 150 studies on risk-taking behaviors showed a similar result. Studies taken before 1980 show a greater gap in the gender difference in risk taking. Men still measure higher on such tendencies, but the gap is higher for risks such as driving and drug and alcohol use. In risk taking on, say, standard decision making, the gap has narrowed considerably. The risk-taking gap narrows even more among the younger cohorts, showing that either girls are getting braver or boys are getting more cautious in a risk-averse, highly protective society.

Increasingly, researchers are finding that qualities we thought of as innate are in fact context-specific, especially for women. To measure rates of competitiveness, anthropologist Uri Gneezy at the University of California, San Diego, compared two distinct societies: the Maasai in Tanzania, who have a patriarchal society, and the Khasi in India, a matrilineal society where families invest mainly in girls. In a ball competition, Maasai men opted to compete twice as much as the women, but in the Khasi, the results were nearly reversed and the women competed much more. At the very least, "it is not universally true that the average female in every society avoids competition more often than the average male in that society because we have discovered at least one setting in which this is not true," writes Gneezy.

Stereotypes are slow to change, but in Western countries the culture is moving into a phase of "new, more conscious acceptance of female aggression," argues Maud Lavin in the 2010 *Push Comes to Shove: New Images of Aggressive Women*. Much of the credit goes to Title IX and its encouragement of vast waves of high school and college girls to play sports. In 1971, about one in twenty-seven girls participated in sports; now that number is up to one in two. Early experience with sports competition allows girls to express behaviors once restricted to men, and also to find a way out of the usual female aggression bind. In sports, violence is not dangerous but orderly, neatly divided into halves and quarters, and part of a larger team goal.

In her essay "Throwing Like a Girl," philosopher Iris Marion Young argues that the early-life failure of girls to use their bodies in lateral space or to throw their whole weight behind physical tasks limits their imagination and sense of potential for themselves. By contrast, the experience of physical competence "ripples through everyday life" and, multiplied by tens of thousands, "causes a behavioral transformation on a mass societal level," writes Lavin. In her book, Lavin traces the evolution of girl sports movies from the prettified territory of gymnastics, cheerleading, and ice-skating to the more brutal soccer and boxing worlds depicted in *Bend It Like Beckham*, *Girlfight*, and *Million Dollar Baby*, which ends in the dismal euthanizing of the boxer played by Hilary Swank.

Slowly pop culture is tuning in to the new wave of female violence. In Roman Polanski's *The Ghost Writer*, the traditional political wife is rewritten as a cold-blooded killer at the heart of an evil conspiracy. In her video for the song "Telephone," Lady Gaga, with her infallible radar for the cultural edge, rewrites *Thelma & Louise* as a story not about elusive female empowerment but about sheer, ruthless power. Instead of killing themselves, she and her girlfriend (played by Beyoncé) kill a bad boyfriend and random others in a homicidal spree and then escape in their yellow pickup truck, Gaga bragging, "We did it, Honey B." Sometimes women take over the roles of men for sheer novelty value. The role of the career assassin Salt in the spy thriller of that name was written for a man but given to Angelina Jolie. Here she is entirely plausible as the reluctant professional killer without a personal life. *Hanna*, directed by Joe Wright, rewrites the male violence trope from its origins. Saoirse Ronan plays a girl raised in the wilderness by her father to be a hunter rather than a nurturer/gatherer. The movie is imbued with myth and fairy tale, and when Hanna ends up in a tutu one night at a concert with a boy, instead of giving her prince a kiss she wrestles him to the ground and nearly chokes him to death.

In teenage books and movies, the mean girl over the last decade has replaced the boy bully as the bane of high school existence. In her latest evolution she goes beyond psychological torture into more lethal territory. Katniss Everdeen from *The Hunger Games*, Lisbeth Salander in *The Girl with the Dragon Tattoo*, and Maximum Ride from the popular James Patterson young adult series of the same name represent an entirely novel kind of girl heroine, damaged but highly effective killers exacting revenge on a demented patriarchy. The new version of boy hero meanwhile is a remarkable wimp, a small bundle of Woody Allen–style neuroses. In many of the popular books and movies for boys these days—*Diary of a Wimpy Kid, How to Train Your Dragon, Alvin Ho, Nerds*—the hero ekes out just enough courage to stumble into a (sort of) happy ending.

For some people the rise in female violence must come as a great disappointment. Many of us hold out the hope that there is a utopia in our future run by women, that power does not in fact corrupt equally. But that vision of a female utopia has always had an air of condescension behind it. The most distinctive trait of women is not necessarily that they are kinder or gentler or will do anything to protect their young. As Twenge discovered, it's that they tend to respond to social cues and bend their personalities to fit in what the times allow.

Women have so far dominated the workforce partly with a traditionally feminine set of traits—social skills, caretaking, and cooperative behavior. But this constellation has only gotten them so far. Now they are realizing that to make it to the very top they will need to play a slightly different game. The greatest barrier to women reaching for the most powerful jobs these days is a set of unspoken assumptions: that women are not competitive, dominant, or hungry enough to make it. But they are breaking through even that last barrier, with the force of the Lady Gagas, Katniss Everdeens, and schoolgirls with cleats and bruises.

THE TOP

NICE-ISH GIRLS GET THE CORNER OFFICE

This is how problems are solved in the workplace of the future: Marissa Mayer, who is the highest-ranking woman at Google, had a bad feeling that one of her top directors, Katy, was going to quit. Katy was hardworking and well liked, but Mayer was picking up rumblings of burnout and resentment. Mayer did not like losing women executives—there were too few to begin with at Google. She figured it was obvious what was causing the strain. Katy was a "soccer mom" of three children, including a set of twins. As the leader of her Google team, she had to participate in a one A.M. call to Bangalore every night. Mayer assumed that with young children at home who did not necessarily sleep through the night, the one A.M. calls were putting Katy over the edge. So she decided to do an intervention.

Mayer called Katy in and explained what she calls her "finding your rhythm" philosophy, which is not an alternative form of birth control but Mayer's home-brewed remedy for burnout. What causes burnout, Mayer believes, is not working too hard. People, she believes, "can work arbitrarily hard for an arbitrary amount of time." But they will become resentful if work makes them miss the things that are really important to them. The key to sustaining dedication and loyalty is having an employee identify what he or she absolutely cannot tolerate missing, and then having the employer accommodate that. She asked Katy to think about it and come back in a month.

Mayer, it turns out, was wrong about the one A.M. phone calls. Katy loved her job and she loved her team and she didn't mind staying up late to help out. What was bothering Katy was something entirely different. Often, Katy confessed, she showed up late at her children's events because a meeting went overly long, for no important reason other than meetings tend to go long. And she hated having her children watch her walk in late. For Mayer, this was a no-brainer. She instituted a Katy-tailored rule. If Katy had told her earlier that she had to leave at four to get to a soccer game, then Mayer would make sure Katy could leave at four. Even if there was only five minutes left to a meeting, even if Google cofounder Sergey Brin himself was midsentence and expecting an answer from Katy, Mayer would say "Katy's gotta go," and Katy would walk out the door and answer the questions later by e-mail after the kids were in bed.

I had always heard that Silicon Valley was the ultimate flexible workplace, so in 2011 I went to visit some of the biggest companies and also some start-ups. Successful women executives there told me stories that would make anyone struggling to manage a high-powered job and a life jealous. As a mother of three, Katie Stanton had found her job at the White House a nightmare. One night at eight P.M., her boss called her at home to ask what she was doing out of the office. "Tucking my kids into bed," she answered. "Why, is there an emergency?" Soon after, she quit and moved back to California, where she went to work for Twitter. As head of international strategy, Stanton asked her new boss if she could leave at five every day—she lives an hour away—and pick up on e-mail again after eight. No problem. "I consider myself incredibly lucky," says Stanton. "Because I can do this job really well and have a family. It's great. This is the place for me and the perfect role for me."

Life for the women I talked to was not exactly perfect; in fact, it sounded exhausting. Stanton works every night—every single weeknight—and never gets to the gym or goes out with her husband. These women work flexibly, but they work all the time. As Emily White, a Facebook executive, put it to me, "Forget the balance, this is the *merge*," meaning that work and play and kids and sleep are all jumbled up in the same twenty-four-hour period. (White came up with this term after she finally managed a night out alone with her husband, and they spent half the dinner staring at their iPhones.) But the work culture was still a revelation. Without a lot of official committees and HR red tape, Silicon Valley is figuring out the single most vexing problem for ambitious working women, a problem everyone thought was unsolvable: how to let them spend time with their children without ruining their careers.

The industry has by no means solved the ultimate problem, meaning that there are just as few female heads of companies as there are in any other elite sector. But it gives us a glimpse of the work culture of the future, where face time isn't so relevant and people take it for granted that women—and men—can be really ambitious and manage a life, too. "Your reputation is based on what you've done," said White. "It doesn't really matter what's in your pants." In a chart comparing the "career cost of family" in various elite workplaces—meaning the price people pay for taking time off—the economist Claudia Goldin floats the tech companies high above the rest, in their own happy cloud. Women and men there can take time off and not take a big salary hit. Other industries, by contrast, suffer from "inertia" or "resistance to change," argues Goldin. She compares them to her husband, who "to this day likes to go into the Whole Foods and go down the same aisle, every time, while I like to wander into new places. These more novel industries step in and they suddenly figure out how to do things differently."

All the problems that companies elsewhere agonize over, the Silicon Valley women seem to workshop informally and on the fly. Worried that the Katy rule stigmatizes mothers? Mayer had it apply to everyone. Now one of her young male executives leaves early every Tuesday for his hallowed potluck dinner with his old college dorm-mates. Life problems are not all that different from technological ones: With enough creative thinking, anything can be solved.

As the first female engineer hired at Google and now one of its top executives, Mayer has become part of the Google legend. She got her master's degree from Stanford in computer science with a spe-cialty in artificial intelligence, and she is so intense in even casual conversation that I found myself tracking whether she ever blinks. She is also tall and blond, with Holly Golightly good looks and a great sense of style, and she regularly appears in local society blogs at fancy parties on the arm of her cute entrepreneur husband. She is well aware that she is an unusual package, and has embraced the extra task of being a role model for aspiring girl geeks everywhere: "I do think it's important for girls especially to know that there is not one way to break through. You can be into fashion and be a geek and a good coder," she says, and then hastens to add, "just like you can be a jock and a good coder. You don't have to give up what you love."

But try to draw Mayer into the morass of issues around

discrimination and she will resist. "I'm not a girl at Google," she likes to say. "I'm a geek at Google." Why aren't there more girl geek computer science majors like her? I asked. "I am much less worried about adjusting the percentage than about growing the overall pie," she told me. "We are not producing enough men or women who know how to program."

The women of Silicon Valley do not live in such a shiny detached bubble that they don't recognize sexism. You would have to be blind to walk through the offices of Facebook or Google every day and not notice the sea of mostly male programmers. It's more that they think of sexism in the same way people in London must think about bad weather: It's an omnipresent and unpleasant fact of life, but it shouldn't keep you from going about your business. The women don't deny sexism, but rather will themselves to ignore it so they can get their work done. Their attitude is neither idealistic nor defiant but highly practical: Better to just workshop these situations one by one, like so many coding glitches, one de-gendered brain to another.

Dwelling on sexism is a "complete waste of time," Lori Goler, Facebook's human resources director, said in a *New Yorker* profile of Sheryl Sandberg, COO of Facebook. "If I spend one hour talking about how I'm excluded, that's an hour I am not spending solving Facebook's problems." Even the stories of outright, obnoxious sexism don't really rate. White told me about an old boss of hers at a different company who told her, "I can't wait for you to quit so I can marry you." But White waved the guy away as "pretty old," a dinosaur no doubt six feet under by now. Her casual assumption was that he was the relic of the *Mad Men* era, exhibiting arcane behavior one might encounter in a retro TV show or a museum. She, conversely, was the future.

* * *

MENTION THE LACK of women at the top of corporate America in certain circles and you will likely get a healthy dose of feminist rage. "I'm sick of hearing how far we've come. I'm sick of hearing how much better situated we are now than before. . . . The fact is that so far as leadership is concerned, women in nearly every realm are nearly nowhere," writes Barbara Kellerman, a professor of leadership at Harvard's Kennedy School, and she cites the familiar statistics: 3 to 6 percent of Fortune 500 CEOs, 17 percent of congressional seats, twenty out of 180 heads of state.

There are, of course, other data points than the ones at the tippy top of the pinnacle. In the levels just below CEO—the top executive officers, or the highest paid—women have been lately inching up about a percentage point a year. The number of women with six-figure incomes is rising at a much faster pace than it is for men. Nationwide, about one in eighteen women working full-time earned $100,000 or more in 2009, according to recent census figures, a jump of 14 percent over two years. Women are now lead TV anchors, Ivy League college heads, bank presidents, corporate CEOs, movie directors, scatologically savvy comedians, presidential candidates— all unthinkable even twenty years ago. The job of secretary of state has been virtually reserved for a woman. The number of female heads of state, although still small, has suddenly doubled in the last several years. And as we learned from Barack Obama, it takes only one person to make the whole picture look different.

But more important than all the data points is the outlook. You can see the current setup as evidence that the top will forever remain in a male iron grip, or you can see it for what it truly is: the last gasp of a vanishing age. Even the way we now frame the issue makes it clear that men's hold on the pinnacles of power is loosening. In business circles, the lack of women at the top is described as a "brain drain" and a crisis of "talent retention." At least half a dozen comprehensive studies have confirmed that losing top women executives is bad for profits. And while female CEOs may be rare in America's largest companies, they are highly prized: In 2009, they outearned their male counterparts by 43 percent, on average, and received bigger raises.

"Women are knocking on the door of leadership at the very moment when their talents are especially well matched with the requirements of the day," writes David Gergen in the foreword to *Enlightened Power: How Women Are Transforming the Practice of Leadership*. The old model of command and control, with one leader holding all the decision-making power, is considered a relic of the midcentury military age. The new model is sometimes called "postheroic" or "transformational," in the words of the historian and leadership expert James MacGregor Burns. The aim is to behave like a good coach, and channel your charisma to motivate others to be hardworking and creative. The model is not explicitly defined as feminine, but it echoes literature about male-female differences. A program at Columbia Business School, for example, teaches sensitive leadership and social intelligence, including better reading of facial expressions and body language. "We never explicitly say, 'Develop your feminine side,' but it's clear that's what we're advocating," says Jamie Ladge, a business professor at Northeastern University.

Julie Gerberding, an infectious disease specialist who was the head of the Centers for Disease Control and is now the president of

Merck Vaccines, calls the new style "meta-leadership" or "horizontal leadership":

> Horizontal leadership takes different skills than vertical leadership. And it requires people to know how to negotiate, to be able to be true and effective partners and collaborators, to find that third path, to be able to walk in someone else's shoes with emotional intelligence and empathy. And while men and women possess those skills, I think some of them are attributes that women are naturally inclined or more socialized to excel in. And in this very complicated world in which we live, that horizontal leadership probably is one of the key success factors for any organization.

A 2008 study attempted to quantify the effect of this more feminine management style. Researchers at Columbia Business School and the University of Maryland analyzed data on the top fifteen hundred US companies from 1992 to 2006 to determine the relationship between companies' performances and female participation in senior management. Firms that had women in top positions performed better, and this was especially true if the organization pursued what the researchers called an "innovation-intensive strategy," in which "creativity and collaboration may be especially important"—an apt description of the future economy.

It could be that women boost corporate performance, or it could be that better-performing firms have the luxury of recruiting and keeping high-potential women. But the association is clear: Innovative, successful firms are the ones that promote women. The same Columbia-Maryland study ranked America's industries by the proportion of firms that employed female executives, and the bottom of the list reads like a roster of the ghosts of the economy past: ship-building, real estate, coal, steelworks, machinery.

Lately, the problem of too few female executives has taken on new urgency. In 2001, as the Internet boom was deflating, MIT's *Quarterly Journal of Economics* published a paper called "Boys Will Be Boys: Gender, Overconfidence, and Common Stock Investment." Two University of California, Davis, researchers compared the trades of men and women over a six-year period. Men, especially single men, traded vastly more frequently than women, and they did so out of a false confidence in themselves and their own judgments, the researchers concluded. (Single men traded 67 percent more times than single women.) The result of this overconfidence, all economic models predict, is many more bad decisions and far lower net returns.

When the economy collapsed several years later, this finding provided one of the few clear guidelines for the future: More women around means fewer pointless risks. What used to be considered a marker of leadership—the ability to act quickly, to remain in a state of pumped-up confidence—was recast as a liability. At the same time, what was long viewed as a feminine weakness—hesitating, waiting for outside feedback and confirmation—now looked like a critical life-saving skill. Researchers have even started looking into the relationship between testosterone and excessive risk-taking, trying to discern whether groups of men, in some basic hormonal way, spur one another to make reckless decisions. We don't yet know with certainty whether testosterone strongly influences business decision-making. But the picture emerging is a mirror image of the traditional gender map: men and markets on the side of the irrational and overemotional, and women on the side of the cool and levelheaded.

"One of the distinctive traits about Iceland's disaster, and Wall Street's, is how little women had to do with it. Women worked in the banks, but not in the risk-taking jobs," writes Michael Lewis in his book *Boomerang*. Halla Tomasdottir was an executive in corporate America before she moved back to her native Iceland and founded a financial services firm. This was in 2007, when Iceland was newly intoxicated by the kinds of complicated investment structures that would soon destroy its economy. Tomasdottir had a "strong feeling in [her] stomach that this wasn't sustainable," so she decided to found a firm with explicitly "feminine values." (This is Iceland, where feminism is not an embarrassing word.) For her this meant giving primacy to some basic concepts, among them risk awareness and emotional capital. Being risk aware means not investing in things you don't understand. And thinking in terms of emotional capital means remembering that it's people who make and lose money, not Excel spreadsheets. Tomasdottir's was one of the handful of firms to come out of the crisis with no losses, and it is now thriving.

In May 2012, when Wall Street was scratching its head about how JPMorgan could have made the disastrous bet that led to a $6 billion loss, *The New York Times* came up with a novel and very relatable explanation. The bank's chief investment officer, Ina Drew, had been overseeing the team responsible for the bet. Drew was a quiet, hardworking mother of two, "as far from a ruthless diva as you can be," according to her friends. Drew had been credited with keeping the bank steady in 2008. Using coachlike "post-heroic" leadership skills, she kept the traders' huge egos in check. In morning meetings she would "huddle" with them and get them to outline the risks they would be incurring in trades that day. "When Ina was there, things ran smoothly," a colleague told the *Times*. But Drew developed Lyme disease in 2010 and missed huge chunks of time at work. The morning meetings turned into "shouting matches" in her absence, her colleagues reported. One of her deputies in New York was at war with another one in London, who came up with the strategy that led to the losing bet. Egos raged and "everything spiraled," leading to a nearly $3 billion loss that almost wrecked the bank.

In *Chasing Stars*, Boris Groysberg, a professor at Harvard Business School, follows a thousand star analysts at Wall Street investment banks. Groysberg had wondered what happens to stars in elite professions when they change jobs, as is common in this era of freelance talent, where no employee is loyal and companies feel free to poach from one another. He found that for the most part, the practice of poaching is disastrous. Stars who change firms "suffer an immediate and lasting decline in their performance," which he judged partly by following their numerical rankings in *Institutional Investor*. But Groysberg discovered a surprising exception: women. The 189 women he followed didn't necessarily trust their firms to support and promote them in the usual ways, so they spent a lot of time securing outside relationships with clients—relationships they could transfer to their new jobs. And the women didn't jump at offers merely because they meant more money or bigger titles; they cautiously evaluated future employers before taking a job. As a result, the women achieved a higher average rank by the end of the study, and more women were ranked first than any other rank. Groysberg guesses the women thrived because in that male-dominated environment, they had to be more intelligent, flexible, single-minded, and ambitious. As one woman analyst told him, "being an average performer was not an option for women." But largely they thrived because they used the traditional "feminine values" of care and caution to their advantage.

If this is the way the world is inevitably moving, why hasn't it arrived yet? What's holding women back from overtaking men at the top? After all, for a woman in her thirties navigating her way through some frustrating corporate hierarchy, thinking about the long sweep of history will probably not cheer her up. But the world does not flip upside down overnight. Men have been in charge for about forty thousand years, and women have started edging them out for about forty. So of course there are still obstacles at the top.

Right now, an ambitious career woman working outside the idyll of Silicon Valley has what we might call a brand identity problem. Women are like the Kia cars of the workforce: They are growing fast, faster than their big brother company, Hyundai. They are known for being nimble, trendy, and much more attuned to customer needs. Once the scrappy underdogs of car manufacturers, they are now ready to play in the major leagues. But they still need to convince everyone else that they belong there.

The top still looks male, so women who make it that far still seem like an anomaly. In fact, they are seen as violating some essential quality of femininity—warmth, maternal instinct, communal feeling. Deep down we—men and women both—are not gender blind. We still expect women to act one way and men to act another. More than that, men and women both resist thinking any differently because it causes too much confusion and cognitive dissonance. We can glimpse the massive paradigm shift just on the horizon but we are not quite ready for it—a resistance that will fade as more and more women reach visible positions of power.

IN 2008, at a time when Citigroup was becoming a model of big bank failure and corruption, its top executives held their regular Monday morning meeting. Vikram Pandit, the bank's new CEO, was about to roll out a controversial new management structure that would shift around control over various geographical territories.

Sallie Krawcheck, who was in charge of global wealth management, was suspicious of the new arrangement. She and Pandit had disagreed about many things, and this time she decided to bring up her objections in the meeting. Unlike the many white-shoe financial institutions, Citigroup was a "let it all hang out kind of place," Krawcheck told me. A meeting that involved yelling and screaming was just another Monday morning meeting. Krawcheck questioned how the new lines of authority would work. "What if I say 'zig' and the guy who runs Asia says 'zag' and we can't agree? Now what happens?" she asked. She hinted that the new system might cause "paralysis."

Until then, Krawcheck, the "Queen of Wall Street," had been a favorite with the business media. For several years she made *Forbes*'s list of the top ten most powerful women in the world. *Fortune* used her as the lead in a 2002 story called "In Search of the Last Honest Analyst"—the ultimate public compliment in an industry second only to Congress in public loathing and distrust. Krawcheck was tall, with blond preppy good looks and a Southern accent, but mostly the media liked her for the same reason I did when I first met her: She was honest and blunt. Krawcheck once joked in an interview, "How do you know when management is lying? Their lips are moving"—a quote that trailed her in nearly every profile. At a Forbes executive forum, she once told a crowd from the podium that her first husband had an affair because she worked too much and he was jealous of her career. But while she was blunt, she wasn't a diva or a screamer. She knew how to put her Southern charm to work, and she was known for her relentless efforts to win over colleagues at the various banks where she worked. She had manners, and she treated people well. "If she cursed, it was only at herself," said one of her former colleagues.

But the following day, the media turned on Krawcheck. *The Wall*

Street Journal reported in a front-page Web story that Krawcheck wasn't supportive of Pandit's micromanaging and that she was challenging him publicly. The word "paralysis" got picked up in blogs and news stories. Krawcheck was chided for being disloyal and out of control. "Son of a bitch," she remembers thinking. "I didn't raise my voice. I didn't scream." The whole incident seemed to her in fact "pretty fricking mild" by Monday-morning standards, particularly given that there was a genuine, substantive disagreement. She was baffled that it had ended up on the front-page of *The Wall Street Journal.*

And then she remembered something that had happened at a Monday morning meeting a few weeks earlier. One of the other female executives had been yelling about something, "and I remember, clear as a bell, the thought forming in my head: B-I-T-C-H." What had happened in her head, she realized, must have been the same as what happened in everyone else's head when she had challenged Pandit. The men could challenge one another at any Monday morning meeting—hell, they could even scream and throw glasses across the room "and I never think, 'jerk' or 'bastard.'" In fact, the tantrum would be forgotten by lunchtime. But if a woman did the same thing, it became front-page news. Not because Wall Street was sexist or biased, exactly, or stuck in the *Mad Men* "pretty little gal" school of women, says Krawcheck, but because of what she came to think of as The Twitch, the instinctive wince we do when a woman unsheathes her sword.

Most working women have probably at some point been victims of The Twitch. In my case, it happened early in my career. As a young writer at *The Washington Post*, I found out one day that a male reporter hired around the same time as me and who had far less experience was making more money. He was actually bragging on the phone to a friend about how much he made, and across the cubicles I heard him. Naturally, I was annoyed. I wrote a reasonably cordial and lighthearted note to my supervisor, asking for a raise, but my sourness crept into it—I may have even used the word "unfair." My supervisor, who was male, responded with outsized horror and disappointment. "I thought we had a good working relationship," his e-mail began, and it went downhill from there. I was so mortified and humiliated that I apologized. Apologized! And because I am not a savvy businesswoman like Sallie Krawcheck, I am ashamed to admit that I never once asked for a raise again.

I now know that this whole incident is fairly standard in the annals of gender workplace fiascos. My victimized whiny note, his shock, my apology, and my career-long reticence are all examples of exactly how women should not conduct themselves in the workplace if they want to speed up that inevitable march to the top.

At the start of the millennium, researchers began to puzzle over why women's earnings seemed to be leveling off. Women were still graduating from college at greater rates than men, and still flooding lucrative jobs in the creative class, but their earnings, especially at the top, had stopped soaring. Economist Linda Babcock hit upon a fairly simple explanation when she was directing the PhD program at Carnegie Mellon University. A group of female graduate students came in to complain that they were stuck teaching for other faculty while the men got to teach their own classes. Babcock tracked down the dean in charge to ask him about it. The women, he told her, "just don't ask," so they don't get assigned their own classes.

Babcock wondered if this might be true in other areas of their lives, so she ran an experiment. She surveyed Carnegie Mellon alumni who had recently graduated with their master's degrees about their starting salaries in their new jobs. It turned out that 57 percent of the men had negotiated their starting salaries, while only 7 percent of the women had, even though the school's career services department strongly advised students to negotiate. As a result, men had starting salaries that averaged 7.6 percent higher than women's.

I can offer anecdotal confirmation of Babcock's findings from my own experience. For the past three years, I have been editing the women's section of *Slate*. About 10 percent of my writers are men. Web magazines do not pay all that much for individual stories anymore, and there isn't much wiggle room in the budget, but sometimes, in certain circumstances, there is a tiny bit. The women, however, would never discover that. In all those years, only four of the dozens of women I work with have asked me for more money. And only two of the men have failed to.

Babcock is an economist, so she played out the math to its logical conclusion: Even if a man never asked for a raise again and he and his female counterpart both got 3 percent raises for the rest of their careers, the man's 7.4 percent higher starting salary would make him half a million dollars richer than her by the time they reached retirement age—the difference between a tiny apartment in a Miami suburb and a luxury condo in Sarasota.

The finding seemed especially urgent given the current nature of the economy. Hardly anyone went to one job and stayed there anymore. In fact, as Babcock pointed out, a quarter of workers in 2000 had been with their current employer less than a year. People moved from job to job, and each time, money and perks were up for grabs. Employers might offer employees different stock options or particular benefits, or special arrangements: working at home, working flexibly, working on contract. The workplace was turning into a big Turkish bazaar, and women might be missing all the deals! Women weren't bad at negotiating in general—on behalf of the company,

say, or for their children or friends. But they were reluctant to negotiate for themselves. As a result, they tended to be blind to their opportunities. They seemed to assume that if they worked hard, the proper
rewards would come their way.

Babcock's research helped spawn an industry of advice books
intended to toughen women up: *Nice Girls Don't Get the Corner Office;
Play Like a Man, Win Like a Woman;* and *Stop Sabotaging Your Career.*
Babcock and Sara Laschever wrote their own version, *Ask For It,* in
which they explain "how women can use the power of negotiation to
get what they really want." The gist of these advice books is obvious
from the titles: If you "worry about offending others" and "back
down too easily" and otherwise insist on workplace displays of "girlish behavior," chides Lois Frankel, author of the *Nice Girls* series,
then you are "sabotaging your career!"

But as the advice books got churned out, the academic research
was taking a curious turn. Study after study was finding that women
who did not conform to female stereotypes—who bluntly asked for a
raise, self-promoted, demanded credit for work they'd done, or failed
to pitch in and help other colleagues—paid a high price in the workplace. People judged them as harsh or unpleasant, did not want to
work with them, did not want them as a boss, and—worse—failed to
grant their requests for a raise or judge them successful. Here was the
evil Twitch, getting in the way of a sisters-take-up-arms plan of attack.
The world, it seemed, was not ready for mean girls at the office.

Researchers all over the country lab-tested different workplace
scenarios, and they always came up with the same result: Women
who speak aggressively get lower marks than women who speak tentatively. Women who self-promote are judged to lack social skills.
Ditto for women who express any kind of anger in the workplace. In
one scenario, some colleagues were about to go to an office party

when a fellow employee showed up in a last-minute panic over a broken Xerox machine. He needed help manually stapling five hundred sets of the pages he had copied. The women who said no and went off to the party were docked mercilessly by the research subjects. Men who did the same in that situation were not judged at all. For men, behaving in a friendly, communal way was optional. For women, it was mandatory.

Perhaps the most dispiriting experiment was conducted in 2004 by Madeline Heilman, a psychologist at New York University. Heilman handed out a packet giving background information about a certain employee who was an assistant vice president in an aircraft company. In some cases, the employee was described as not yet having received a performance review. In other cases, the employee had gone through the review and been deemed a "stellar performer" or a "rising star." The only other difference was that in some cases, the employee described in the packets was "Andrea" and in others, "James." Among those who believed the employee had not yet received a review, Andrea and James were judged equally likeable, with Andrea being judged less competent. But among those to whom the employee had been described as a "rising star," people finally judged Andrea to be as competent as James but far less likeable and more hostile.

You'd think that a woman who managed the impressive feat of rising to the top at an aircraft company would get gold stars. Not at all. People judged rising star Andrea as far less likeable and far more hostile than James; in fact, the Andreas were judged to be "downright uncivil," explains Heilman, even though there was no information provided to support that view. Subjects merely assumed that "Andrea" must have behaved too much like a man, which was socially unacceptable. The implications were depressing. All women had to do was be stellar performers in what was considered a male arena in order to bring on The Twitch. Clearly it was time to workshop a new strategy.

A few years later, Heilman came up with a successful makeover for Andrea. Heilman reran the Andrea/James experiment, only this time she added some extra descriptions. Andrea/James "demands a lot from her/his employees" and is also "caring and sensitive to their needs" or encourages "cooperation and helpful behavior." These extra feminizing descriptions did the trick for Andrea ("fair minded" was too neutral), making subjects like her as much, be happy to have her as a boss, and consider her competent. Heilman even tried the mother card. She mentioned that Andrea was a mother, and that had the same effect. Surely a mother couldn't be mean, goes the thinking. A little bit of sugar seemed to go a long way.

So what were women supposed to do, bake brownies for their colleagues, give noontime massages, and generally spread sunshine around the office? It still seemed like they were caught in a trap. How could a woman be nice enough not to trigger The Twitch, but not so insipid that she would never get a promotion?

In 2011 researcher Hannah Riley Bowles at the Harvard Kennedy School took up the challenge. Bowles was a protégé of Linda Babcock, but she started with a premise opposite that of her mentor, that "it does hurt to ask." Working with Babcock, she picked the simple scenario of an employee receiving a job offer and then asking for a higher salary. Each subject saw a video of different employees, played by hired actors, asking for a raise using a different script. Her working hypothesis was that in order to be successful, the performance had to fulfill two different criteria: It had to be girlish enough not to trigger a backlash (The Twitch), but it had to be aggressive enough to convince the research subjects that the woman should be given a raise.

"I think I should be paid at the top of that range. And I would also like to be eligible for an end-of-the-year bonus."

Nope. Too aggressive.

"I hope it's okay to ask you about this. I'd feel terrible if I offended you in doing so."

No again. Too girlish.

"I don't know how typical it is for people at my level to negotiate, but I'm hopeful that you'll see my skill at negotiating as something important that I bring to the job."

Bingo.

When the actress used this script, research subjects were both willing to work with the woman and to give her a raise. The key, it turned out, was to fit the stereotype just enough to avoid social backlash. The party at the other end of the table accepted her advocating for herself when she portrayed her needs as aligned with the needs of the company. She could negotiate for herself in order to prove she could negotiate for the company later. And one other thing: It might be more effective not to act aggrieved, as I was in my note to the *Washington Post* editor. "You want to get past the initial outrage phase," counsels Bowles. "As a persuasion strategy it might have worked twenty-five years ago, but it doesn't work today." Bowles adds that it might be the honorable thing for women to speak out if they have been wronged. But her research is pragmatic, and just confirms a reality that they might pay a price for doing that. "If you are intent on showing that you've been treated wrongly, that you have been treated like a lower-status person, then too often you just end up persuading them that you are in fact a lower-status person."

The formula is maddening in its tightrope specificity and insulting in the capitulation it requires, Bowles admits. "If we could change the results of our experiments," she writes in the study, "we would choose a more liberating message." But it is also extremely pragmatic and, in its own way, liberating. When women negotiate, emotions tend to get in the way: excess humility, shame, resentment, outrage. Those feelings are not so helpful in building a reasonable case. The Bowles strategy gives women something else to focus on, something that may even fall more in their comfort zone: creating a convincing narrative that explains why her own needs match up with the company's.

A senior executive Bowles once counseled found out that one of the male subordinates on her team was paid more than her. Her instinct was to march into the CEO's office and tell him how unfair and outrageous that was—because it was unfair and outrageous. But with Bowles's help, they mapped out a different script, one that would convey "unfair" without screaming it, and would refer to general standards rather than personal fury: "I know this is not the kind of company that wants to set up a structure where subordinates are paid more than their superiors." She practiced the script several times, keeping her voice even. She got the raise.

Another woman Bowles was advising was asked to run her law firm's diversity initiative. She suspected that this was merely a way to sidetrack her off a successful career path. She wanted to go to her boss and tell him that the new assignment would damage her career. Bowles suggested she should try a different tack: "If I'm hearing you right and you want the position to have the authority you describe, I think it should be paid at ____ level and require a new title." She didn't complain, she got the promotion, and the diversity initiative was elevated to a new level of importance and authority.

In her book *Knowing Your Value*, MSNBC host Mika Brzezinski, who has consulted with Bowles, describes her own inept attempts at asking for a raise. In her first attempt, she apologized over and over to Phil Griffin, president of MSNBC. "I'm sorry." "I don't want to be a problem." "I really don't want to be a diva." Nothing. In her second attempt, she tried a combination of outrage and swagger, channeling her coanchor Joe Scarborough. "This is ridiculous, and I'm not going to put up with it anymore!" she said, jabbing Phil in the shoulder the way she'd seen Joe do. Griffin just looked at her like she was bonkers and jabbed back. Finally she got it right, by "not venting. Not whining. Just talking in my own words: 'You are a bad boyfriend. Do you know what that is, Phil? You take and take and take, but never give. Start giving.'"

As I interviewed women executives, I learned that many of them had picked up some version of this advice along the way, and most of them gritted their teeth and followed it. Indra Nooyi, the CEO of PepsiCo, recalled an executive meeting she attended when she first came to the company. Someone was presenting a dubious three-year plan. Most people objected, along the lines of, "That's very interesting, but you might want to look at it differently." Nooyi said in the meeting, "That's crap. It's never going to happen." Afterward, one of the male executives called her aside and explained that if she wanted to get along at the company she might tone it down a bit. "He was helping edge me along to a different place," she said. "The whole organization is not going to meet you. That's just not realistic." It was her first lesson, she recalls, in learning how to survive in a male-dominated environment.

Facebook executive Sheryl Sandberg has always advised women to negotiate with nearly the exact same language that Bowles settled on in her study. Sandberg's version of the script goes something like: "You realize you are hiring me to run the business development team, so you want me to be a good negotiator. Well, here goes. I am about to negotiate." Sandberg understands that some women might consider this more pragmatic approach a cop-out, or a missed opening for change. "But I say, you have to put your ego aside and play by the rules so you can get to the top and change things. Look, here I am at Facebook, at a company that gives four months of paid maternity and paternity leave. Isn't that worth it?"

Emily White is one of Sandberg's young protégés, and she has reluctantly adopted Sandberg's mandate that she play by the rules as well. "I am a really aggressive person. I have really strong views and I'm very competitive, and I expect people around me to be the same way," White explains. "But I've definitely tried to change my style and hold my tongue a lot more. I always actively ask for other people's opinions even when I don't care about their opinions. And I hedge a lot more and use softer language." Then she adds, "It drives me nuts. I'm not sure how long I can keep it up." From White's resentful attitude about the forced makeover, you get the hopeful feeling that this painful transition phase won't last forever, that we are closer to the tipping point than we realize, and one day soon there will be enough Emily Whites in power that they won't have to tread so lightly anymore.

WOMEN MAY IN TIME learn to walk this line perfectly. In their limitless capacity for morphing and adjusting, they may strike just the right balance between feminine and aggressive to move ahead without triggering any suspicion. But even if they get past these external barriers, there are still other, and in some ways deeper, ones holding them back.

Women carry psychological baggage with them into the workplace: a lingering ambivalence about their ambition, a queasiness about self-promotion, a duty to family that they can't or won't offload onto their husbands, a catholic notion of satisfaction that encompasses much more than climbing the corporate ladder, and a general feeling of vulnerability they seem to drag with them up the ranks no matter how powerful they get. It's all understandable, given that most workplaces are structured in such a rigid, unaccommodating way that women are always made to feel as if they are asking for special favors. Still, these are the reasons women end up leaving behind $10,000 every year on the table, as Claudia Goldin puts it. They are not, as the women's magazines like to say, "bad habits" women have to conquer; more like biases women should be aware of before they decide what to do about their careers.

We know, from a long-term study of Chicago business school graduates, the basic trajectory of the elite professional woman, in this case the average female MBA. Straight out of business school, she earns slightly less than her male counterparts, $115,000 compared to $130,000. Five years out, the men and women start to diverge. The women start to work fewer hours, and some stop working altogether. Nearly a decade out, the women are earning $250,000 and the men are earning $400,000.

Why? What happens? How does a giant gap get created out of a small one?

The first clue is that there is hardly any earning gap between women who don't have children and men. Mostly what happens is obvious: Women with children start cutting back hours or seeking out situations that are more family-friendly. This is a perfectly reasonable response to an American workplace that barely acknowledges that the same adults showing up at the office every day also raise children at home.

But children are not the whole story, or maybe children are a proxy for the general drift and disaffection that often starts to weaken women's resolve to fight somewhere in their late twenties and takes full hold of them in their thirties and forties.

Do women lack ambition? psychologist Anna Fels asked in a 2004 *Harvard Business Review* article. She opens with a poignant vignette of a woman who confesses a dirty secret from her childhood: She'd once had a diary littered with the letters "IWBF"—for "I will be famous." This was a dirty secret because it now caused this forty-year-old great shame to think about that. What kind of woman walks around saying she wants to be famous?

Fels concludes that women have this bravado beaten out of them over the years. They retain their early girlish pride in their own mastery of skills, but they lose the drive to demand recognition for that mastery: They lose ambition itself. "In fact the women I interviewed hated the very word," she writes. "For them 'ambition' necessarily implied egotism, selfishness, self-aggrandizement, or the manipulative use of others for one's own end. None of them would admit to being ambitious. Instead, the constant refrain was, 'It's not me. It's the work.'"

Imagine a video game called Ambition Killer. A girl would start out life with a certain amount of ambition points and then run into various obstacles that would knock some out of her—husband, children, a pigheaded boss, an inflexible workplace, the lure of a lazy weekday afternoon. There are multiple ways that women tread old feminine ground and lose the will to fight for what they want. Sometimes women end up marrying into a situation that sets them up as the traditional wife, whether they planned to become that or not. Sometimes women feel the pressure of parenting culture that defines their desires for success as selfish, and against the interests of their children. Sometimes—and this is the hardest one—women can see no greater appeal in spending their middle years climbing a corporate ladder rather than, say, being a mother, or even reading a book in a café.

The study of University of Chicago MBA students showed a very curious split. The women set out earning their average of $115,000, and subsequently many of them married, some to men who earned more or less what they did, others to men who earned a lot more. Those who married a "high" earner, defined in the study as making more than $200,000 a year, and then had children were much more likely to stop working as women with a spouse who earned less. They also described themselves as responsible for a much greater percentage of the child care—52 percent, versus 32 percent for women with lower-earning spouses.

The underlying tragedy of such a dynamic was perfectly articulated in a column by Michael Lewis, "How to Put Your Wife Out of Business," which ran in the *Los Angeles Times* in 2005. It was almost satire, but not quite. "There was a brief time, from about 1985 to 1991, when high-powered males demonstrated their status by marrying equally high-powered females with high-paying jobs. That time has passed. The surest way for a man to exhibit his social status—the finest bourgeois bling—is to find the most highly paid woman you can, working in the most high-profile job, and shut her down."

A long time ago, the high earner would not have married an MBA in the first place. He'd have married a flight attendant or a secretary or the high school girlfriend who had worked to put him through business school. But these days people of equal education tend to pair up. For the pashas of Wall Street, it's not enough to marry a model; you have to marry the most impressive woman in business school—and then, as Lewis says, put her out of business. To feminists this should be an outrage: countless potential future female CEOs sacrificed to their husbands' greed and selfish demands.

Women who would be king would do well to heed this advice: If you meet a man in business school and suspect he might strike gold, don't marry him. Go for the middle manager instead.

Or at least she might go for someone who will understand that her career counts as much as his. One would expect that a powerful woman would downplay her husband's role in her success, that she would insist that she'd made it *despite* the man in her life. But in a new twist on an old trope, the powerful women I spoke to all admitted being utterly dependent on their husbands. All described this as the first rule of success: "Choose your spouse or partner carefully. I often say this as a joke, but there is almost no other choice that you can make that will have as much of an impact—positive or negative—on your career," says Sallie Krawcheck. Sheryl Sandberg tells women at every speech she gives that "your most important career decision is who you marry." And then sometimes she adds, depending on the crowd, "If you can be a lesbian, definitely do it." Many of the most successful women—former HP CEO Carly Fiorina, Indra Nooyi, *The Daily Beast* and *Newsweek* editor in chief Tina Brown—credit their husbands with making their success possible. "I lucked out at home," says Nooyi, who was born into a traditional Indian family and married an Indian man, Rajkantilal Nooyi. "He supported me massively. I don't think I could have worked the way I did if I hadn't had that kind of support at home."

In my midtwenties, I had a serious boyfriend I'd met right after college. We traveled together, traded novels, and talked about politics. I was just starting out as a journalist, and he generously praised my writing. If I had asked him how he felt about his wife working, he would have said he fully supported it. But I could tell that wasn't quite true. I could tell by the way he talked about his mother and her attempt, late in life, to create a career for herself. I could tell by the way he talked about what his future kids would be doing over the summer. I could tell by his large ambitions, which left little space for any distractions. I was right to pay close attention to these cues: Today he is fabulously wealthy, and his highly credentialed wife does not work.

This is an economy where single childless women under thirty make more money than single childless men. This means that among the elite, who tend to marry later, there is a high chance that the woman is making more than the man when they first get married. Women can learn to let that early start set the rhythm of the marriage and to resist the impulse to defer. As a frustrated friend with a baby once said of her husband, like her a corporate lawyer, "It's not that his job is less flexible. It's that he is less flexible about his job."

Before they married, Emily White's husband assumed that she would probably be the one taking care of most things around the house. But he's learned to be accommodating. He runs a private equity firm, which is a demanding job but still leaves him more space than she has. He now "does the majority of house stuff," White says—paying bills, fixing leaks, getting dinner, planning the rare vacations. She takes their child to school in the morning but he does the evening nanny handoff—"arguably the bigger sacrifice," she admits, so she can work later. White chose him consciously, because whatever his worldview was when they met, she could tell he was the kind of guy who was "open to having that worldview rocked." White's personal experience has left her with the impression that "the men around here"—meaning in Silicon Valley—"are becoming more comfortable with all that. There's no shame here if you're the one doing more of the child care."

A few years ago I wrote a story in *The Atlantic* called "The Case Against Breast-Feeding." The title is a slight exaggeration—I understand perfectly what the proven health benefits of breast-feeding are.

But my point was, those benefits are not so tremendous that they should automatically outweigh all the factors on the other side of the ledger. My conclusion was:

> Overall, yes, breast is probably best. But not so much better that formula deserves the label of "public health menace," alongside smoking. Given what we know so far, it seems reasonable to put breast-feeding's health benefits on the plus side of the ledger and other things—modesty, independence, career, sanity—on the minus side, and then tally them up and make a decision. But in this risk-averse age of parenting, that's not how it's done.

I've seen so many friends nearly quit their jobs because they did not want to stop breast-feeding or deal with the stress of pumping breast milk at work. In that myopic, desperate moment of early motherhood, women demote their own ambition to the near moral equivalent of starving your baby.

Even after all these years in the working world, women tend to portray parenting decisions as a choice between the mother's selfish desire and the baby's needs. But this is a very narrow way of looking at things. It might surprise people to learn that over the course of the century, as women have flooded the workforce, time-use studies show they spend at least as much or even more time with their children than women did in earlier decades. In fact, one study found that since 1995, women have almost doubled the amount of time they spend directly caring for their children, to 21.2 hours a week. I've seen this statistic come up in several different studies and I still do not understand how it's possible. But it does confirm one thing without a doubt: The sin of our parenting generation is definitely not neglect.

As a reporter I was once assigned to cover a comprehensive 2006 study by the National Institute of Child Health. My editor had described it to me as a study showing that the kids in day care had more temper tantrums, because this is how early news stories had summarized it. In fact, the study—one of the most long-term and comprehensive ever done—shows that there are virtually no differences in either cognitive development or behavior between children raised at home with mothers, at home with nannies, or in day care. A small minority who spent long hours in day care showed a few behavioral problems, but the study found that they resolved over time. Yet the storyline about selfish mothers persists no matter what the data.

Too often, what's left out of the conversation over child care are the benefits a mother brings back to the house when she works; not just her paycheck and her own professional satisfaction, but her example of a woman engaged with the outside world. A mean story: When my first child was in preschool, I overheard a conversation between another mother and her child in the same class. The mother was a prevalent type in the school, a corporate lawyer who had married a lobbyist in the high-earning category and then quit her job. The mom was explaining that they would be going to look at some elementary schools that afternoon, because it was important to pick the right school for the daughter so she could get a great education and love to learn. "Why is that important" the daughter asked, "if I'm just going to grow up and be a mommy like you?" Ouch.

Often there are obvious solutions to the mother time crunch, but women won't use them. Like a husband, for example. As I am writing this chapter, my husband is packing to take our three children away to his parents' summer house in Vermont. He is taking them without me because my deadline is approaching and he wants to give me space and time to work. It's an act of great generosity and love. Still, the thoughts forming in my head are not driven by gratitude:

He's taking the wrong boots for the youngest child, the wrong pair of gloves for the middle one, and the eldest is about to forget her pile of books. He's taking the water bottle with the busted top and a giant bag of pretzels instead of little baggies he can easily distribute in the car. I am already imagining the little frozen fingers and toes and the moment when, having fought over who gets to keep the pretzels on their lap, they let go of the bag and all the pretzels tumble out and gleefully nestle under the floor mats.

But I am disciplining myself to wipe those images from my mind and say nothing. For one thing, it's not fair. I would never go up to a colleague and tell him a story he'd worked hard on, which I had asked him to do, was all wrong just because I would have done it differently. Secondly, it doesn't matter. Eleven years of parenting and three children have taught me that it honestly and truly doesn't matter. Cold fingers and smushed pretzels are not what vacation memories are made of. They can borrow boots from the neighbors and turn the visit into an opportunity to enlist them in a snowball fight. They will probably drop the pretzels out the window and stop at a great diner. And in the meantime, I will get my work done, simple as that.

Once you start calling the baby "my baby," you have a problem. If diversity is good in the workplace, then it's also good at home. In her book *Getting to 50/50*, Sharon Meers, a former managing director at Goldman Sachs and now an executive at eBay, points out that a father's involvement is the critical factor in a child's success. In a massive Department of Education study, a child's grades were more closely correlated to how many times the dad showed up at a school event than any other factor. Children with involved fathers measure as having higher IQs by age three, higher self-esteem, and in the case of daughters, grow up to be less promiscuous.

Deciding on more equitable child-care arrangements is not just a

logistical matter; it's about rooting out deep and crippling assumptions women hold long before they even have children.

Sheryl Sandberg at Facebook beautifully reframed the issue of
women and work in her 2010 TED talk with her memorable phrase
"Don't leave before you leave." The phrase was attached to a story
about a young woman at Facebook who came into her office agonizing
about how she would balance work and a child. The woman looked
very young, so Sandberg asked her, "Are you and your husband thinking about having a baby?" It turned out that the woman didn't have a
husband. She didn't even have a boyfriend. She was just doing that
thing that young women tend to do, which is hesitate before she'd even
gotten started. "I watch it all day long," Sandberg told me. "Women
are making room for kids they don't have, years before they try and
get pregnant. Then when they do get pregnant, they would be coming
back to a job they no longer want." The men, meanwhile, are "super
aggressive and focused. They are in your office every day. 'Can I do
that? Can I lead this?' They don't have to be talked into things."

Women tend to be fatalistic about children and work, so even if
there are possible solutions to the problem, they don't look for them.
At Facebook, Sandberg forces optimism on her employees by giving
them the opposite of the usual advice. Recently Sandberg offered a
woman a new job in business development. The woman came into
her office worried that she might not be able to handle it. Why?
asked Sheryl. She was pregnant, the woman confessed. "Congratula-
tions," said Sandberg. "That's all the more reason for you to take this
job. Then you'll have something exciting to come back to." The
logic is, it's hard to leave for work in the morning when your warm,
delightful toddler is clinging to your leg, so what's at the other side
of that better be pretty compelling or you'll just give up. Sandberg

herself leaves work at five thirty and then like most of her colleagues tunes back in after her children have gone to bed.

Gone are the days when hard-driving women had to hide their pregnancies from their bosses. In the 1960s, Barbara Walters went back to work a day after her miscarriage. When she finally adopted a baby girl, she didn't mention it, and she didn't slow down. "There was no having it all," Walters has said about her situation. If Walters were a news anchor today, she would do a series on adoption and live-tweet the moment she picked up her daughter from the orphanage. She would show her baby pictures on air, as Fox's Megyn Kelly did, getting into vicious arguments with any viewers who complained. Kelly also got into one with a fellow conservative TV host who complained that her maternity leave was a "racket." Earlier she had squeezed her milk-enhanced boobs into a tight black dress for a sexy photo shoot for *GQ*.

A space has opened up for women—and yes, we are talking mostly about professional women (and men) here—to get creative about how they conduct themselves in the workplace as parents. High-profile companies have begun to adopt radical flexibility programs. Best Buy recently instituted a Results-Only Work Environment for managers and executives, which goes by Silicon Valley rules. As long as you get your work done, you don't have to show up; you can conduct meetings by cell phone from your fishing boat if you want. The top accounting firms—KPMG, Deloitte, Ernst & Young, PricewaterhouseCoopers— are in a PR race to see who can come up with more creative options for flexibility, and now financial firms are joining in, too. The key is not to place pressure on individual women to ask for special deals, but to make flexibility the default option, for everyone.

If a company doesn't have a blanket flexibility policy, then the same strategy that works for women negotiating pay raises works for negotiating a flexible schedule: Present your solution as good for yourself and the company. When Sukhinder Singh Cassidy had her first child, she was working at Google. "I went into Eric's office"—meaning then-CEO Eric Schmidt—"and I said I need to pay for my nanny and my daughter to travel business class around the world." This was, on its face, an outrageous request, even for the permissive culture of Silicon Valley. "Why did I do it? Because I love my daughter and I love my job and I have the energy to manage them both. And at that point I had earned that flexibility," she said. Cassidy made her case with a spreadsheet showing that the extra cost "is nothing compared to what it would cost to recruit another person who you know can perform in this job." Her boss assented.

Sallie Krawcheck has referred to being a mother on Wall Street as an "extreme sport." In the early years she managed it by choosing her firm, and what she calls her "microclimate"—meaning her specific boss and assignment—carefully. She became a research analyst, which was a job she could do largely on her own time. Although she is a Southern WASP, she sought out firms where the culture was renegade outsider, which in this case meant essentially Jews. One of the firms she worked for was most proud of having hired a former taxi driver as an analyst, "not the typical Joe from Harvard." One weekend she and her husband were packed up to move when she got a call from her boss, who wanted to review an earnings model she'd drawn up. Krawcheck called a colleague, panicked—all her work clothes were boxed up and being shipped to her new place. "Don't worry," her colleague told her. "All he will see is your brain." Krawcheck went to the office in sweatpants and a T-shirt and nobody cared. She got her first promotion when she was six months pregnant. "There was none of this 1970s thing of pretending I don't have kids. Every Friday afternoon I went to the mommy and me sing-along. I never missed a single one."

Many great working women reach the point where they stop and wonder whether the mad daily rush is worth it. Sometimes the moment is forced on them by some job frustration or layoff, but sometimes it starts to preoccupy them for no apparent reason at all. The typical male midlife crisis tends to hit out of the blue and take men by surprise, but for women it's been lingering there all along. They might have felt it during maternity leave, or on the day they walked into the fourth meeting of the morning and desperately wanted to walk back out and find some quiet place to sit and read a magazine. What they need is not a room of their own—they probably have one at home, even if it's called an office—but just more *room*, in the crammed minute-by-minute calendars that are their lives. Maybe they think, I could get away with slipping away—not for an hour, with a magazine, but for good. There are, after all, usually children to tend to and a household to manage; it could be justified.

In Tina Brown's case, the moment arrived unbidden. Brown had been a celebrity editor since she was in her midtwenties and revived the British society magazine *Tatler*. She had always had a constant eye on the news, had always been in the news. Several stints later, she was put in charge of her own new magazine, *Talk*, but the magazine lasted barely four years and Brown, in her forties, found herself for the first time free of a workday calendar. She pottered around the house, had breakfast with her husband, Harry Evans, had ice cream and tea with her daughter, and helped her son with his homework. I have over the years read many profiles of Brown, but none had quite the wistful tone of this recent one in the British magazine *The Lady*, where she reflected on those years.

"I had," she recalled, "become very happy. For the first time in my entire working life as a mother I wasn't conflicted anymore. The conflict gets very tiring. Just suddenly to be free of that—to be able to come to the school—to be there when you're supposed to be there—or if plans change that you weren't immediately thinking how to do this or juggle that. All those conversations with yourself had stopped. I was able to pick up my children from school and gain proper insights into their day. It was really lovely. I was immensely rejuvenated. I looked about five years younger. People said I looked so relaxed—and I was!"

I recently asked Brown about this period, and why she thinks women are so tempted to leave their jobs. "A lot of women have been battered around in traditional structures and they just don't find it satisfying or edifying, and not particularly stimulating," she told me. "They don't want to go through the thing of being at the traditional top. They want to go off and be creative." In Brown's case, it worked out. During that hiatus she wrote her best-selling book, *The Diana Chronicles*. And now she is once again back in the news cycle, running *Newsweek* and *The Daily Beast*, e-mailing her editors at two in the morning.

Brown says she makes her peace with the "traditional structure" by sticking to what are essentially the same rules Marissa Mayer follows to ward off burnout. In her negotiations with new bosses, Brown always insists on a single thing: not more money, or a wardrobe, or a driver, but creative freedom. "I love working on magazines. I love writing. I love being in an office and seeing projects come to fruition. If I wasn't able to do my work I'd get depressed. I think you either have that passion or you don't—and those of us who do are very lucky, because in the end our children do grow up, so actually I'm glad I have it."

Krawcheck has seen plenty of Wall Street women succumb to the temptation to jump ship. They make it through their first career plateau, where they don't get promoted or don't like a boss, and then a few years later they hit a second one. "The men continue to make it through, but I've seen numerous women who at that point say, 'I'm out. It's not worth it. I have two beautiful children at home, and it's socially acceptable to be home. It's more fun at home.'" But, she adds, "if we can get women past their second career plateau, you'll find more making their way to the top—because it does get a lot easier when the kids are in school. It's a lot easier for me, with kids who are twelve and fourteen, than when they were four and six."

A recent McKinsey survey on women and the economy uncovered an admirable and also frustrating trait common to women. Much more than men, women tend to derive their satisfaction and moral identity from aspects of work—and life—that are unrelated to lockstep promotion. Women stay at jobs rather than move up to new ones because they might "derive a deep sense of meaning professionally," the report concluded. They don't necessarily want to "trade that joy for what they fear will be energy-draining meetings and corporate politics" that come along with a bigger title.

There is, of course, nothing wrong with a deep sense of meaning. The Netherlands, for example, is right now gripped by an epidemic of meaning. Despite various government incentives, Dutch women do not want to work full-time, because they would rather have their afternoons free for coffee with friends.

I asked Sheryl Sandberg about this once. What if it's innate that women are allergic to a certain kind of ambition? What if women are somehow programmed to ease their way through life at a different pace? What if the resistance from the ruling patriarchy in the American workplace is still so overpowering that only a brave and exceptional few—only women like Sheryl, essentially—can keep up the will to fight it? "I think it might be innate and I still don't care," she said. "We need to get over it. We might be biologically programmed to get obese, but we don't give in to that, too." The external barriers are decreasing every day. Pretty soon women will take up 30 percent of spots at the top, which most people say is the tipping point, after which their presence there no longer seems unusual. But the internal barriers are likely to be the harder fight.

Often Sandberg is accused of blaming women for not advancing more quickly, of being blind to the realities of the average working woman (she stands to gain $1.6 billion in the Facebook IPO). But this again is a narrow reading of the situation. If Sandberg is watching over Facebook's maternity leave policy, the receptionist has as much to gain from that as Sheryl does. If women want the future to contain fewer energy-draining meetings and a more family-friendly workplace, you need more women to make it to Sheryl Sandberg's level. Not just for Sheryl Sandberg's benefit, but for the millions of women who have a lot less power to make demands. You need women at the top to remake the workplace in their own image.

THE GOLD
MISSES

ASIAN WOMEN TAKE
OVER THE WORLD

One of the propositions considered by the Asian Debate Institute held in Seoul in the winter of 2012 is whether quotas are necessary for women to advance in Asian society. The college students assembled in this downtown university classroom provide strong evidence for the negative. These students have traveled from all over Asia to the South Korean capital for this weeklong debate camp, held over their winter break, and about three-quarters of them are women. Some have come just to practice speaking English but most are here to "get more aggressive," as Hitomi Nakamura, a Japanese freshman who goes by the nickname Miki, told me. "This will help me get ahead in life."

Yeeun Kim, a student-teacher and 2011 national debate champion, is teaching this class of beginners how to develop and deepen their arguments so they are more "powerful." She calls on Miki for an example of utilitarian logic, and Miki gives her answer in a kitten whisper. Miki has never debated before, and her English is halting. It's unclear whether she even understands what "utilitarian" means. She turns her head slightly away and covers her mouth with her hands when she talks. "Louder," says Yeeun. Miki raises her voice half a notch. "I said *louder*," Yeeun repeats. "I can barely hear you up here." She rests her hands on her waist in the universal sign for growing impatience.

With her chunky sweater and short plaid skirt, Yeeun looks like a lot of the other college girls walking around Seoul, shyly holding hands with boys, leaning against each other, or talking on cell phones dangling with little dolls or stuffed bears. But Yeeun has none of the girlish giggle left in her. She started debating two years ago, after breaking up with a boyfriend who was turned off by her reluctance to lower her voice, to back down from an argument, or generally to behave like the "ideal, feminine Korean woman." Yeeun was looking for a "challenge, a fresh feeling to life," and a friend introduced her to a school debate club. There she found her role models, women and men who were "so confident and so intelligent!" At the time her English wasn't that fluent, but within a year she was winning top speaking awards and placing in international competitions, beating back all-male teams with calm, methodical confidence.

Around 2003, debate clubs began popping up at all the elite Korean universities in Seoul, as the activity became the nation's latest marker of academic success and future achievement. Teams from all over Asia traveled to Korea for competitions, and pretty soon one school began to dominate those competitions: Ewha, the all-women's university in Seoul. This surprised most people but not Peter Kipp, an American who teaches English at Ewha and runs the debate institute.

During his fifteen years of teaching, Kipp has seen a remarkable transformation in the women at Ewha. When he started, they were fairly shy and dutiful, coming to school in shirts with Peter Pan collars, never missing a class, always grateful. This kind of deference is not a quality Kipp especially admires. He is an American bohemian type who settled here after marrying a Korean woman. He was initially attracted to his wife because she was wearing combat boots (it turned out they were more fashion statement than punk). He liked Ewha because there was a sweet feminist sisterhood to the place, a group of women striving together to stay ahead of The Man. Now the aura of togetherness is gone, and the vibe is more cutthroat. Ewha women are known as the most competitive students in Korea, a country famous for killer academic competitors. In fact, the Ewha women these days are so "über-competitive" that they have started to seem almost "arrogant" and "entitled" to Kipp. The women in his English classes lobby him for higher grades and rarely help their fellow students. Their new attitude is "It's my natural right to be a future global leader," he says. "They fight to the end." By this winter, Kipp admits, some of the other Korean debate teams were so weary of Ewha's dominance that they were secretly rooting for the Japanese teams to win the regional competitions.

OVER SEVERAL CENTURIES, South Korea constructed one of the most rigid patriarchal societies in the world. A series of authoritarian leaders imposed their Confucian-inspired power structure on every aspect of society, including individual households. Men held all the property, and when women married, they were formally transferred to their husbands' families. Eldest sons were responsible for taking care of all their relatives, and for seeing that the ancestors were properly respected. These rules were enshrined in the Korean Civil Code in 1958 as the Family Laws, which specified that eldest sons headed their families, and inheritance passed down male lines. When President Park Chung-hee began to rebuild Korea's economy in the

1960s, he did it largely by promoting large conglomerates, called *chaebol* (Samsung Electronics, Hyundai Motor) and putting them in the hands of a small number of powerful patriarchs.

In the 1970s and 1980s, the government embraced an industrial revolution, and Korea became perhaps the most miraculous of the Asian miracle stories. A country that had ranked as poor as Ghana, where children chased after US army trucks to gather stray biscuits, transformed itself into the thirteenth-largest economy in the world. Because Korea is not especially resource-rich, it managed this feat by making its workers its main asset. ("Work hard," was Park's theme for the country one year. The next year it was "Work harder!") The government set up extremely difficult national exams to determine which university students would go to and where they would eventually work—another Confucian legacy. The system tacitly encourages extreme academic competition, and most high school students attend private "cram" schools six days of the week that prepare them for the exams and can go until midnight or later. As a result, Korea climbed into the top five international rankings in math and reading scores and has remained there.

The government encouraged women to educate themselves, too, and they did. Women moved to the cities and went to college. They proved themselves to be perhaps the most plastic women in the world, advancing through the labor force with uncanny speed. They went through their *Mad Men* era in the early 1990s, when women were expected to serve tea and coffee to their male colleagues, and in many offices, to wear a uniform that made them look like stewardesses. But that phase passed quickly. Last year the percentage of women enrolling in college surpassed the percentage of men, and the newly educated women are trying their best to push into once exclusively male fields—medicine, law, technology, and finance. In

jobs for which exam scores are the only criterion—primarily government jobs—women have sailed past men. In the last few years they
have made up 55 percent of those who passed the extremely difficult
foreign service exam, causing the Korean Foreign Ministry to establish a minimum quota for men.

Pretty soon, without anyone anticipating or planning for it, these
changes started to erode the traditional patriarchal order. In 1991,
the country's laws were revised so that women could keep custody of
their children after a divorce and inherit property. In 2005, the government abolished the law making men the automatic head of the
family and allowed mothers to register children under their own
family names. As recently as 1985, about half of all women in a national
survey said they "must have a son." That percentage fell slowly until
1991, and then plummeted to just over 15 percent by 2003. In the
latest national study in 2010, about 40 percent of mothers and fathers
said they would prefer a *daughter*, about 30 percent said a son, and
the rest said they had no preference. Male preference in South Korea
"is over," says Monica Das Gupta, a demographer and Asia expert at
the World Bank. "It happened so fast. It's hard to believe it, but it is."

Now South Korea is in economic and cultural crisis. The extremely modern, test-based meritocracy the government established
was embedded in an old-fashioned patriarchy, and the two systems
are at last at war. At the center of that war are Korea's women, caught
between society's mixed messages that they should study hard and
work like killers but somehow still remain dainty women and old-
fashioned wives.

I chose South Korea to visit because it's so blatantly on this colli-
sion course, but I could have chosen any number of countries in
Asia, Latin America, the Middle East, and probably, in a generation
or so, Africa. Women worldwide are educating themselves and

accumulating credentials. Economies everywhere are becoming dependent on the women's success, even their unfettered ambition despite resistance from local versions of macho culture.

In Latin American countries, women's rapid entry into the educated workforce over the last twenty years is credited with lifting several countries out of poverty, according to a recent United Nations report. But Latin machismo has kept them out of top spots—for now. A recent report found that Latin American companies had fewer women in senior positions than companies in almost any other region. In Mexico, two legislators recently tried to introduce a law *requiring* women with children to stay home a certain number of hours a week, but that seemed a shade too desperate; a women's executive group squashed it.

In fact, a country's comfort level with the rise of women is becoming a marker of global success. In 2006, the Organization for Economic Cooperation and Development devised the Gender, Institutions and Development Database, which measures the economic and political power of women in 160 countries. With few exceptions, the greater the power of women, the greater the country's economic success. Aid agencies have started to recognize this relationship and have pushed to either funnel aid through women or institute political quotas in about a hundred countries, essentially forcing women into power in an effort to improve those countries' fortunes. In many countries, advancing women requires delicately tiptoeing around local customs that put men in charge of money or trust only men to be leaders.

But women are in fact advancing, and their success is causing cultural upheaval all over the world. Spanish demographer Albert Esteve has been tracking the global rise of women and its effects on marriage patterns. Historically, women have tended to marry men with more education or status than they have. But as women get more credentialed, that trend is halting virtually all over the world, and in some countries has even started to reverse itself. In France, Hungary, Israel, Portugal, Brazil, Belarus, Mongolia, Colombia, among a handful of others, the majority of women now marry down, meaning marry men with less education than they have.

In Spain, some men have found a way to end-run this unsettling new phenomenon for the moment. Instead of marrying a successful Spanish woman, they find a wife among the new wave of Latin American or Eastern European immigrants. "When a man here marries a woman from Colombia he is marrying the kind of woman he would have married fifty years ago in Spain," says Esteve. The ambitious Spanish women, meanwhile, find a husband among the German or Swedish men coming to Spain. "I suppose the women are marrying the kind of man they will find fifty years from now in Spain. The Spanish men," he adds, "are looking for a woman from the past, while the women are looking for men in the future."

The problem with this strategy is that the Colombian women don't stand still, either. Latin America is delayed in this trend because there is less economic opportunity and urban rents are high, but women there are also going to university more and starting to delay marriage. "In so many of these countries men don't realize that women's expectations have changed," says Esteve. "Women are working and having education and economic independence and they are not willing to settle for the old kinds of marriages where they are expected to take care of everything, and this is creating a mismatch in the marriage market."

In Asia that mismatch is extreme. Like most Asian countries, Korea has a fast-aging workforce with a very low birthrate. The country has infinite potential to grow its economy, but it can't do that without future workers. And at the moment, Korean women, newly liberated to work and spend and live as they please, have no incentive to produce those future workers. For three years running, South Korea has had the world's lowest birthrate, according to the World Health Organization. Among the ten countries with the lowest birthrates, half are in Asia.

Korean women have started to avoid marriage in droves, another remarkable shift in a country that has clung to the Princess Bride fantasy longer than most. In 2010, the average age for first marriage for Korean women was twenty-eight, about two years higher than in the United States. Divorce, still taboo in Asian society, has tripled in Korea since the 1990s. One in five Korean and Taiwanese women in their thirties is single. In Japan, it's one in three, and demographers guess that half of those will remain unmarried.

The Asian media is filled with faintly condescending and sometimes hostile articles about the new breed of Asian power woman. In Korea she is known as the alpha girl, the King Kong girl (a term invented by French feminist Virginie Despentes), or the "dried fish" woman, dessicated and lonely. The most common term is the semi-official "Gold Miss," defined by Korean government agencies as a professional, single woman over thirty who makes the equivalent of about $40,000 or more. "All that glitters is not gold," one article that originally ran in *The China Post* explains about the Gold Misses. They "typically spend their money on fashion, cosmetics, plastic surgery, travel or marriage agencies," the article goes on to explain, and then ends with a warning from a life planner: "Housewives will be with children and husband even if she lacks money. Gold Miss will find her life empty if she has no money."

Since Yeeun Kim broke up with her boyfriend and started debating, she has tried to date other men. But the same dynamic always unfolds. At first, when she's attracted to someone, she tries to impress him. "I behave to his expectations," she says. "I am very quiet and when I do speak, I lower my voice. If we go out to dinner I let him choose the dishes and I eat small amounts. I pretend, 'Oh, this is what I really want.'" But she can't keep it up. Eventually, she tries to persuade him to change his expectations, "but it's almost impossible. And then I start to lose interest." Once I asked Yeeun to show me how she does it, how exactly she lives up to a potential boyfriend's expectations across the table at dinner. She put the back of her hand to her mouth and giggled softly, but then quickly put her hand down in disgust. "I can't do it anymore." She's clear in her mind that she wants a child, but marriage? "I'm afraid of it."

Yeeun is not one of the spoiled, entitled women of Ewha university. The daughter of an army chaplain who has known hard times, she has "always felt a certain desperation to boost myself up." When she was a little girl, her mother told her she should grow up to be an "international leader" or a "female CEO," without really knowing what that meant. Her parents did not speak English and never traveled out of the country. Only after she started debating did she recognize herself as "someone who can win over many great, intelligent people. So, I told my father that I wanted to be a more successful woman."

How would a husband fit into her new dream? "I'm afraid he might restrict my lifestyle and the goals I want to pursue," she says. "If I get married and live a very unhappy life, what is the point?"

I AM A BAD WOMAN

The headline appeared across a full-page ad in several Korean newspapers in 2009. The text of the ad read like a private diary, or some kind of written confession or cry for help. The plea was unsigned, and many people who read it assumed that it was a clever campaign for some new deodorant or makeup or one of the daytime soap operas that run on Korean television. But there was a little too much realism in the ad, and not all that much romance.

> I may be a good employee, but to my family, I am a failure. In their eyes, I am a bad daughter-in-law, a bad parent, a bad wife and a bad mother. Do the benefits of working rationalize carrying all these labels? . . .
>
> I want to share my burden with others. I am desperate to hear words of support—that I am on my way to achieving greater things, that I shouldn't give up now. I need a family who can lead me through difficulties. I need a family who can be there for me always.

Eventually the Korean media made their way to the author, thirty-six-year-old Hwang Myeong-eun, who took out the ad with her own money for exactly the reasons she wrote: She was "desperate," she told me when we met in her office in the winter. At the time, Hwang's son was four, and she was the chief financial officer at a major advertising firm in Korea. She was working sixteen-hour days, leaving before her son woke up and coming home after he was in bed every day. She was making more money than her husband, but this fact went unacknowledged between them, and did not change the usual household dynamics. He never helped out at home, and she was still the one who got the scolding calls from the mother-in-law: "Have you forgotten today is the day of your father-in-law's memorial service? Your other family members are already here. I understand you are talented and all, but do you ever fulfill your family obligations?" What eventually broke her, Hwang told me, was the morning her son woke up before she left for work and caught her as she was walking out the door. He wanted to sing her his favorite song before she left, "and I had to cut him off in the middle. I had to leave."

Working mothers the world over may complain, but in Korea the pressures on them are unimaginable. Work hours in Korea are the second longest of any advanced nation, after Japan. Office workers typically stay until eight or nine at night, and then are usually expected to go out drinking with their colleagues or clients—the Korean extreme-sport version of bonding and networking. As women have begun flooding the workforce, they have disrupted these elaborate post-work rituals, but they haven't fundamentally transformed them. The drinking sessions still involve several rounds of high-proof *soju*, a sweet, vodka-like drink. Employees are asked on applications how many bottles of *soju* they can down in a session, and the newly ambitious working women feel pressure to keep up with the boys. Sometimes the colleagues will decamp to a "salon," a Hooters-like club where sexy waitresses serve the drinks. Most of the working women peel off at this point, but a few sigh and follow along, then spend the night sitting awkwardly with the group or trying to make conversation with the waitresses.

Asian society is stereotyped as family centered, but the stereotype only applies in an era where women stayed home full-time. Workplaces in much of Asia are distinctly incompatible with any kind of home life. Flextime or part-time arrangements are unheard of, and women are usually reluctant to take advantage of maternity leave for more than a month or two. At the same time, the domestic burdens on a Korean wife haven't changed much since the turn of the century: She is expected to cook, clean the house herself, and take care of both sets of in-laws. And in the modern era of ultra-competitive schooling, she also has to manage her children's unbelievably complicated roster of extracurricular activities. And have I mentioned that nannies are frowned upon? Mothers use them, but always with apologies, and often they end up cobbling together child care using the more acceptable combination of relatives and trusted neighbors.

Hwang is an unlikely person to have become a poster girl for the impossible situation of the modern Korean woman. She is pretty in an old-fashioned, feminine way, with a perfect bob framing her delicate face, and the day I met her she had light blue nails that perfectly matched her cashmere sweater. She seems reserved and cautious and not at all the type to opt for a public confession. But somebody had to do it. Korea does not have a tell-all kind of culture. There is no equivalent of *Oprah* or *The View*, no public space for girlfriends to keep it real. Magazines are not full of wrenching essays by young women frustrated by the dating scene or working mothers agonized by the time squeeze. Self-help and chick-lit have only penetrated the publishing market in the last couple of years. When newspapers mention the dilemmas of the new alpha girls, they generally enlist experts to supply withering diagnoses of their psychological weaknesses: "obsessed with having to excel in everything and more likely to form unsuitable relationships," or "unconsciously dislike men they have to compete with, so they gravitate toward men with lowlier jobs than theirs or even no job at all."

Two thousand nine should have been a tremendous year for Hwang. She was thriving in her job, making more money than ever, and she had a beautiful son. But instead, she found herself full of intense, conflicting emotions with nowhere to put them. What made it worse was she had no role models to follow. A generation earlier, Korean women barely worked, so mothers had only vague advice to offer, and probably a dose of disapproval. And in this culture, shrinks are unheard of. So Hwang fell apart. "I was making excuses at home and excuses at work and I was so stressed out," she says. "The guilty feeling that I couldn't be with my kid was the worst thing I'd ever experienced. I wanted to be with him, to take care of him the right way, and I couldn't."

Why didn't she quit her job? "Because I had to make money. Nowadays if you don't have a double income you can't properly educate your child and send him to the right schools." She was a bad mother if she failed to stay home and take care of her child, and a bad mother if she failed to work and help pay for her child's schooling. How could a woman win? Her dilemma would have been a familiar one to Americans, but in Korea it was a novelty to have someone say it aloud.

When I caught up with Hwang a year and a half after she ran the ads, she had finally quit her job and started her own company. Now she is head of a small boutique advertising firm, Ark & Pancom. She is a rare female CEO in the industry, but she is not intimidated by the competition. Advertising, she figured, values creativity and attention to detail, qualities she believes women have in abundance. Since she made her confession, her husband started helping around the house more. On weekends if she is tired, he will sometimes watch their son by himself. But she still has to tiptoe around him. "I have to be cautious, to make sure he does not feel inferior to me." She makes a point of asking his advice about small domestic decisions, new clothes for herself or a fish for their son's aquarium. If he wants to have sex she complies, no matter how tired she is, because "I don't want to wound his pride," she says.

Hwang received hundreds of letters after her ads ran and was invited to speak at many public forums. She gives herself some credit for helping to change the climate for working women. After the ads ran, the government expanded child-care options for lower-income women, and more actively encouraged companies to offer flexible work schedules. And she is hopeful that younger men will change their ideas about working women and help out more around the house. But what about her life? Had it changed all that much?

Not really. In fact, Hwang's family schedule would probably strike even hardworking Americans as alarming. She leaves the house at seven A.M. and returns home sometime between eleven P.M. and one A.M. "Most Korean companies expect us to work very late," she says. "I'm the boss now, so I have to take care of everything." I asked about her son's schedule, and this was the only time I saw the flash of sadness that could have prompted her dramatic public confession. He comes back from kindergarten at three thirty each day and then goes straight to two cram schools, where he studies some combination of art, painting, music, tae kwan do, English, Korean, Chinese, and mathematics. "I manage the cram schools through the nannies," she says. She still doesn't see him during the week, but she tries to spend most of her time on the weekends with him if she's not too tired.

"I hope my son sees me as a good mother when he grows up," she says. "I hope he sees me as someone who accomplished important things for his future."

WHAT'S THE ANSWER? How does a new generation of Korean women fulfill their ambitions without destroying their souls? One solution bubbling up is something Korean authorities don't want to discuss, something that wounds their deep sense of national pride and makes them panic about their future. Elite Koreans these days almost always spend some time abroad to improve their English, either in high school, college, or graduate school. Per capita, Korea exports a larger percentage of students than almost any other nation. Families who can afford it move to the United States or Australia for a few years, and those that can't, send children to live with relatives.

The idea is that the students will come back and enrich the national economy. They will help the Korean conglomerates grow and better export their products. They will help exalt their country's place in the global culture. They will transform the average Korean's identity from one of provincial pride to that of sophisticated citizen of the world. But for the women especially, this is not always how it happens. When they travel abroad they realize that women in other countries live differently, that women in other countries do not pay such a high price for their ambitions. There is a reason that the top ambition for young Korean women these days is "foreign diplomat" or "global leader." Even as early as high school, they must sense that they will need an escape.

Yongah Kim went to college at one of Seoul's most prestigious universities, and then got her MBA at Harvard Business School. When she graduated in 2001 she interviewed with a large Korean conglomerate, a Korean bank, and several foreign firms, including a few investment banks and consulting firms that had expanded their business in the country after the economic crisis of the 1990s. At the foreign consulting firms she was asked very specific, logic-driven questions: How would you solve the traffic problem in Seoul, for example. At the Korean firms the questions were more generic, and also intrusive: What are your strengths? Do you have a boyfriend? If you get married, would you continue to work? One interviewer said, "Let's assume your boss asked you to fetch coffee. Would you do it?" Yongah answered: "Only if he would fetch coffee for me."

"Just the fact that they were asking me those questions tipped me off that there would be limitations," she said. "At a Korean firm there is so much hierarchy. I would have to start out copying documents. I went to a very good school. I can do better than copying documents." At a foreign firm, an entry-level executive might be in the same meeting with the CEO, or working on teams with much more senior executives—a configuration unheard of at a Korean company.

Yongah took a job at McKinsey Consulting and has been there over a decade. She is married now, and has a son, She starts her day at eight or nine and leaves around eight, which is still long but reasonable by Korean standards. She feels free to skip out on some after-work drinking sessions and instead invite certain clients to lunch or tea, or send them a book. She finds that some of them actually appreciate these alternatives, which give them a few evening hours to themselves. Now, when she talks about her work/life juggling, she sounds like any ambitious American woman, stressed out but not desperate. "It's up and down. If I have to go to my son's school to meet a teacher I can leave at four and finish my work in the evening, or do a conference call from home. If it's an unavoidable family event I try to make it. But at the same time I don't want to jeopardize my professional life. In each case it comes down to my own personal judgment."

A research team at Harvard Business School led by economist Jordan Siegel noticed that in the last several years, foreign firms not just in Korea but in many industrial and emerging economies in Asia, Latin America, and Eastern Europe have begun to hire large numbers of local women executives. After looking at Korean examples more closely, Siegel figured out why. The sudden interest in women executives was not driven by a sense of justice or equity, but by a keen eye for a new kind of competitive edge. Every year these countries are churning out female graduates from colleges and professional schools, but relatively few of them find jobs. In Korea, for example, only 60 percent of college-educated women work, the lowest rate in any OECD country. And once they do find a job at a local firm, they have trouble climbing the corporate ladder.

Foreign firms have begun to take advantage of this disparity, hiring the most qualified female executives at lower salaries, and hanging on to them with more humane work policies. Why are they only doing this now? Fifteen years ago, the consequences of hiring women would have been too damaging. Local clients would have been resistant to doing business with a woman. Their sexism and condescension are typified by the response one Korean financial executive gave Siegel when asked about his own hiring practices (and this is the mildest insult in the report): "I have no female managers. . . . I found that women are limited by emotional decision-making and that it causes problems." These attitudes haven't disappeared, but they have softened just enough that foreign firms in Korea can get away with hiring a few more women. The world, in other words, is at a transition point, grudgingly aware that women are poised to be powerful but not quite ready to accept it. For the companies who take the risk, by Siegel's analysis, it pays off. Siegel found that increasing female managers makes a firm more profitable over time. More specifically, increasing female managers by 10 percent raises profitability by 1 percent, partly because they pay women less, and partly because the firms hiring more women are more nimble and responsive to trends, Siegel guesses.

When Yongah took her first job at an American investment bank in the bank's Seoul office around 1997, women were still a rarity in boardrooms and clients did not know how to treat her. She would hold out her hand and no one would shake it. Male executives would not look her in the eye. Most assumed she was the secretary or the translator. She heard stories of clients who absolutely refused to work with teams that included a woman. Now fifteen years later, clients have gotten used to her; in fact, after years of excellent work they have begun requesting her—if nothing else, a woman on a team is memorable. Last year, a few Korean companies asked her to give talks at their firm on how they can recruit and retain female workers. Lately, clients have started asking Yongah how their daughters can grow up to be more successful like her. In Korean universities, women now make up about half of all business majors and last year McKinsey was flooded with impressive female applicants. "Women have the drive and the persistence to excel," says Yongah. "It's just that so many things get in their way."

Here and there, Korean business leaders, like business leaders all over the world, are slowly starting to loosen up. In my visits to many Korean companies, Yuhan-Kimberly, a paper goods and pharmaceutical company, stood out from the minute my translator and I walked into the waiting room. The office could have been in Silicon Valley: no cubicles, only tables and cushy chairs in friendly Ikea colors. A man met us and offered us tea and water while we waited for his boss, who was a woman. Yuhan-Kimberly was named one of Korea's Most Admired Companies in 2011 for its humane workplace policies and corporate ethics. Although it's a joint venture with a British company, many of the innovations originated with Moon Kook-Hyun, the former CEO and failed presidential candidate from the Creative Korea party. Executives at Yuhan work eight- or nine-hour days and can choose flexible schedules, working from seven to four, for example. At seven thirty, the company turns off the lights to force any remaining employees to go home. New mothers are encouraged to take a full six months of maternity leave. You might even argue that the company goes too far in its sensitivity to women, isolating pregnant women in a corner with a special ergonomically designed chair and desk, and reserving for them a resting lounge that calls up a Victorian fainting couch.

When economists assess a country's future, they see this ambivalence over women's role as the critical factor blocking its progress. Korea thrived so quickly under an era of severe discipline and rigid hierarchy. But now, decades in, those same qualities are stalling the country. In order to move forward, South Koreans need to create a more nimble economy, focused on innovation, design, knowledge, and service. They need to prove to the world that they have joined the twenty-first century. And a large part of that transformation involves empowering women workers, who are now kept just below middle management and behind the scenes. As executives at companies such as Kia (which is owned by Hyundai) try to expand their share of the global market, they face what in part amounts to an image problem: Sending a solid block of middle-aged men in suits as the company's ambassadors to France or Canada, say, does not convey cool car of the future. It conveys that the company is stuck in another era.

The more Korea wants to be part of the global culture, the more the country's leaders will have to bend—if not out of a sense of fairness and justice than out of a desire to succeed. In 2000, Korea set its heart on hosting the Winter Olympics. This would have been a major coup because until that point hosting the Games had generally been the province of northern Europe or the United States, and implied being rich enough that a significant portion of your population enjoyed expensive leisure activities and patronized luxury resorts. The Korean emissaries tried for a decade to win over the International Olympic Committee, without much luck. After evaluating past bids and polling international members they finally figured out why: The Korean team was stocked with senior businessmen who spoke very little English and could not really mingle at the networking parties. They needed to present a more "modern face of Korea," to look "more approachable."

Actually what they said to Theresa Rah, the TV anchor they finally chose to be their communications director, was, "we need a woman," she told me when we met in a Seoul coffee shop. Raised by a diplomat father and fluent in Korean, English, and French, Rah was drafted as the face of the PyeongChang 2018 Winter Games Bid Committee. At the final meeting, she gave a public presentation that won over committee members and made her an instant celebrity in Korea, the symbol of the "perfect working woman," as one Korean newspaper put it. Youthful and utterly charming, Rah gave a speech that could have just as easily served as a plea to Korea's leaders on behalf of the nation's women. The committee should give "people with desire and talent the tools they need to succeed," she urged them. "This is a race about dreams, about recognizing human potential." At one of the press conferences announcing that Korea had beaten out France and Germany for the Winter Games, a young woman showed up dressed in the Korean national costume and insisted on shaking hands with Jacques Rogge, president of the International Olympic Committee. She was a university student now but "in the future I want to be president of the IOC," the girl told him.

Women such as Yongah Kim at McKinsey or Theresa Rah remain a rare, privileged breed in Korea. They are buffeted by impressive foreign diplomas and worldly diplomat friends, and fluency in several languages. If they get truly frustrated, they can escape to Switzerland or California. But for the average Korean woman—as for the average woman in most recently industrialized countries—appearing too cosmopolitan, or cosmopolitan in the wrong ways, can backfire. Perhaps the most insulting of the expressions for the new breed of power woman used regularly by the Korean press is "soybean paste" girl. The label implies that she eats soybean paste stew for her meals because it's cheap and she wants to save the rest of her money to buy foreign luxury products—a Louis Vuitton bag, Chanel sunglasses, and a six-dollar Starbucks coffee to go with her one-dollar stew. In other words, as a consumer she is a national traitor.

In a wonderful unpublished paper, University of Chicago graduate student Vivien Chung compared the soybean paste girl with her vaunted counterpart, the fashionista. In the Korean media, the former is portrayed as an embarrassing mimic of other people's styles. She wears whatever she sees on *Sex and the City* or *Gossip Girl* and carries around English magazines that she can't really understand. The latter—the fashionista—is a true artist, the ideal modern Korean woman who creates a personal style that's locally inspired. In the fashionista, Koreans see a nation that can hold its own with France or the United States, a nation whose cultural prestige genuinely matches its economic power. In the soybean paste girl, Koreans see what they fear they have become—an arriviste nation, with economic power but no panache or respect, a mimic of other nations' modernity.

In her paper, Chung quotes from a series of popular stories that imagine a romance between soybean paste girl and hot pepper paste man. He is a hardworking student fresh out of the military and preparing for his grueling national exams. He does not have much money, so he eats a frugal lunch and drinks water. Along comes a pretty soybean paste girl, who convinces him to buy her a fancy meal and a Starbucks coffee. He blows all his remaining money on a single meal. In the parable, hot pepper paste man is the old, noble Korea and she is the shallow temptress leading the nation down a dangerous path.

It's easy to recognize the soybean paste girl on the streets of

Seoul—a young woman in sunglasses with a designer bag on line at Starbucks. But in my experience she was not usually nursing her cappuccino, or madly texting her friends about which mall they would meet at next. What seemed most off to me about the stereotype was the impression that she was in any way frivolous—crass and commercial, maybe, but not a woman with endless time on her hands. Initially I had written a few contacts saying I wanted to "hang out" with some young Korean women and maybe go shopping with them. I got this idea from reading about what was known a few years ago as the new class of "parasite girls" in Japan—young super-shoppers who idled all day at department stores, changing their look every two weeks and living off their parents. But then one of my contacts corrected me: "I know plenty of women here who shop," she said. "But I can't think of a single Korean friend who 'hangs out.' That's just not something they do." Instead they are generally rushing somewhere, to study or to work.

The real danger to hot pepper paste man these days is not soybean girl; it's something like her opposite: a woman who doesn't tempt him away from his exams because she is so busy studying herself, a woman who a few years later has no need of his money to buy her lunch or a fancy designer bag, because she is making enough money to buy them for herself. Asia's looming problem right now is not the dangers of seduction but the threat of industrial-scale sexual indifference. In a host of Asian countries, including Korea, the new woman and the same old man have looked each other over and each has deemed the other a wholly unsuitable life partner, creating a region of "lonely hearts," as *The Economist* recently called them. Japan, a few years down the road in this phenomenon, is now into comic territory. Sixty-one percent of single Japanese men between ages eighteen to thirty-four said in a government survey they have no girlfriend, and nearly half said they did not want one. The travel industry has begun to adjust honeymoon resorts to accommodate single-sex groups. The men often show up with a handheld device containing a virtual girlfriend who is a customized digital being, or with a body-length pillow on which is painted a picture of a woman.

Stephanie Kim and Kirsten Lee have been friends since they went to college together in Seoul. I met Stephanie through a friend and she brought along Kirsten because she was a typical "Gold Miss," Stephanie informed me: thirty-four, successful, and decisively single. We met in a slouchy tea house that doubled as a theater and served Korean takes on American vegan (tofu cheesecake, for example). They were both consciously stylish but in no way unserious; Kirsten carried all her work papers in a backpack, not a designer bag. She works as a producer of soap operas for the main Korean television station; you could say both had sacrificed domestic stability for independence and work satisfaction.

Kirsten has had the same boyfriend for three years. They don't live together, because very few couples in Korea do. Theoretically she would like to get married one day, but in fact she does nothing to encourage it. Her life right now is "perfect," she told me. "I make good money and I do whatever I want." Whatever she wants means working from seven A.M. to midnight most days on the set, but that's fine by her. She's already told her boyfriend that she'll never stop working, not even when she has a child, although a child at this point is just a word she throws out, nothing close to a concrete possibility.

Kirsten knows what the culture makes of hardworking mothers because she casts them in her soap operas all the time. A recent series features a working mother who is always frantically fielding calls from her autistic son's school. But the audience reaction to her was so hostile that they had to make the woman quit her job. That experience in her professional life only made Kirsten dig in deeper in her personal one. "I really don't see any reason to get married. If I do get married, I'll just have to do all the work. All my married friends complain about life, so my only conclusion is, there's no better life after marriage, only worse."

"*They* complain?" asks Stephanie, and she is joking, since her own story may be the cautionary tale most responsible for keeping Kirsten single. A few years ago Stephanie married someone she thought was the "new Korean man," a cool fashion photographer who seemed like he understood what she wanted. Now, she summarizes her decision as: "I was totally deceived." As soon as they got married he reverted to old Korea, she says. He would not do any housework or cooking; he just went to his room to work. When she went away on work trips three times a year, he shipped their son to her parents. "I was doing everything myself. I was the breadwinner and the housekeeper, and it seemed pointless to stay married," she says, and they divorced. "I feel like I fired him."

"Our generation was educated to compete with men. We go to equally good schools and get equally good jobs and have careers almost the same as a man. And then we get married and the men expect us to revert to an entirely different mental system," Stephanie told me. "Once only the sons were brought up like kings. But now we are brought up like queens. And when the kings and the queens are in the same house, they collide."

Perhaps the most depressing stories I heard in Korea were about what happens to successful women in the dating market. Young men and women frequently use dating sites and matchmakers, and like everything else in Korea potential candidates are ranked. Women lose points if they are not working at all, but they lose even more points if they are overeducated or have the potential to work too hard. As a result, a woman with a PhD or a Fulbright scholarship, say, will lie, and downgrade herself to a master's. ("They told me my schoolbag strap was too long," one PhD in sociology told me, meaning she'd been in school too long.) A newly minted doctor I met said the last service she applied to "told me I'm unmarketable, because I went to a top university and I'm thirty." Potential spouses were ranked as A, B, C, or D, I was told, and when people paired up, the A women and the D men often got left out.

By one estimate, nearly one in ten marriages in Korea involves foreign women. This is largely because there are so few women left in category D. They have all skipped up a notch, leaving the rural farmers or urban construction workers—the category D—without suitable brides. The men wind up importing brides from the Philippines or Vietnam. But the groom importation business having not yet taken off, the A women stay single.

Lacking a homegrown heroine, the lonely hearts take solace in *Sex and the City*, or in the surprise local hit by French feminist theorist Virginie Despentes, *King Kong Theory*, about her own rape and prostitution and the idea that "when it comes to sex today, everyone's getting screwed." Not meant for comfort, exactly, Despentes's manifesto at least helps unleash the rage.

Because this ideal of the attractive but not whorish white woman, in a good marriage but not self-effacing, with a good job but not so successful she outshines her man, slim but not neurotic over food, forever young without being disfigured by the surgeon's knife, a radiant mother not overwhelmed by diapers and homework, who manages her home beautifully without becoming a slave to housework, who knows a thing or two but less than a man. . . . I for one have never met her, not anywhere. My hunch is that she doesn't exist.

But there are more hopeful signs as well, even in Korean media. A recent popular drama, *My Name Is Kim Sam-soon*, starred a charming, pudgy pastry chef who always speaks her mind. She falls for a younger man who, after much drama, chooses her over his younger and more classically feminine ex-girlfriend—a vindication for the King Kong girls. Kirsten Lee recently worked on a soap opera, which features a working woman who insists that her husband, who can't find a job, take care of the children and cook. The woman had gotten the idea from her sister-in-law, who was a typical Gold Miss and intended to be the villain of the show; in one scene, the man's mother bursts into tears when she discovers her Cinderalla son wearing an apron. But Kirsten's viewers ended up being much more sympathetic to the Gold Miss, Kirsten told me, because at least "she was working hard, and she symbolized a good work ethic."

I HEARD HOPEFUL STORIES of the intimate kind, too, although they tended to involve the persistence and patience of a Confucian parable, like that of an ant pushing a boulder up a hill. Generally, they featured a woman slowly and slyly teaching her husband to notice when she needed help, and a husband pliant and loving enough to start noticing. One of the women I most enjoyed meeting in Korea was a senior official at one of the government ministries. If she'd been a decade younger, she could have been a Gold Miss; she wore a fur vest and chose as our meeting place a French café on the top floor of a posh department store. Over the twenty years of her marriage, her husband had changed, she swore, but at a "glacial pace." In the early years, family rituals would proceed in the usual Korean fashion. They would visit his family for the holidays and she would spend all day preparing food for neighbors she'd never met while the men watched football. "It really got under my skin," she told me. "After every holiday I came back in a nasty temper."

Then slowly she started making small requests, adding a new one each year. "Oh, honey, can you hand me that bucket?" "Oh, honey, I need more flour." "Guys, could you crack the walnuts?" "Pass the coffee?" Rice-flour dumplings are the staple of Korean holiday meals, and generally making them is solely a woman's job. Eventually she recruited her husband to help with even that detailed and tedious work, instead of just shooting him "bullets with my eyes." Just before the holidays, she will remind him that a "happy wife means a happy husband," and after two decades he has learned to take the hint. "Now, as soon as we step through the door at my mother-in-law's house he starts rolling up his sleeves." She has also taken steps to ensure that her son's wife won't have to go through that twenty-year reeducation process. She makes him clean up his breakfast dishes and do his own laundry.

Yeeun Kim, the young debater, may not have had any dating luck yet but she did have a breakthrough with her debate partner. For a year she debated with two men and one in particular always left her out of the strategic planning. "He was a very traditional Korean guy and whenever we would prep together he would try to dictate what we would do." He would say she was "too strong" and compare her to other girls he knew. Yeeun got fed up and at one tournament, burst out crying from fury, and said she would no longer debate with him.

But then she set her mind to reforming him. She tried to strike just the right note between deferential and confrontational. She argued with him but without being too aggressive. Eventually she won him over, and they began to operate like true partners. Now she says that's the closest model she has to a good relationship, and the reason she still has hope she might find someone she can marry.

You can understand why Korean men are in a state of shock. Korean women have gone from housewives to manic superwomen in just one generation. But the shock needs an equally strong counter-shock. A recent best seller loosely translated as *Things of a Man* by a local academic advises Korean men to change their habits because their form of patriarchy belongs to a dying era. In what might count as the most monumental change, Korea's leading presidential candidate at the time I visited was a woman: Park Geun-hye is the daughter of a political dynasty, but her candidacy is still an amazing development in a country that effectively does not believe in female leadership. With any luck, Korea might go the way of some other formerly patriarchal, even militaristic cultures, and recognize the value of women leaders as a sort of maternal rescue team—Liberia's president, Ellen Johnson Sirleaf, for example, who portrayed her country as a sick child in need of her care during her 2005 campaign. Or post-genocide Rwanda, which elected to heal itself by becoming the first country with a majority of women in parliament.

Despite her bad experience or maybe because of it, Stephanie Lee is doing her part to make sure the next generation of men will make a clean break. She has taught her son to speak softly, and she buys him pink stuffed animals and enrolls him in cooking and ballet instead of tae kwan do, even if he's the only boy in the class, even if the teachers object. "I think machos really can't survive in this new era," she says, "and if I want him to thrive he needs a more feminine side."

CONCLUSION

B y the end of my research for this book I had gone a few months without talking to Calvin, the man I mentioned in the introduction—the boyfriend of Bethenny, the man who'd set off my curiosity about the fate of men. I gave him a call to catch up. I was happy to hear his deep, slow voice again, and as always he had plenty of time to talk, although not as much time as he'd had when we first met. Calvin was seeing his daughter much more regularly these days; he had just dropped her off at a friend's house when I called. She was a preteen now, which he acknowledged is not the easiest time for a father to reconnect. (He and I have daughters about the same age, so we relate on that front.) But better late than never, right?

Calvin told me his next stop was the unemployment office, but not just to inquire about his check this time. He was looking into applying for a tuition subsidy. A few weeks earlier, he had wandered over to the local community college. It offered classes in engineering and various mechanical skills that might have seemed like a natural fit for Calvin, especially now that manufacturing jobs were trickling back into the region, as everywhere else in the United States.

But Calvin had decided to check out the nursing program—the same program Bethenny had just completed. His own mother had been a nurse, and he'd seen Bethenny "grow up about twenty years" while completing the program, he told me. Even though the classes looked like "all skirts" to him, he'd decided to give it a try. I could almost see it. Calvin was big but pretty gentle and not all that intrusive, qualities that might be soothing in a nurse. I could imagine patients feeling safe in his presence, particularly since "safe" in a hospital context does not entail long-term commitment. I told him I could not be more delighted, which is the truth. If he had started out as my muse for the "end of men," Calvin was now showing that "end" might not be a permanent state of existence.

AS PART OF MY RESEARCH, I have read and reread the prophets of brain difference, particularly the popularizers such as Simon Baron-Cohen and Louann Brizendine, who argue that the male brain works this way and the female brain works that way and that those distinctions ordain the sexes to permanently work and love and live in diametrically opposite ways. But at this point at least, I just don't find that line of research all that convincing. I'm sure that in the future neuroscientists will discover important differences between the male and female brains, but I suspect it's less likely that those differences will decide matters so complicated as whether we choose to better ourselves by studying, to work in fulfilling jobs, or to be dedicated parents.

At this moment in history, Plastic Woman and Cardboard Man

are at their most divergent. Over this century, women have proven themselves adept at shifting and remaking and sometimes contorting themselves to fit the times, and that very flexibility and responsiveness has come to define success in our era. Men, by contrast, seem much more resistant and rigid. But that might just be the case at this particular moment. In my heart of hearts I believe that men, even some of the most discouraged men I've written about in this book, will eventually learn to decode the new flexibility, and will begin to adopt it for themselves. This doesn't mean they will all go to nursing school or become teachers or get straight As in AP English, but it does mean that they will learn to expand the range of options for what it means to be a man. There's nothing like being trounced year after year to make you reconsider your options. Bethenny had laughed when Calvin told her he was considering following in her footsteps. But when he asked, "You got any other ideas?" she admitted that she didn't.

There are not only Calvins out there, but also plenty of men considerably further along in helping with Project Plastic Man. I chose not to focus on them in this book because there didn't yet seem to be enough of them to constitute a definite trend. But some men I came across make it obvious that plasticity is not necessarily limited by gender. A few men I interviewed for my *Slate* survey on breadwinner wives, in particular, sounded like voices from the future. Here, for example, is Robert from Portland:

The fact that my wife makes more money than I do is never a topic of conversation in our house and is in no way an issue in our relationship. I'm proud of her accomplishments, and since everything we earn and spend is "ours," I never feel like I'm not pulling my weight. I've read a few articles about this topic and find the idea of jealousy or emasculation completely foreign.

Robert lives in a city so progressive that it's the subject of an extended TV comedy sketch on organic food–loving, DIY-ing, bike-lane-nazi progressives (*Portlandia*), and I suspect that his neighbors admire his open-mindedness. But my hope is that men in Calvin's slice of America will also adjust their attitudes.

A subtle shift in their behavior is already underway. In 2009, sociologists Carla Shows and Naomi Gerstel published a study comparing child-care habits of men who were high-earning, highly educated physicians and men who were low-income, less-educated emergency medical technicians. Because the hours of the EMTs were generally more flexible than their wives', the EMTs ended up being fairly active participants in their children's daily routines, the researchers found. They picked up the kids from day care, fed them dinner, and traded shifts with other EMTs to stay home when a child was ill. Their self-image might not have included "active dad" but that is exactly what they were. The physicians, by contrast, had very little to do with the routines of family life. Instead, they saw themselves as "good fathers" because they attended their children's special events, such as soccer games or performances that took place on weekends. Living closer to the bone, it turns out, provides a certain impetus to inhabit new kinds of masculine roles. The EMTs did not have the luxury to consider what someone might think of them staying home with a sick baby or making dinner. In a world where their wives were working hard and earning as much or more, they had to step into new roles to keep their families afloat.

But it's not just the men who have to adjust. In "The Seesaw Marriage," I mentioned that I was "startled" at the sight of a stay-at-home dad at my youngest child's preschool making hand-printed T-shirts for the teachers. When I confessed to that reaction in introducing my female-breadwinner-couple survey in *Slate*, a stay-at-home dad who guessed I was talking about him approached me to ask what exactly was so "startling." I had to think about that one for a while. In fact, he was one of the saner parents I knew. He brought in instruments to play for the kids, concocted cool art projects, biked his toddler daughter to school in all weather, and generally seemed to radiate the energy of someone who considered himself lucky. Obviously it was not just men restricting themselves to a narrow set of acceptable roles, but the rest of us colluding to keep them imprisoned. He was right. Why should I, after all my research, be "startled"? Why should I be anything but delighted?

Slowly, our attitudes seem to be shifting, the surest sign being that pop culture is starting to pick up the signal. In the TV sitcom *Up All Night*, the character played by Will Arnett starts out as a doltish stay-at-home dad, playing video games and ignoring the baby. But over the course of the series he evolves into the competent, sensible parent reining in his wife's crazy competitive instincts. The series' main accomplishment is creating a stay-at-home dad whose wife wants to sleep with him. The movie *What to Expect When You're Expecting* focuses on a "dude's group," where the dudes confess that their kids eat cigarettes or play in the toilet, but still there they are, a crew of dads and babies at the park. One of them confesses to a reluctant would-be father: "We love being dads. When I was young I used to think I was happy but now I *know* I'm happy." This seems to be about as far as the culture can go right now, although a few trailblazers are helping to move things along. A recent Huggies campaign showed a group of guys too transfixed by a football game to change a baby's diaper. ("Hand him some diapers and wipes and watch the fun," one promotional ad condescended.) Chris Routly, a stay-at-home father of two boys, started an online campaign complaining that the ad was "encouraging mockery of dads" and got Huggies to take the ad off the air.

The changes are starting to show up in younger men even before they have children. Anthropologist Helen Fisher studies what she calls the science of love—how people meet, the laws of attraction, what they long for when they date. Lately, she has started to notice something curious in the online dating population. The men want children more than the women do. In her recent study of over 5,000 singles, 51 percent of unattached men aged twenty-one to thirty-four wanted children, compared to just 46 percent of single women that age. In older age groups (ages thirty-five to forty-four), 27 percent of single guys wanted to have children, and only 16 percent of women. Fisher theorized that maybe as women "gain self-confidence, self-worth, money, and experience through work," men are becoming more needy and "broody," much like the old female stereotype. But why is that "broody"? Maybe the men are just making a sane and healthy adjustment to a new economic reality. Maybe they are even copping to longings they have always felt but were not expected or permitted to express.

There have long been theorists who claim that masculinity is entirely a social construct, a kind of warrior mask or armor men have insisted on wearing, down through the generations, partly because they fear that if it slips away their softness will be revealed. And although "masculinity" has taken many forms over the centuries and in different cultures, one of its constants—dating even to the epic of Gilgamesh—is being "steeped in nostalgia for lost masculinity," writes Leo Braudy in his book *From Chivalry to Terrorism: War and the Changing Nature of Masculinity.* Maybe we are approaching the moment when men stop looking back, fretting that all the "real men" are dead, and allow themselves to go soft, a little.

In 2010 I edited a story for *Slate* by an American father who was living in Sweden and just ending his extended paternity leave. Over the last decade, the Swedish government had piled on incentives designed to force fathers to actually take the allotted leave, and now 80 percent of them do. The writer, Nathan Hegedus, described indoor play centers full of dads acting just as moms would, talking about "poop, whether their babies sleep, how tired they are, when their kid started crawling or walking or throwing a ball or whatever." By filling the sidewalks with men pushing strollers, the country had achieved what Hegedus called a subtle redefinition of masculinity, where the notion that nurturing and caregiving is unmanly was "melting away." Now if a man refuses to take the time off, he is judged negatively by his family and even his guy friends. Sweden has gone the furthest to orchestrate such a shift, but other countries are trying. The Japanese government has recently started to offer paid paternity leave, and newspapers have tried to make celebrities of the new *Iku-men*, or men who stay home with their kids.

Sociologist Amy Schalet, who studies the culture of young boys and romance around the world, reports that Dutch teenage boys are extremely comfortable saying they've been in love, because the culture in the Netherlands encourages them to do that. But she also finds that American teenage boys are moving more in that direction. The American teenage boys she interviews have started to use "strong, almost hyper-romantic language to talk about love," she reports. Chalk it up to *Twilight*, maybe, or the influence of teenage crooner Justin Bieber. One boy she interviewed whose condom broke during sex was not callous or dismissive but distraught, she writes. The most important thing to him was being in love with his girlfriend, he told Schalet, and "'giving her everything I can.'" Maybe the Dutch will lead the way and transport us all into a new era of sweeter teenage romance.

Homogenous, social welfare–minded Nordic countries may be the global equivalents of Portland, but the effort to reengineer masculinity is cropping up in some surprising places—even more surprising than the average American high school. Over the last few decades, the company that controls a couple of offshore oil platforms nicknamed "Rex" and "Comus" in the Gulf of Mexico has made a systematic effort to transform their work culture. The goal was to reduce the unusually high number of workplace accidents, but the method they chose involved basically leaching the macho out of the workplace culture. In the old system, "the field foremen were kind of like a pack of lions. The guy that was in charge was the one who could basically out-perform and out-shout and out-intimidate all the others," one of the workers explained to two researchers from Stanford and Harvard who did an anthropological study of the worksites. The old macho culture encouraged the workers to be man enough never to wear a hard hat, for example, or ask for help, or otherwise show a shred of vulnerability. The aim was to be the "biggest, baddest rough-necks" around, one worker explained.

The new initiative, called Safety 2000, identified this macho behavior as the root source of the accident rate and tried to discourage it in every way possible. Management put up signs everywhere with reminders like NO ONE GETS HURT, PEOPLE SUPPORTING PEOPLE, and RESPECT AND PROTECT THE ENVIRONMENT. They held regular meetings where they encouraged workers to share their mistakes so others could learn from them. If a man needed extra help carrying a heavy load, say, or navigating a dangerous situation, he was encouraged to ask for it. If a man was having a hard time at home—if he was facing a divorce or had a sick child, for instance—he was encouraged to ask his coworkers to take it easy on him and to give him emotional support. At one point, the researchers overheard two of the crew talking about how much a worker named Joe missed his baby. One of them confessed that he had "sent home a tape of that Mozart and Chopin for Joe's baby, because it's real important for them babies to listen to music like that. Real soothing."

In an interview with the researchers, a production operator described how the workplace culture had changed. At first, he acknowledged, he and his peers had to be taught "how to be more lovey-dovey and more friendly with each other and to get in touch with the more tender side of each other type of thing. And all of us just laughed at first. It was like, man, this is never going to work, you know? But now you can really tell the difference. Even though we kid around and joke around with each other, there's no malice in it. We are a very different group now than we were when we first got together—kinder, gentler people."

Ultimately the new rules of operation seeped into the men's definition of their own masculinity, the researchers concluded. One worker told them that being a man "doesn't mean I want to kick someone's ass." Another said, "I don't want to be a superhero out here. I don't want to know everything." A third admitted, "A man is a man when he can think like a woman," which meant "being sensitive, compassionate, in touch with my feelings; knowing when to laugh and when to cry."

Rex and Comus are basically closed working environments where men live for some period isolated from their family and friends. In this way, they serve as perfect sites for social engineering, and are not all that similar to the actual world. Still, if a pack of lions can be tamed in this way, taught to cry and laugh and pray together, then there might be hope for everyone else. As the researchers theorized, Safety 2000 probably worked because the payback was greater. Striving to be the biggest, baddest redneck was just chasing after an image, like trying to catch the glow from the TV. But being this new kind of man meant forging actual human connections, which tend to hold us—all of us—longer.

We live in a world that privileges nimbleness and flexibility, the willingness to adapt and bend to a fast-changing economic landscape, to be responsive to social cues. At the moment, Plastic Woman manifests those qualities better than Cardboard Man does—at the moment. Yes, it's possible that Plastic Woman has some innate configuration of traits that ideally suit her to today's world. But it's just as possible that after so many years of lagging behind men, she is simply supercharged with underdog intensity. Or perhaps centuries of raising children have made her an expert at doing several things at once.

In the future—perhaps after his own long spell as underdog and chief caretaker for children—Cardboard Man may become more plastic, too. In the course of my reporting, I have met a few men who are leading the way to this future. And my research has caused me to start raising my two sons differently. Even if it's against their "nature," I want to teach them to bend. To my relief, I've discovered that with a little creativity on all our parts, it's not all that hard.

TWO MONTHS BEFORE I reached him, Calvin had been in a car wreck and had broken seven bones. The experience "just opened my eyes," he said. He thought of the wearying "muscle jobs" he'd held, and wondered, "What do I really want to do for the rest of my life? Do I really want to spend my last days smashed between two guys in the front seat of a truck?" He found himself thinking back to a time when he was eleven, about the same age as his daughter was now. His favorite uncle—his mother's brother—had gotten seriously sick but refused to go to the hospital. So Calvin's mother, the nurse, took him in and expertly cared for him at home. He was a difficult patient and would sometimes act out by smashing his pills with a hammer. But eventually he got better, and from then on he'd served as a second father to Calvin, coming to see him, taking him on hunting trips, and teaching him carpentry. Calvin figured the memory of that time came back to him after the car wreck to remind him how far a little nursing could go in mending people, relationships, and families.

In our conversation Calvin kept looping back to the moment he'd finished "putting up the papers," meaning turning in the application for college. This pretty perfunctory task had settled on him as a profound moment in his life. He'd found the process of walking into the admissions office and handing in his big manila envelope terrifying. Twice he'd gone home to get a new envelope because he noticed a crease in the one he was about to turn in. He'd been "more scared than I've ever been, even in that car wreck." But once he actually crossed the threshold into the office, "I also got this little thrill," he said. "Like I'm finally doing it."

AFTERWORD

You would think that a book called *The End of Men* would be, prima facie, an insult to men. But one of the great surprises I've had while speaking about the book over the past year is how little resistance I have gotten from the aggrieved sex. Yes, I have been to a forum or two where dude-bros from the men's rights movement fired their talking points at me, about how feminists like me have destroyed American manhood. And yes, I have still failed to completely win over my elder son, who has only recently started to yield in his belief that the title is "mean." But for the most part, the men I've encountered at my events or on radio call-in shows all over the world have approached me with surprising openness and curiosity.

My guess is that men sense the ground shifting beneath them and are not quite sure how to react, so they are relieved to have a space to talk about it. Men do not have magazines or TV shows or advice columns instructing them how to be a man in a changing world, and so they can ask me. "I lost my job and I discovered that I kind of like staying at home. Is that okay?" (One man even confessed that he likes staying at home even though he's a trained architect and he and his wife have no children; the project of keeping house so he and his wife don't have to live the usual frantic double-income life intrigues him.) "I'm dating a woman who makes more money than I do and she keeps suggesting fancy restaurants. What do I tell her?" Or the opposite: "I'm dating a woman who seems threatened by the fact that I'm more successful than she is. How do I handle that?"

When I've encountered resistance to my observations and analysis, it's come mostly from women—not from working-class women, who seem to find what I'm describing painfully familiar, if not totally obvious, but from the kinds of women in a position to suggest the fancy restaurants. There comes a point in nearly every book event I've done when a little feminist revolt stirs inside the crowd. I can feel it coming when an audience saves its wholehearted applause for the first moment I mention a sin committed against the women of America—say, our appalling lack of paid maternity leave (which is appalling!). Or when a questioner quotes to me in a triumphant tone statistics about the tiny percentage of female CEOs, as if I had never heard them before.

"Let's call it what it is: THE PATRIARCHY." This was a comment from a young woman who came to an event I was moderating. The event was centered on Anne-Marie Slaughter's 2012 Atlantic article, "Why Women Still Can't Have It All." Slaughter and I were on stage, and about six hundred people were in the audience. Although Slaughter and I have many points of agreement, we tend to draw a different crowd, or mood. Women come to hear her when they feel like they've hit a wall and need to commiserate. They want to vent about their frustrations, not to hear how they've triumphed.

"Can you say that word? PATRIARCHY?" This woman was not gunning for a laugh; she was dead serious, and pretty angry. She looked to be thirty or so, and from the way she spoke seemed well educated—exactly the type of woman I portray in the book as benefiting from the new era of female dominance, when women are better prepared for the current economy and have more independence to choose their life path.

As the woman spoke, I started to think of my own Slaughter moment, when, after the birth of my first child, I decided to work four days a week, a capitulation that sank me into a terrible depression. (If only Sheryl Sandberg had been around then to tell me to "Lean in!") I tried to figure out who, in the series of events that led up to that decision, had played the role of the patriarch. My husband? He couldn't care less how many days I work. My employer? Relatively benevolent and supportive—willing to let me work four days or five, willing to let me leave early. I suppose the patriarchy was lurking somewhere in my subconscious, tricking me into believing that it was more my duty to stay home with our new baby than my husband's. But I didn't see it as a "duty." I wanted to stay home with her, and I also wanted to work like a fiend. It was complicated and confusing, a combination of my personal choices, the realities of a deadline-driven newsroom, and the lack of a broader infrastructure to support working parents—certainly too complicated to pin on a single enemy.

I said some version of this out loud from the stage, partly because I was looking for sympathy, and partly because I wanted to convey that the "patriarchy" was not a fixed monolith we could never get around but something shifting and changing and open to analysis. But that confessional approach only brought down more ire on me. "Lucky for you that you have the luxury to agonize about your choices," the young woman said. "What about the woman who picks up your trash after you leave at five?"

This is when I knew I was dealing with some irrational attachment to the concept of unfair. For my book I'd interviewed plenty of women who might find themselves picking up the trash, likely as a second job after a full day of school or another job, or both, because their husbands—or, more likely, the fathers of their children—were out of work. These women, on the other side of the class divide from where I (or, I was willing to bet, my questioner) stood, know all about the end of men and what it looks like.

They are the ones who wrote me letters like this one, from Cindy, a forty-nine-year-old Hispanic woman who has worked her way up to becoming a manager for a clothing company, and who just got back together with an ex who was once a fireman, but is now struggling to find work:

> This is my life and the life of so many of my friends. The majority of the women I know are the primary (and often only) breadwinner in their family. None of us expected to end up in this scenario, but it's our reality. After six months of unemployment, I recently started a new job. One day, as I sat at my desk, multitasking in a lively office, I realized that as smart and hardworking as he is, my husband simply does not have the skills to perform the kind of job that is proving so lucrative for me: the ability to concentrate in a distracting environment, the kind yet firm empathy I need to lead my team, the instinctive understanding of different viewpoints and how to effectively build consensus. . . . Sometimes I find myself thinking condescending thoughts when he tries to give career advice, much the way my dad probably thought when my mother tried

to help him out in the sixties. I bite my tongue when my husband says wistfully that it would be nice to have a larger house. . . . Yet I feel very powerful and at the top of my game, and he contributes a great deal to my getting there. Thank you for giving voice to the quiet revolution that is going on around us.

You can hear many of the strains I describe in the book in Cindy's voice: ambivalence, for one. What she's witnessing at home is a microcosm of a national tragedy, probably the biggest one our nation faces: millions of men who find themselves unable to adapt to changes in the economy, losing their old roles in the home and having a hard time finding new ones. Mixed with that is pride at having found her own way, having discovered that she can carry the weight alone if it comes down to that.

Finally, Cindy is experiencing this situation much as I did. She did not go looking for it; neither did I. We both started out with one set of assumptions until reality showed us something quite different. I stumbled on this story of shifting power dynamics between men and women pretty much by accident, as the statistics and personal stories began to reveal that Americans were living very different lives than we ever expected to.

And I don't pretend that the world I'm describing is paradise, not even for the women who are rising on its tidal shifts. Change, even when it comes with benefits, is uncomfortable for everyone, and it takes a very long time to settle into new roles. (Cindy told me a friend to whom she gave the book would only read it on her Kindle, because if her boyfriend saw it on her nightstand he would be "devastated.") We don't just wake to find women turned executives and men transformed into housewives, and there, it's settled! The whole landscape looks different and uneven. Women settle into some power roles easily; others not so readily. Women give up some of their domestic duties, but not enough to balance the new loads they take on. Men pick up some of the slack, but not all, and often with resentment. All too many men pick up nothing; they just drop off the map.

And naturally, there is a lot of nostalgia. My young interrogator might be annoyed to learn that many of those women who pick up the trash—or even strivers like Cindy—yearn to bring back at least some aspects of the patriarchy. They generally appreciate their new economic independence and feel pride at holding their families together, at working and studying and doing things on their own, but sometimes they long to have a man around who would pay the bills and take care of them and make a life for them in which they could work less. Even their motives are complicated: It's partly that they want to work less, and partly that they want the men in their lives to be happy. No, it's elite feminists like me and my questioner who make up the vast majority of the audience at forums like the one where we were sparring, who cling to the dreaded patriarchy just as he is walking out of our lives.

A few months after my book came out, sociologist Stephanie Coontz published an editorial in the *New York Times* that was headlined "The Myth of Male Decline," which summarized many of the responses to my book in order to support her argument that the end of men was nowhere in sight. Many of the points made by Coontz and other members of what Liza Mundy, author of *The Richer Sex*, calls the academic "Fempire" are true, in a selective sort of way that elides other truths. I notice they often choose the statistics that make women look the most beleaguered. For example, one figure that both Mundy and I cite in our books, and that has provoked much angry dissent, is how many wives earn more money than their husbands. We all agree that the proportion of female breadwinners leapt from only 4 percent in 1970 to nearly 30 percent in 2010. Coontz, however, discounts this gain by arguing that when we look at *all* married couples, not just dual-earner couples, the numbers look much weaker because some wives don't work at all.

This is a fair point. But if we are going to add on extra data samples, then I offer another, more relevant one: the growing number of single mothers. The United States is undergoing an explosion not of full-time stay-at-home mothers but of single mothers who are often, for better or worse, the main breadwinners for their families by default. We recently passed the threshold, for example, at which more than half of all births to mothers under thirty were to single mothers. I'm not sure this counts as feminist progress, but it does count as a profound shift in the traditional power dynamics of the American family.

Coontz also makes the broader point that women, even college-educated women, continue to flock to less prestigious, lower-paid jobs. She points out that woman are even more concentrated now than they were before in the professions of legal secretary or "managers of medicine and health occupations."

First, let's put women's relatively lower wages in the context of this much broader trend: As a whole, men's wages have been steadily declining for three decades, and their role in the family has been dramatically eroded as women increasingly decide to go it alone—to educate themselves and work and raise children without the thought of a man in their lives. That's the radical transformation in American society, and the one most worth paying attention to.

Then let's look at the nature of the work itself. We can call the pattern of women's jobs by its old, disparaging name, "gender segregation," and insist on seeing it as a choice that is imposed on them. But we can also see it through a new paradigm—as Coontz in her own work has so successfully encouraged us to do about marriage—that acknowledges women as agents making intelligent decisions about what jobs are available in this economy. (You can see this decision making at work in community colleges, the training camps for the current workforce, where women typically make up about 70 percent of the student body.) As I observed in my research, of the top fifteen job categories projected to grow in the next several years, twelve are dominated by women. Maybe women are choosing health occupations because the health-care field is booming, not because they are blindly walking—or being led—into a female ghetto.

There is a pretty clear pattern to the professions where women tend to gravitate now, as Harvard economist Claudia Goldin points out. Women tend to thrive in jobs where some structural or technological innovation has made it possible for workers to succeed without sacrificing their personal lives. Women are dominating the field of pharmacy because pharmacists now work in shifts and no longer have to shoulder the 24/7 responsibility of owning a business. This shift has made the profession a viable choice for women looking to scale back for some years while raising young children, or otherwise aiming for control over their time. Other high-paying jobs women are lately dominating—veterinarian, accountant, certain medical specialties—have their own versions of this story.

While we could argue about whether it's fair that women are still the ones who make time management their priority—men would enjoy the same flexibility as pharmacists, but they don't choose the profession as often as women do—I don't think we should automatically conclude that women are drawing the short end of the stick. An equally plausible interpretation is that women are taking over professions that *allow* them to be decent parents *and* that are likely to last in the new economy. They are acting with an eye to both their ambition and the well-being of their children and mates, not to mention their own sanity. The most hopeful interpretation of what's going on is that women are helping to remake the workplace in an era when both men and women increasingly want greater flexibility, the freedom to be present for a kid's school assembly or doctor's appointment.

Women's rise in the workforce will look very different from men's. They may always choose jobs that allow for some control over their lives. They may always shy away from jobs that demand slavish dedication to the office. This does not mean they will never have power; it just means they will amass and exercise it in different ways, ways we may not be able to imagine or predict yet.

What surprised me most about Coontz's piece was not its content but the collective sigh of relief it seemed to generate. "Marry me, Stephanie Coontz," tweeted one young writer. "Stephanie Coontz is a national treasure and I wish her work were required reading for everyone in the world," blogged a second, and went on to explain how all this "women are dominating . . . stuff" is not quite true. The women who seemed to be reveling in Coontz's insistence that reports of the end of men have been greatly exaggerated were by and large young and quite successful, and as far as I could tell hadn't been held back all that much in their careers by "the patriarchy." Many of them are in positions of influence of their own, widely published and widely read; one is an admirably aggressive reporter and a star of her generation. If a male boss of hers ever did anything sexist or even condescending, I have no doubt she would gleefully skewer him in one of her many online outlets. These were exactly the types of women I had portrayed in the book as benefiting from the new age of female dominance. Why should they feel reassured to be told that men were still on top, that the old order had not been shaken?

The 2012 elections inspired a similar reaction in some quarters, which was greeted with a similarly satisfied response. A record number of women were elected to Congress, bringing their number to a third of the membership, the level many sociologists cite as a tipping point when a minority becomes normalized and starts to enter the mainstream. In other words, it's no longer big news when a woman gets elected; it's expected. Another big story was how critical women had been to Obama's reelection, particularly single women. And yet the day after the election, the *New York Times* published as its lead op-ed a study by two academics showing that women would not truly reach parity or be in a position to pass women-friendly policies until they controlled half of all congressional seats.

This seems true enough, if a little obvious. But it entirely missed the revolutionary shift the moment marked. There was a group marginalized in the election: white men. They voted en masse for Mitt Romney, and lost. It was the first time a president had been elected without their support, a development that entirely upset our notion of who is the majority in America, and who holds the power.

In the early days of the feminist movement, every small victory was celebrated. Women fought for the cultural space to publish the word *fuck* in a novel and then published exuberant, triumphant novels about self-knowledge through fucking. Women earned the right to sign their own name on a lease in a Southern state, and the nation celebrated. Women stood on a stage cursing at brooms and then practically masturbated with those brooms to show what they were good for. (Okay, maybe only Germaine Greer did that.) Still, there was an exultation, a liberation, a sense of celebration at women's progress that seems largely absent today. Somehow the mood of the movement seems to have shifted into reverse: The closer women get to real power, the more they cling to the idea that they are power-less. To rejoice about feminist victories these days counts as betrayal.

Recently I was part of a panel on the fiftieth anniversary of Betty Friedan's *The Feminine Mystique*. A big part of the discussion centered on why young women today don't want to call themselves feminists, which dismayed the other panelists. This was right after Marissa Mayer, now the CEO of Yahoo, declared in a PBS documentary on the women's rights movement that she would never call herself a feminist because they were "militant" and had a "chip on the shoulder." Afterward, a high schooler in the audience stood up to ask a question. She said that in her progressive school the girls were "creaming" the boys at virtually everything. She said they were better at sports and got better grades and ran all the extracurricular clubs. But the one thing she and her friends could not get anyone to do was join the feminist club.

At first, like the other panelists, I was dismayed, as I had been at Mayer's comments. But after a while a new realization dawned: Maybe if all these smart young women, Mayer among them, can't settle comfortably under the old banner of "feminism" then it's time to find a new framework; maybe the old one is just too freighted with history and it's time to shift the lens to reflect the new realities. I'm not sure what that term should be; I'll leave it to those high school go-getters to figure it out.

A month after my book came out, I was invited to an academic conference dedicated largely to rebutting the claims I had made in it. The participants came from many fields—law, sociology, anthropology—but were people who had spent their careers exploring social inequality. This issue is probably the most important one the United States and a number of other countries face, ever more so as the gap between rich and poor expands. But as I sat through the conference I realized that the study of inequality has an occupational hazard: After decades of looking for certain patterns, they may become all you can see. It's not that you're hallucinating or making them up; it's that you may be ignoring the larger play of elements of which the smaller patches you're studying are only elements. The phenomenon reminds me of the famous study in which researchers asked subjects viewing a video clip to count how many times basketball players wearing a certain color shirt passed a ball. A giant gorilla walked across the court in the course of the video, but many subjects failed to see it, so focused were they on the patterns they'd been instructed to watch.

History does not march in a single prescribed direction. If it did, who would be directing it—the Male Trilateral Commission? It often switches course, throws us surprises. We are living in such a moment. This doesn't mean no fights remain to be fought. Women do in fact get paid less than men, and do tend to choose lower-paying professions. Women don't yet occupy most of the top jobs. But other things are happening at the same time. Women are moving into new professions, new roles in their families. Men are straying off the old path, and every once in a while finding a new one. And mainstream media—like the NBC sitcom *Guys with Kids*, featuring a new generation of sexy, respectable, BabyBjorn-wearing men—is helping to legitimize those choices.

Much of the public discussion sparked by the golden anniversary of Friedan's book centered on how much a part of the fabric of women's lives her ideas had become. Once Friedan had anatomized "the problem that has no name," it seemed people just instantly absorbed it into their bloodstream. Of course women didn't want to sit around matching slipcovers and futzing with blender buttons! Wasn't that obvious?

But that's not in fact exactly how The *Feminine Mystique* was greeted when it was published. Here is a sample of her early reviews:

> [Friedan] demands that all women find a life purpose or career which will give them an independent identity and what she calls fulfillment. In that, she surely goes too far. How many women—and, for that matter, how many men—find that kind of career or purpose? Rather than be a file clerk, the average girl will continue to stay home and cream her face as long as society sanctions it.

"Cream" her face? Isn't that giving the verb a little too much robustness? Nowadays, if the average woman has time to *put* cream on her face, she is probably doing it on her way to work, in the car or on the subway, because a good 75 percent of women are in the workforce, according to the latest census, and an even higher percentage of the college-educated women Friedan was writing about. But that trajectory, so obvious in retrospect, wasn't at all obvious at the time.

I understand that the phrase "the end of men" gets under some women's skin, because it doesn't reflect their daily experience of life. Maybe they have an overbearing husband or a retrograde boss or just a lingering problem that has no name. But as a collective I sometimes feel that women tend to look too closely at the spot right in front of us. This is a moment, unprecedented in history—and also pretty confusing—when young women who work how they want and have sex how they want may also quilt and can fruits. When working-class women who quietly leave the only steady paycheck on the kitchen table every week may still believe that a man is the God-ordained head of the household. When Beyoncé, a near-perfect icon of this age of female dominance, launches a nostalgically named

"Mrs. Carter Show World Tour." In music, we call this sampling. History is jagged like that; it does not proceed in a slow and steady march but moves in unexpected, tangled, sometimes hard-to-detect patterns. So I want to tell these women who are seeing only oppression: Stop working so hard to connect the dots to the past, because they are leading to the future too—in a whole new direction, lots of new directions, in a landscape whose every detail we can't yet make out.

ACKNOWLEDGMENTS

Now it's time to thank all the good men who have helped me to trumpet their demise. I owe my greatest intellectual debt to Don Peck, my editor at *The Atlantic*. Don has the editor's equivalent of thrift-store genius. He is able to sift through heaps of disconnected thoughts and ideas and hone in on the gems hiding somewhere in the pile. I was staring at bits and pieces of this idea for months and there is no chance I would have clarified it into an *Atlantic* cover story without Don's help. I also thank James Bennet, editor of *The Atlantic*, for giving me a fun and supportive writing home for many years and for letting me temporarily hijack his magazine for a gender war which has, to some degree, continued there to this day. (Some would say that *The Atlantic* has become the best women's magazine around.)

Now, the women. I got enough heat for the magazine story that I probably would have stopped there if not for a phone call from Becky Saletan, who edited my first book. Becky convinced me to go back at the idea and expand it, and part of the reason I said yes was for the chance to work with her a second time. There were moments during this process when I felt she was sweating every phrase and paragraph as much as I was, which seems impossible given everything else she does. On top of that, she's been a great friend and general all-around life guru. My agent, Sarah Chalfant, is the toughest, most loyal guardian angel a writer could ask for. I always feel safe while she's on my side. Geoff Kloske believed in the book, with enthusiasm and good humor, despite its message. Jynne Martin and the rest of the Riverhead publicity team have worked hard to help it succeed. Sarah Yager saved me from many a minor embarrassment.

My colleagues at *Slate*'s DoubleX, the women's section I cofounded, created for me the rollicking women's studies seminar I never had in college. Jessica Grose, Emily Bazelon, and Julia Turner—and early on, Meghan O'Rourke, Sam Henig, and Noreen Malone—helped make meetings, podcasts, and projects seem like anything but work. Day after day we pored over lady news ranging from dumb to deadly serious until a coherent picture began to emerge for me about a larger story happening to women and men. Thanks also to Jacob Weisberg for having the vision for the section, and trusting us to carry it out.

Many fellow journalists, academics, and luminaries I have spoken to and argued with along the way—most of whom have been thinking about these subjects a lot longer than I have—forced me to rethink or expand or delete: Nancy Abelmann, Dan Abrams, Elizabeth Armstrong, Jeffrey Arnett, Kathleen Bogle, Kate Bolick, June Carbone, Meredith Chivers, James Chung, Alice Eagly, Kathy Edin, Albert Esteve, Susan Faludi, Garanz Franke-Ruta, Claudia Goldin, Michael Greenstone, Daniel Griffin, Metta Lou Henderson, Gregory Higby, Christina Hoff Sommers, Ann Hulbert, Arianna Huffington, Maria Kefalas, Laurel Kendall, Michael Kimmel, David Lapp, Maud Lavin, Lori Leibovich, Daniel Lichter, Wendy Manning, Amanda Marcotte, Marta Meana, Sharon Meers, Tom Mortenson, Linda Perlstein, Zhenchao Qian, Mark Regnerus, Amanda Ripley, Katie Roiphe, Sheryl Sandberg, Amanda Schaffer, Larry Summers, Rebecca Traister, Bruce Weinberg, Richard Whitmire, Brad Wilcox, Philip Zimbardo. Each has in some way, either through their writing or in conversation, helped shape my thoughts. Thank you also to Evan Ramstad, Krys Lee, Frank Ahrens, and SungHa Park for making Korea seem like the most exciting country ever.

As with every project, I owe the most to the people who agreed to be written about. Even the ones who chose to remain anonymous allowed themselves to be prodded and scrutinized and reexamined to a degree that can only be called brave. They include the students at the unnamed Ivy League business school (you know who you are); the students at the University of Wisconsin School of Pharmacy; the citizens of Alexander City; the men and women in Kansas City; the couples who spoke to me for my breadwinner wives survey; the women of Silicon Valley and Wall Street; the girls at PACE; and the various young women and men I interviewed in Korea. I thank them for trusting me and I admire them for their willingness to be open and honest.

I barely feel human without my crew of Washington girlfriends, each of whom has rescued me in one way or another at the drowning moments of book writing: Nurith Aizenman, Meri Kolbrener, Jessica Lazar, Alix Spiegel, Margaret Talbot. I wish I lived a Carrie Bradshaw life in which I could see each of them on successive nights of the week. Meri especially has gone through more during the last year than any mother should and yet still manages to be an anchor for an improbable number of people (Mark Leibovich, you're not a girl but you belong here too). If not for her, I don't think I would understand how to be a friend. The same appreciation goes to Tonje Vetleseter on the West Coast.

My mother, Miriam, is the reason why I was able to recognize the phenomenon I wrote about in the first place. I come from a long line of matriarchs who dominated their husbands in one way or another (I am not one of them). My mother is of an era and social class where women were never officially in charge, but in fact she was, in every way that mattered. She was the self-appointed neighborhood watchdog, known for being able to intimidate men three times her size. She is smart and tough and big-hearted and doesn't let anything intimidate her or distract her from doing the right thing. I love my dad, Eli, and my brother, Meir, for many reasons, including their not asking too many questions about the title of my book. And I love them for keeping an eye on Dalila, Tiago, Talles, Kyla, and Chloe.

My in-laws, Judith and Paul, I come to appreciate more every year. I realize it's not supposed to be that way, but it is. They are like grandparents, friends, colleagues, and intellectual sparring partners all in one. John, Lisa, Nelly, and Daria, I love you all and wish you lived closer. Holy Ramampandrison, you never let me down and you bring so much extra love into our house every day.

My daughter, Noa, has been a ray of sunshine streaming into my attic in the midafternoon, except when she's not (she's nearly a preteen). She's grown up so much in the time I've been writing this book, but still managed to hold on to her curiosity and core of confidence. She's also become one of the funniest people I know. My son Jacob asks me every day why I would write a book with such a mean title. I always tell him that I want to convince people that some men out there need our help, since it's not always so easy for them to ask for it. He doesn't quite believe me yet, but maybe one day he will. My son Gideon is thankfully too young to read the title, and too busy with his cars. But he is candy at the end of a long day. I kind of wish he'd never grow up.

How can I thank a husband who puts up with a wife who writes a book called *The End of Men*? Just imagine the potential for embarrassing tableaux: on the basketball court, at the gym, at the office. "Hey, what's your wife up to?" Yet David has been nothing but proud, so proud that I always hear from his friends the nice things he says about me. When I interviewed top executives about the most important decision they made in their lives, most of them said: I married the right man. I completely agree.

NOTES

A few notes on sources: All of the characters mentioned in the book are real people I met or interviewed in the course of reporting this book. However, sometimes I used only their first names, and sometimes I changed their names entirely. I used pseudonyms mostly in cases when I was revealing particularly intimate details about relationships: Tali, Shannon, Troy, Hannah, Billy, and Dian are pseudonyms, as are Stephanie Kim and Kirsten Lee. Quotes from experts generally come from interviews I conducted, unless a different source is noted below. Quotes in text that do not have sources noted below come from interviews conducted by the author in the research for this book.

INTRODUCTION

Page 1 This world has always belonged to males: Simone de Beauvoir, *The Second Sex* (New York: Vintage Books, 2011), p. 71.

Page 4 three-quarters of the 7.5 million jobs: Between June 2007 and December 2009, according to Pew Research Center's analysis of Bureau of Labor Statistics data, men lost 5.4 million jobs and women lost 2.1 million. http://pewresearch.org/pubs/2049/unemployment-jobs-gender-recession-economic-recovery.

Page 4 worst-hit industries: Mark J. Perry, "The Great Mancession of 2008–2009," Statement before the House Ways and Means

Committee Subcommittee on Income Security and Family Support on "Responsible Fatherhood Programs," June 17, 2010. http://democrats.waysandmeans.house.gov/media/pdf/111/2010Jun17_Perry_Testimony.pdf.

Page 4 In 2009, for the first time: According to revised employment data from the Bureau of Labor Statistics, women outnumbered men in the workforce in February, March, November, and December of 2009.

Page 4 Women worldwide dominate: OECD, *Education at a Glance 2011: OECD Indicators* (OECD Publishing, 2011). http://www.oecd.org/dataoecd/61/2/48631582.pdf.

Page 4 for every two men who will receive a BA: According to "Gender Equity in Higher Education: 2010," a report by the American Council on Education, women have consistently earned around 60 percent of bachelor's degrees for the last decade.

Page 4 Of the fifteen job categories: "The 30 Occupations with the Largest Projected Employment Growth, 2010-20," Bureau of Labor Statistics, February 2012. http://www.bls.gov/news.release/ecopro.t06.htm.

Page 5 more than 40 percent of private businesses in China: "41 Pct of China's Private Businesses Run by Women," *People's Daily*, September 17, 2004.

Page 9 the new "ornamental masculinity": Susan Faludi, *Stiffed: The Betrayal of the American Man* (New York: HarperCollins, 1999).

Page 9 "fixed in cultural aspic": Jessica Grose, "Omega Males and the Women Who Hate Them," *Slate*, March 18, 2010.

Page 10 In her iconic 1949 book: Beauvoir, *The Second Sex*, p. 562.

Page 11 "Women of our generation": Genevieve Field, "Girl Crazy," *Cookie*, August 2008.

Page 12 "You have to be concerned": Louise Lague, "Shopping for a Boy Baby? Ron Ericsson Can Help, but Critics Say He Shouldn't," *People*, September 17, 1984.

Page 13 a national survey of future parents: Jaeseon Joo, "Statistical Handbook: Women in Korea 2011," Korean Women's Development Institute, 2011.

HEARTS OF STEEL
SINGLE GIRLS MASTER THE HOOK-UP

Page 17 "Yale's sexual culture" itself: Bijan Aboutorabi, Eduardo Andino, and Isabel Marin, "Change the Climate, End Sex Week," *Yale Daily News,* September 20, 2011.

Page 19 In 1988 half of boys: Tara Parker-Pope, "The Kids are More Than All Right," *The New York Times,* February 5, 2012.

Page 19 Teen pregnancy rates dropped 44 percent: Brady E. Hamilton and Stephanie J. Ventura, "Birth Rates for U.S. Teenagers Reach Historic Lows for All Age and Ethnic Groups," National Center for Health Statistics, Data Brief No. 89, April 2012. http://www.cdc.gov/nchs/data/databriefs/db89.pdf.

Page 20 "A lot of them": Kathleen A. Bogle, *Hooking Up: Sex, Dating, and Relationships on Campus* (New York: New York University Press, 2008): pp. 43–44.

Page 21 In 2004, Elizabeth Armstrong: Laura Hamilton and Elizabeth A. Armstrong, "Gendered Sexuality in Young Adulthood: Double Binds and Flawed Options," *Gender & Society* 23, no. 5 (2009): 589–616; study results originally published in Elizabeth A. Armstrong, Laura Hamilton, and Brian Sweeney, "Sexual Assault on Campus: A Multilevel, Integrative Approach to Party Rape," *Social Problems* 53, no. 4 (2006): 483–499.

Page 29 Hakim has identified: Catherine Hakim, *Erotic Capital: The Power of Attraction in the Boardroom and the Bedroom* (New York: Basic Books, 2011).

Page 29 "Properly understood, erotic capital": Catherine Hakim, "Have You Got Erotic Capital?" *Prospect,* March 24, 2010.

Page 30 people labeled "attractive" earned: Markus M. Mobius and Tanya S. Rosenblat, "Why Beauty Matters," *American Economic Review* 96, no. 1 (2006): 222–235.

Page 31 "worst sin imaginable": Meghan Daum, *My Misspent Youth: Essays* (New York: Open City Books, 2001), p. 20.

Page 34 We've been taught: Lois P. Frankel, *Nice Girls Don't Get the Corner Office: 101 Unconscious Mistakes Women Make That Sabotage Their Careers* (New York: Warner Business Books, 2004), p. 2.

Page 37 In 2011, psychologist Roy Baumeister: Roy F. Baumeister, "Cultural Variations in the Sexual Marketplace: Gender Equality Correlates with More Sexual Activity," *Journal of Social Psychology* 151, no. 3 (2011): 350–360.

Page 37 "Societies in which women have lots of autonomy": Christopher Ryan and Cacilda Jethá, *Sex at Dawn: The Prehistoric Origins of Modern Sexuality* (New York: HarperCollins, 2010), p. 133.

Page 38 "Tell it to our mothers": Helena Andrews, *Bitch Is the New Black* (New York: HarperCollins, 2010), pp. 6–7.

Page 38 More of them turn: Mark Regnerus and Jeremy Uecker, *Premarital Sex in America: How Young Americans Meet, Mate, and Think about Marrying* (New York: Oxford University Press, 2011).

Page 39 "Erotic capital," Regnerus writes: Mark Regnerus, "Sex Is Cheap," *Slate*, February 25, 2011.

Page 39 In their 1983 book: Marcia Guttentag and Paul F. Secord, *Too Many Women?: The Sex Ratio Question* (Newbury Park, CA: Sage Publications, 1983).

Page 40 On the cover of Guyland: Michael Kimmel, *Guyland: The Perilous World Where Boys Become Men* (New York: HarperCollins, 2008).

Page 40 Stanford psychology professor Philip Zimbardo: Philip Zimbardo, "The Demise of Guys?" TED Talk, March 2011. http://www.ted.com/talks/zimchallenge.html.

Page 41 This is the argument: Barbara Ehrenreich, Elizabeth Hess, and Gloria Jacobs, *Re-Making Love: The Feminization of Sex* (New York: Anchor Press/Doubleday, 1986).

Page 41 More recently, Baumeister put that theory: Roy F. Baumeister, "Gender Differences in Erotic Plasticity: The Female Sex Drive as Socially Flexible and Responsive," *Psychological Bulletin* 126, no. 3 (2000): 347–374.

Page 42 writer William Saletan points out: William Saletan, "The Ass Man Cometh," *Slate*, October 5, 2010.

THE SEESAW MARRIAGE
TRUE LOVE (JUST FOR THE ELITES)

Page 48 In 1970 women in the United States: Richard Fry and D'Vera Cohn, "Women, Men and the New Economics of Marriage," Pew Research Center, January 19, 2010. http://pewsocialtrends.org/files/2010/11/new-economics-of-marriage.pdf.

Page 48 Now the average American wife: Heather Boushey, "The New Breadwinners," *The Shriver Report*, Maria Shriver and the Center for American Progress, p. 36. http://shriverreport.com/awn/economy.php.

Page 48 also known as "alpha wives": "Alpha Wives: The Trend and the Truth," *The New York Times*, January 24, 2010.

Page 49 For the 70 percent of Americans: 30.4 percent of Americans twenty-five and over hold a bachelor's degree or higher, according to data from the 2011 Current Population Survey.

Page 49 In Washington, DC, for example: Heather Boushey, Jessica Arons, and Lauren Smith, "Families Can't Afford the Gender Wage Gap," Center for American Progress, April 20, 2010. http://www.americanprogress.org/issues/2010/04/pdf/equal_pay_day.pdf.

Page 49 But for the elites: W. Bradford Wilcox, ed., "When Marriage Disappears: The Retreat from Marriage in Middle America," The National Marriage Project at the University of Virginia and the Center for Marriage and Families at the Institute for American Values, December 2010. http://stateofourunions.org/2010/when-marriage-disappears.php.

Page 49 the "private playground of those already blessed with abundance": Wilcox, ed., "When Marriage Disappears," p. xii.

Page 49 Sylvia Plath described: Sylvia Plath, *The Bell Jar* (London: Heinemann, 1963; New York: Harper Perennial Modern Classics, 2005), p. 4. Citations refer to the Harper Perennial Modern Classics edition.

Page 54 In 1965 women reported: Suzanne M. Bianchi, "Family Change and Time Allocation in American Families," Focus on Workplace Flexibility Conference, November 29–30, 2010. http://workplaceflexibility.org/images/uploads/program_papers/bianchi_family_change_and_time_allocation_in_american_families.pdf.

Page 54 Only 2.7 percent of Americans: America's Families and Living Arrangements data for 2010 report an estimated 154,000 stay-at-home dads—married fathers with children younger than fifteen who have been out of the labor force for at least one year primarily to care for the family while their wives work outside the home.

Page 55 In Spain, marriages with foreigners: Albert Esteve, Alberto Del Rey, and Clara Cortina, "Pathways to Family Formation of International Migrants in Spain," XXVI IUSSP International Population Conference, October 1, 2009. Abstract: http://iussp2009 .princeton.edu/download.aspx?submissionId=92078.

Page 55 what Jessica Grose at Slate *dubbed:* Jessica Grose, "Omega Males and the Women Who Hate Them," *Slate*, March 18, 2010.

Page 61 She published the results: Mirra Komarovsky, *The Unemployed Man and His Family: Status of the Man in Fifty-Nine Families* (Walnut Creek, CA: AltaMira Press, 2004). Originally published in 1940 by Estate of Mirra Komarovsky.

Page 63 as Barbara Ehrenreich outlines: Barbara Ehrenreich, *The Hearts of Men: American Dreams and the Flight from Commitment* (New York: Anchor Books/Doubleday, 1983).

Page 63 No wonder then that a young college-educated bourgeois male: Philip Roth, *My Life as a Man* (New York: Holt, Rinehart and Winston, 1974), p. 170.

Page 64 Midway through Richard Yates's 1961 novel: Richard Yates, *Revolutionary Road* (New York: Vintage Books, 1961, 2008). Citations refer to the 2008 Vintage edition.

Page 65 "Prostitutes don't sell their bodies": Flo Kennedy, *Color Me Flo: My Hard Life and Good Times* (Englewood Cliffs, NJ: Prentice Hall, 1976), pp. 5–6.

Page 65 America's divorce rate began going up: National Vital Statistics.

Page 66 when a wife works: Nancy R. Burstein, "Economic Influences on Marriage and Divorce," *Journal of Policy Analysis and Management*, 26 (2) (Spring 2007): 387–429.

Page 67 earns you playground pity: Katie Roiphe, "Single Moms Are Crazy!" *Slate*, October 5, 2011.

Page 67 On the verge of retirement: Maggie Gallagher, "Why Marriage Is Good for You," *City Journal*, Autumn 2000.

Page 68 A recent study conducted by the Canadian Medical Association: Clare L. Atzema et al., "Effect of Marriage on Duration of Chest Pain Associated with Acute Myocardial Infarction before Seeking Care," *Canadian Medical Association Journal* 183, no. 13 (2011): 1482–1491.

Page 68 Statisticians Bernard Cohen and I-Sing Lee: Bernard Cohen and I-Sing Lee, "A Catalog of Risks," *Health Physics* 36, no. 6 (1979): 707–722.

THE NEW AMERICAN MATRIARCHY
THE MIDDLE CLASS GETS A SEX CHANGE

Page 85 Since 2000, the manufacturing economy: Total manufacturing employment in the United States was 17.3 million in January 2000, and hit a low of fewer than 11.5 million in January 2010, according to the Bureau of Labor Statistics. In 2011, the number of manufacturing jobs grew by 1.2 percent, the industry's first increase since 1997.

Page 85 The housing bubble masked this new reality: Lawrence Katz, "Long-Term Unemployment in the Great Recession," Testimony for the Joint Economic Committee, US Congress, April 29, 2010. http:// www.employmentpolicy. org/topic/ 10/research/ long-term-unemployment-great-recession-0.

Page 85 During the same period, meanwhile: More than two million people are now employed in education and health services, up from less than 1.5 million in January 2000, according to seasonally adjusted data from the Bureau of Labor Statistics.

Page 86 In 1967, 97 percent of American men: Michael Greenstone and Adam Looney, "The Problem with Men: A Look at Long-Term Employment Trends," Brookings Institution, December 3, 2010. http://www.brookings.edu/opinions/2010/1203_jobs_greenstone_looney.aspx.

Page 86 New York Times *columnist David Brooks:* David Brooks, "The Missing Fifth," *The New York Times*, May 9, 2011.

Page 86 In 1950, roughly one in twenty men: According to data from the Bureau of Labor Statistics Current Population Survey, the employment-population ratio for men between twenty-five and fifty-four was 95.3 percent in 1950 and 81.4 percent in 2011.

Page 86 When asked by **The New York Times:** Andrew Goldman, "Larry Summers, Un-king of Kumbaya," *The New York Times Magazine*, May 12, 2011.

Page 87 reveals the real McDowell County: Bill Bishop, *The Big Sort* (New York: Houghton Mifflin, 2008), p. 128.

Page 88 Starting in the 1970s: William Julius Wilson, *When Work Disappears: The World of the New Urban Poor* (New York: Knopf, 1996).

Page 88 African-American boys whose fathers: Keith Finlay and David Neumark, "Is Marriage Always Good for Children? Evidence from Families Affected by Incarceration," *Journal of Human Resources* 45, no. 4 (2010): 1046–1088.

Page 88 the greatest gender gap in college graduation rates: Ralph Richard Banks, *Is Marriage for White People? How the African American Marriage Decline Affects Everyone* (New York: Dutton, 2011).

Page 90 This is the first time that the cohort: Richard Fry and D'Vera Cohn, "Women, Men and the New Economics of Marriage," Pew Research Center, January 19, 2010. http://pewsocialtrends.org/files/2010/11/new-economics-of-marriage.pdf.

Page 91 The divorce statistics alone tell: "Ups and Downs: Americans' Prospects for Recovery after an Income Loss," Pew Economic Mobility Project, January 2012. http://www.economicmobility.org/assets/pdfs/EMP_Ups_and_Downs_FactSheet.pdf. In 1970, 67 percent of divorced women experienced an income loss of at least 25 percent. By the early 2000s, just 49 percent of women—and 47 percent of men—suffered a comparable loss. Income increases by at least a quarter for 20 percent of women and 16 percent of men.

Page 91 one of the highest proportions of citizens: Pew's Religious Landscape Survey found that 49 percent of adults in Alabama affiliate with the Evangelical Protestant tradition, compared to a 26 percent national average. http://religions.pewforum.org/maps.

Page 91 Yet despite a steady increase in population: Household marriage data taken from "Population Trends," published by the Alabama Policy Institute, and from the 2010 Census. http://www.alabamapolicy.org/issues/gti/issue.php?issueID=255&guideMainID=8.

Page 92 The sociologist Kathryn Edin: Kathryn Edin and Maria Kefalas, *Promises I Can Keep: Why Poor Women Put Motherhood Before Marriage* (Berkeley and Los Angeles: University of California Press, 2005).

Page 92 After staying steady for a while: The National Center for Health Statistics reports that 41 percent of children are now born to unmarried parents. In 2002, that figure was 34 percent, according to Stephanie J. Ventura, "Changing Patterns of Nonmarital Childbearing in the United States," NCHS Data Brief No. 18, May 2009. http://www.cdc.gov/nchs/data/databriefs/db18.pdf.

Page 92 now the "new normal": Jason DeParle and Sabrina Tavernise, "Unwed Mothers Now a Majority Before Age of 30," *The New York Times*, February 17, 2012.

Page 94 chronicle in a groundbreaking report: Wilcox, ed., "When Marriage Disappears."

Page 96 As Albert Mohler, president of the Southern Baptist Theological Seminary: Dr. R. Albert Mohler, Jr., "The End of Men? A Hard Look at the Future," AlbertMohler.com, June 22, 2010. http://www.albertmohler.com/2010/06/22/the-end-of-men-a-hard-look-at-the-future.

Page 97 mulling over a passage in Proverbs: Proverbs 31:10–23 (NIV).

Page 106 James Chung stumbled on a data set: Interview with James Chung, September 2010.

Page 106 Chung's findings made the cover of Time magazine: Belinda Luscombe, "Workplace Salaries: At Last, Women on Top," *TIME*, September 1, 2010.

PHARM GIRLS
HOW WOMEN REMADE THE ECONOMY

Page 114 Pharmacy is one of the many middle-class professions: Women now hold 55 percent of pharmacy jobs, according to 2011 data from the Bureau of Labor Statistics Current Population Survey.

Page 117 In 2009, for the first time in American history: According to revised employment data from the Bureau of Labor Statistics, women outnumbered men in the workforce in February, March, November, and December of 2009.

Page 117 About 80 percent of women: Claudia Goldin, "The Rising (and then Declining) Significance of Gender," National Bureau of Economic Research Working Paper No. 8915, April 2002. http://www.nber.org/papers/w8915.pdf.

Page 117 According to the Bureau of Labor Statistics: Job data for 2011 from the Bureau of Labor Statistics Current Population Survey. Law firm associates data from "Women in Law in the U.S.," *Catalyst*, January 2012. http://www.catalyst.org/publication/246/women-in-law-in-the-us.

Page 117 In the UK, women are poised: Mary Ann Elston, "Women and Medicine: The Future," The Royal College of Physicians, June 3, 2009. http://www.learning.ox.ac.uk/media/global/wwwadminox acuk/local-sites/oxfordlearninginstitute/documents/overview/women_and_medicine.pdf; and subsequent lecture by Jane Dacre, "Medicine: Sexist or Overfeminised?" The Royal College of Physicians, 2011 (quoted in http://careers.bmj.com/careers/advice/view-article.html?id=20006082.)

Page 118 Women made up about 8 percent: U.S. Census of Population and Housing, 1960: "Occupational Characteristics: Data on Age, Race, Education, Work Experience, Income, Etc., for the Workers in Each Occupation" (Washington: Government Printing Office, 1961). http://www.worldcat.org/identities/nc-united%20states$bureau%20of%20the%20census$18th%20census%201960.

Page 119 dubbed this the typewriter paradox: Interview with Alice Kessler-Harris, 2009.

Page 119 Harvard economist Claudia Goldin uses a different term: Claudia Goldin, "A Pollution Theory of Discrimination: Male and Female Differences in Occupations and Earnings," National Bureau of Economic Research Working Paper No. 8985, June 2002. http://www.nber.org/papers/w8985.

Page 119 the editor of the **American Journal of Pharmaceutical Education** *wrote:* Rufus A. Lyman, "The Editor's Crime," *American Journal of Pharmaceutical Education* 1, no. 209 (1937).

Page 120 Una Golden, the heroine: Sinclair Lewis, *The Job* (New York: Harper & Brothers, 1917).

Page 124 Of the thirty professions projected to add the most jobs: Comparison of 2011 employment data from the Bureau of Labor Statistics Current Population Survey and BLS occupations with the largest projected employment growth, 2010–2020.

Page 125 In 2009, men brought home $48,000 on average: Michael Greenstone and Adam Looney, "Have Earnings Actually Declined?" Brookings Institution, Up Front blog, March 4, 2011. http://www .brookings.edu/opinions/2011/0304_jobs_greenstone_looney.aspx.

Page 125 the truth is even more dismal: Greenstone and Looney, "Have Earnings Actually Declined?"

Page 125 But this polarization has affected men: David Autor, "The Polarization of Job Opportunities in the U.S. Labor Market: Implications for Employment and Earnings," The Center for American Progress and The Hamilton Project, April 2010. http://www.amer icanprogress.org/issues/2010/04/job_polarization.html.

Page 127 "practically noiseless [sic], and pours out": Arthur Colton Company catalog (Detroit, Michigan, 1902).

Page 128 As novelist Sherwood Anderson would write: Sherwood Anderson, *Perhaps Women* (New York: Liveright, 1931), p. 45.

Page 128 An 1893 article discussing the prospect: Metta Lou Henderson, *American Women Pharmacists: Contributions to the Profession* (New York: Haworth Press, 2002), pp. 11–12.

Page 128 this love-struck and utterly condescending poem: Henderson, p. 21.

Page 129 the first commencement speaker opened the graduates' eyes: Henderson, p. 7.

Page 129 "We [will not accept] the weakling cry": Gregory J. Higby, "Emma Gary Wallace and Her Vision of American Pharmacy," *Pharmacy in History* 40, no. 2/3 (1998): 67–76.

Page 129 Just as they do today, they graduated: Claudia Goldin, "America's Graduation from High School: The Evolution and Spread of Secondary Schooling in the Twentieth Century," *The Journal of Economic History* 58, no. 2 (1998): 361.

Page 130 who "would be dissatisfied": Goldin, "Rising."

Page 130 essentially acquired "secondary sex characteristics": Goldin, "Rising."

Page 130 Can you type? Goldin, "Rising."

Page 130 A 1939 report on what was known: Arthur T. Sutherland, "Wages and Hours in Drugs and Medicines and in Certain Toilet Preparations," *Bulletin of the Women's Bureau*, no. 171 (1939).

Page 132 Miss and other women's magazines: Henderson, p. 87.

Page 132 for pharmacy school the tipping point: According to data from the American Association of Colleges of Pharmacy, 1985 was the first year that female first professional degree recipients outnumbered males: 53.9 percent to 46.1 percent.

Page 132 "Where would a sense of maleness": Elliott J. Gorn, *The Manly Art: Bare-Knuckle Prize Fighting in America* (Ithaca, NY: Cornell University Press, 1986, 2010), p. 192 (2010 edition).

Page 132 Joel Garreau picks up on this phenomenon: Joel Garreau, *Edge City: Life on the New Frontier* (New York: Doubleday, 1991).

Page 133 "Once pharmacy shed the Victorian view": Henderson, p. 106.

Page 134 Robots can count tablets more accurately": Albert Wertheimer, foreword to *Social Pharmacy: Innovation and Development* (Philadelphia: Pharmaceutical Press, 1994), p. ix–xi.

Page 135 In a 2005 international study: Lex Borghans, Bas Ter Weel, and Bruce A. Weinberg, "People People: Social Capital and the Labor-Market Outcomes of Underrepresented Groups," IZA Discussion Paper Series No. 1494, February 2005.

Page 135 Now they also wanted to be innovative: Ruth Shalit, "The Name Game," *Salon*, November 30, 1999.

Page 137 A 2002 study of the pharmacy workforce: David A. Mott et al., "A Ten-Year Trend Analysis of Pharmacist Participation in the Workforce," *American Journal of Pharmaceutical Education* 66, no. 3 (2002): 223–233.

Page 138 full-time women pharmacists do work: Surrey M. Walton and Judith A. Cooksey, "Differences Between Male and Female Pharmacists in Part-Time Status and Employment Setting," *Journal of the American Pharmacists Association* 41, no. 5 (2001): 703–708.

Page 139 a close breakdown of medical professions: Claudia Goldin and Lawrence F. Katz, "The Cost of Workplace Flexibility for High-Powered Professionals," *The ANNALS of the American Academy of Political and Social Science* 638, no. 1 (2011): 45–67.

Page 140 they pay a low "career cost": Claudia Goldin and Lawrence F. Katz, "The Career Cost of Family," Sloan Conference Focus on Flexibility, November 30, 2010. http://workplaceflexibility.org/images/uploads/program_papers/goldin_-_the_career_cost_of_family.pdf.

Page 140 Surveys of Generation Y reveal: Sylvia Ann Hewlett, Laura Sherbin, and Karen Sumberg, "How Gen Y and Boomers Will Reshape Your Agenda," *Harvard Business Review*, July 2009.

DEGREES OF DIFFERENCE
THE EDUCATION GAP

Page 145 The chart, which had originally appeared in **U.S. News & World Report:** Alex Kingsbury, "Many Colleges Reject Women at Higher Rates Than for Men," *U.S. News & World Report*, June 17, 2007.

Page 147 Heriot wrote up a proposal: See full text of the proposal in "A Professor Proposes to Examine Gender Bias in College Admissions," *The Chronicle of Higher Education*, October 31, 2009.

Page 148 The public reason they gave was "inadequate" data: See Daniel de Vise, "Federal Panel Ends Probe of College Gender Bias," *The Washington Post*, March 16, 2011.

Page 149 Women earn almost 60 percent: See "The Condition of Education 2011," NCES 2011-033, National Center for Education Statistics, 2011. http://nces.ed.gov/pubsearch/pubsinfo.asp?pubid=2011033.

Page 149 Between 1970 and 2008: See David Autor, "The Polarization of Job Opportunities in the U.S. Labor Market," Center for American Progress and The Hamilton Project, April 2010. http://economics.mit.edu/files/5554.

Page 149 Among college graduates sixty-five and over: See "Field of Bachelor's Degree in the United States: 2009," American Community Survey Reports, February 2012.

Page 150 Women now earn 60 percent of master's degrees: See Nathan E. Bell, "Graduate Enrollment and Degrees: 2000–2010," Council of Graduate Schools and Graduate Record Examinations Board, September 2011.

Page 150 about half of all law and medical degrees: Women earned 47.2 percent of JDs in 2009-2010, according to the American Bar Association, and earned 48.4 percent of MD degrees from US medical schools in 2011, according to the Association of American Medical Colleges.

Page 150 about 44 percent of all business degrees: See Nathan E. Bell, "Graduate Enrollment and Degrees: 2000–2010," Council of Graduate Schools and Graduate Record Examinations Board, September 2011. http://www.cgsnet.org/ckfinder/userfiles/files/R_ED2010.pdf.

Page 150 In twenty-seven of those countries: OECD, Education at a Glance 2011: OECD Indicators, Organisation for Economic Cooperation and Development, (OECD Publishing, 2011). http://www.oecd.org/dataoecd/61/2/48631582.pdf.

Page 150 The same is true: Philip G. Altbach, Liz Reisberg, and Laura E. Rumbley, "Trends in Global Higher Education: Tracking an Academic Revolution," Report Prepared for the UNESCO World Conference on Higher Education, 2009. http://unesdoc.unesco.org/images/0018/001831/183168e.pdf.

Page 151 women in Saudi Arabia: See "Higher Education: The Path to Progress for Saudi Women," World Policy Institute blog, October 18, 2011. http://www.worldpolicy.org/blog/2011/10/18/higher-education-path-progress-saudi-women.

Page 151 In Brazil, 80 percent of college-educated women: See Sylvia Ann Hewlett and Ripa Rashid, "The Battle for Female Talent in Brazil," Center for Work-Life Policy, December 15, 2011. http://www.worklife-policy.org/documents/CWLP_BattleForFemaleTalentInBrazil_copyright2.pdf.

Page 151 as the economists: Claudia Goldin, Lawrence F. Katz, and Ilyana Kuziemko, "The Homecoming of American College Women: The Reversal of the College Gender Gap," *Journal of Economic Perspectives* 20, no. 4 (2006): 133–156.

Page 152 As Adlai Stevenson told a Smith graduating class: Adlai Stevenson, "A Purpose for Modern Woman," Smith College Commencement Speech, 1955.

Page 152 In 1957 the average boy: See Goldin, "Homecoming."

Page 153 Between 1968 and the late 1970s: See Goldin, "Homecoming."

Page 153 By 1973, only 17 percent of female college freshmen: See Goldin, "Homecoming."

Page 153 Now, according to the Census Bureau: Data for the population twenty-five and over with a bachelor's degree or higher, from the 2011 Current Population Survey.

Page 158 In 2005, a study: Sandy Baum and Eban Goodstein, "Gender Imbalance in College Applications: Does it Lead to a Preference for Men in the Admissions Process?" *Economics of Education Review* 24, no. 6 (2005): 665–675.

Page 158 Jennifer Delahunty Britz, the dean of admissions and financial aid at Kenyon College: Jennifer Delahunty Britz, "To All the Girls I've Rejected," *The New York Times*, March 23, 2006.

Page 159 In a 2006 paper: Claudia Buchmann and Thomas DiPrete, "The Growing Female Advantage in College Completion: The Role of Family Background and Academic Achievement," *American Sociological Review* 71, no. 4 (2006): 515–554.

Page 160 Christina Hoff Sommers caused a storm: Christina Hoff Sommers, "The War Against Boys," *The Atlantic*, May 2000.

Page 160 Boys, writes Michael Gurian: See Kelley King, Michael Gurian, and Kathy Stevens, "Gender-Friendly Schools," *Educational Leadership* 68, no. 3 (2010): 38–42.

Page 160 In a Newsweek story: Peg Tyre, "The Trouble with Boys," *Newsweek*, January 29, 2006. http://www.thedailybeast.com/newsweek/2006/01/29/the-trouble-with-boys.html.

Page 160 But as neuroscientist: Lise Eliot, "Stop Pseudoscience of Gender Differences in Learning," ASCD Community Blog, November 3, 2010. http://ascd.typepad.com/blog/2010/11/myth-of-pink-blue-brains.html.

Page 161 In the latest assessment: "The Nation's Report Card: Reading 2011," NCES 2012-457, National Center for Education Statistics. http://nces.ed.gov/pubsearch/pubsinfo.asp?pubid=2012457.

Page 161 nearly one in four white sons: Richard Whitmire, *Why Boys Fail: Saving Our Sons from an Educational System That's Leaving Them Behind* (AMACOM, 2010), p. 25.

Page 161 In math, scores of both boys and girls: National Assessment of Educational Progress 1990, 1992, 1996, 2000, 2003, 2005, 2007, 2009 and 2011 Mathematics Assessments, National Center for Education Statistics.

Page 161 "The world has gotten more verbal": Whitmire, *Why Boys Fail*, p. 28.

Page 162 ninth-grade bulge: Whitmire, *Why Boys Fail*, p. 21.

Page 162 They are more likely than boys: See tables 157 and 159 in "Digest of Education Statistics: 2010," National Center for Education Statistics. http://nces.ed.gov/programs/digest/d10/.

Page 162 University of Michigan study: Jerald G. Bachman, Lloyd D. Johnston, and Patrick M. O'Malley, "Monitoring the Future: Questionnaire Responses from the Nation's High School Seniors, 2010," University of Michigan Institute for Social Research, 2011.

Page 163 "What for?" George Eliot, *The Mill on the Floss* (Harper & Brothers, 1860), p. 32.

Page 163 "Monitoring the Future": Jerald G. Bachman et al., "Monitoring the Future."

Page 163 up from 19 percent: Lloyd D. Johnston and Jerald G. Bachman, "Monitoring the Future: Questionnaire Responses from the Nation's High School Seniors, 1975," University of Michigan Institute for Social Research, 1980.

Page 165 A lawmaker in China recently proposed: Gao Changxin and Wang Hongyi, "Bars Should Be Lowered for Boys in Exams, Lawmaker Says," *China Daily*, March 9, 2012.

A MORE PERFECT POISON
THE NEW WAVE OF FEMALE VIOLENCE

Page 168 an "attempt to assert power": Joyce Carol Oates, "The Witchcraft of Shirley Jackson," *The New York Review of Books*, October 8, 2009.

Page 168 After poisoning the sugar bowl: Shirley Jackson, *We Have Always Lived in the Castle* (New York: Viking/Penguin, 1962), p. 161.

Page 170 "My impression was that Mrs. Schuster": Chris Collins, "Psychiatrist Says Schuster Had Battered Spouse Syndrome," *The Fresno Bee*, November 15, 2007.

Page 171 Brett Steenbarger, who gives advice: Brett Steenbarger, "Four Overlooked Qualities of Successful Traders," blog entry on TraderFeed, January 11, 2007. http://traderfeed.blogspot.com/2007/01/four-overlooked-qualities-of.html.

Page 172 The bravest and most skilled fighter: Simon Baron-Cohen, *The Essential Difference: Male and Female Brains and the Truth about Autism* (New York: Basic Books, 2003), p. 124.

Page 172 Such evolutionary origins "have important ramifications": Kingsley Browne, *Divided Labours: An Evolutionary View of Women at Work* (London: Weidenfeld & Nicolson, 1998), p. 3.

Page 172 global homicide statistics show that men: "2011 Global Study on Homicide," United Nations Office on Drugs and Crime, 2011, p. 70. http://www.unodc.org/documents/data-and-analysis/statistics/Homicide/Globa_study_on_homicide_2011_web.pdf.

Page 172 Neuroscientist Lise Eliot explains: Lise Eliot, *Pink Brain, Blue Brain: How Small Differences Grow into Troublesome Gaps—and What We Can Do About It* (New York: Houghton Mifflin Harcourt, 2009), p. 260.

Page 172 attributes the historical decrease in violence : Steven Pinker, *The Better Angels of Our Nature: Why Violence Has Declined* (New York: Viking, 2011).

Page 173 Jesse Prinz points out in his recent influential article: Jesse Prinz, "Why Are Men So Violent?" *Psychology Today*, February 3, 2012.

Page 174 As best-selling crime writer Patricia Cornwell: Sam Tanenhaus, "Violence That Art Didn't See Coming," *The New York Times*, February 24, 2010.

Page 174 The share of women arrested for violent crimes: "Women in America: Indicators of Social and Economic Well-Being," White House Council on Women and Girls, March 2011, p. 54. http://www.whitehouse.gov/sites/default/files/rss_viewer/Women_in_America.pdf.

Page 174 arrests of girls for assault climbed: FBI data analyzed by Meda Chesney-Lind, "Girls and Violence: Is the Gender Gap Closing?" National Resource Center on Domestic Violence, 2011. http://www .vawnet.org/applied-research-papers/print-document.php?doc_id=383.

Page 174 juvenile male arrest rate for simple assault: "Juvenile Arrest Rates for Simple Assault by Sex, 1980–2009," Office of Juvenile Justice and Delinquency Prevention, Statistical Briefing Book, October 2011. http://www.ojjdp.gov/ojstatbb/crime/JAR_Display .asp?ID=qa05241.

Page 175 In that age group, arrests for violent crimes : Data taken from FBI Uniform Crime Reports.

Page 175 But in the latest cohort, that trend: In 2009, there were 144,007 estimated drug- and violence-related arrests for women under eighteen, and 928,500 for women eighteen and over, according to "Arrest in the United States, 1980–2009," Bureau of Justice Statistics, September 2011. http://www.bjs.gov/content/pub/pdf/ aus8009.pdf.

Page 175 From 1985 to 2002, girls' juvenile court cases: Elizabeth Cauffman, "Understanding the Female Offender," *Juvenile Justice* 18, no. 2 (2008): 119–142.

Page 175 During about the same period, the detention: Meda Chesney-Lind, Merry Morash, and Tia Stevens, "Girls' Troubles, Girls' Delinquency, and Gender Responsive Programming: A Review," *The Australian and New Zealand Journal of Criminology* 41, no. 1 (2008): 162–189.

Page 175 what some criminologists call "vengeful equity": Meda Chesney-Lind, "Women in Prison: From Partial Justice to Vengeful Equity," *Corrections Today* 60, no. 7 (1998): 66–73.

Page 176 "The uncomfortable fact is that for all": Tanenhaus, "Violence."

Page 176 TMZ posted a video of her punching: "'Teen Mom' Star in Brutal Catfight—On Tape," TMZ, March 25, 2011. http://www.tmz .com/2011/03/25/teen-mom-2-jenelle-evans-catfight-video-footage- britany-truett-fist-brawl.

Page 177 If there is any relevant ethnography to apply: Cindy D.

Ness, *Why Girls Fight: Female Youth Violence in the Inner City* (New York: New York University Press, 2010).

Page 180 A 2010 White House report on women and girls: "Women in America: Indicators of Social and Economic Well-Being," p. 53.

Page 181 A recent British study showed: Marianne Hester, "Who Does What to Whom? Gender and Domestic Violence Perpetrators," University of Bristol in association with the Northern Rock Foundation, June 2009. http://www.nr-foundation.org.uk/wp-content/uploads/2011/07/Who-Does-What-to-Whom.pdf.

Page 181 One British study found: John Mays, "Domestic Violence: The Male Perspective," *Parity*, July 2010. http://www.parity-uk.org/RSMDVConfPresentation-version3A.pdf.

Page 182 One of the bombers was "emotionally distressed": Andrew E. Kramer, "Russia's Fear of Female Bombers Is Revived," *The New York Times*, March 29, 2010.

Page 182: "Women, we are told, become suicide bombers": Lindsey A. O'Rourke, "Behind the Woman Behind the Bomb," *The New York Times*, August 2, 2008.

Page 183 In her dissertation, O'Rourke discovered: Lindsey A. O'Rourke, "What's Special about Female Suicide Terrorism?" *Security Studies* 18, no. 4 (2009): 681–718.

Page 183 sociologists at Princeton conducted an experiment: Jenifer R. Lightdale and Deborah A. Prentice, "Rethinking Sex Differences in Aggression: Aggressive Behavior in the Absence of Social Roles," *Personality and Social Psychology Bulletin* 20, no. 1 (1994): 34–44.

Page 185 the "hot sauce" study: Holly A. McGregor et. al, "Terror Management and Aggression: Evidence that Mortality Salience Motivates Aggression against Worldview-Threatening Others," *Journal of Personality and Social Psychology* 74, no. 3 (1998): 590–605.

Page 185 women "increasingly reported masculine-stereotyped personality traits": Jean M. Twenge, "Changes in Masculine and Feminine Traits Over Time: A Meta-Analysis," *Sex Roles* 36, no. 5/6 (1997): 305–325.

Page 185 In 2001, Twenge analyzed personality tests: Jean M. Twenge, "Changes in Women's Assertiveness in Response to Status and

Roles: A Cross-Temporal Meta-Analysis, 1931–1993," *Journal of Personality and Social Psychology* 81, no. 1 (2001): 133–145.

Page 186 A 1999 analysis of 150 studies on risk-taking behaviors: James P. Byrnes, David C. Miller, and William D. Schafer, "Gender Differences in Risk Taking: A Meta-Analysis," *Psychological Bulletin* 125, no. 3 (1999): 367–383.

Page 186 To measure rates of competitiveness: Uri Gneezy, Kenneth L. Leonard, and John A. List, "Gender Differences in Competition: Evidence from a Matrilineal and a Patriarchal Society," *Econometrica* 77, no. 5 (2009): 1637–1664.

Page 186 a phase of "new, more conscious acceptance:" Maud Lavin, *Push Comes to Shove: New Images of Aggressive Women* (Cambridge, MA: MIT Press, 2010), p. 16.

Page 187 In her essay "Throwing Like a Girl": Iris Marion Young, "Throwing Like a Girl: A Phenomenology of Feminine Body Comportment, Motility, and Spatiality," in *On Female Body Experience: "Throwing Like a Girl" and Other Essays* (New York: Oxford University Press, 2005), p. 27.

THE TOP
NICE-ISH GIRLS GET THE CORNER OFFICE

Page 193 the "career cost of family" in various elite workplaces: Claudia Goldin and Lawrence F. Katz, "The Career Cost of Family," Sloan Conference Focus on Flexibility, November 30, 2010. http://work placeflexibility.org/images/uploads/program_papers/goldin_-_the_career_cost_of_family.pdf.

Page 195 a "complete waste of time": Ken Auletta, "A Woman's Place," *The New Yorker,* July 11, 2011.

Page 196 "I'm sick of hearing how far we've come": Barbara Kellerman, "The Abiding Tyranny of the Male Leadership Model—A Manifesto," *Harvard Business Review,* April 27, 2010.

Page 196 Nationwide, about one in eighteen women: Carol Morello and Dan Keating, "More U.S. Women Pull Down Big Bucks," *The Washington Post,* October 7, 2010.

Page 197 "Women are knocking on the door of leadership": David Gergen, foreword to *Enlightened Power: How Women Are Transforming the Practice of Leadership*, ed. Linda Coughlin, Ellen Wingard, and Keith Hollihan (San Francisco: Jossey-Bass, 2005), p. xxi.

Page 197 "post-heroic" or "transformational": James MacGregor Burns, *Leadership* (New York: Harper & Row, 1978).

Page 198 calls the new style "meta-leadership": Rebecca Blumenstein, "Tales from the Front Lines," *The Wall Street Journal*, April 10, 2011.

Page 198 A 2008 study attempted to quantify the effect: Cristian L. Deszö and David Gaddis Ross, "'Girl Power': Does Female Representation in Top Management Improve Firm Performance?" Robert H. Smith School Research Paper No. RHS 06-104, August 2008.

Page 199 as the Internet boom was deflating: Brad M. Barber and Terrance Odean, "Boys Will Be Boys: Gender, Overconfidence, and Common Stock Investment," *The Quarterly Journal of Economics* 116, No. 1 (February 2001): 261–292.

Page 199 "One of the distinctive traits about Iceland's disaster": Michael Lewis, *Boomerang: Travels in the New Third World* (New York: W. W. Norton & Company, 2011), p. 37.

Page 200 a "strong feeling in [her] stomach": Halla Tomasdottir, "A Feminine Response to Iceland's Financial Crash," TED Women Talk, December 2010. http://www.ted.com/talks/halla_tomasdottir.html.

Page 200 **The New York Times** *came up with a novel and very relatable explanation:* Jessica Silver-Greenberg and Nelson G. Schwartz, "Discord at Key JPMorgan Unit is Faulted in Loss," *The New York Times*, May 19, 2012.

Page 201 follows a thousand star analysts: Boris Groysberg, *Chasing Stars: The Myth of Talent and the Portability of Performance* (Princeton, NJ: Princeton University Press, 2012).

Page 203 **Fortune** *used her as the lead in a 2002 story:* David Rynecki, "In Search of the Last Honest Analyst," *Fortune*, June 10, 2002.

Page 203 Krawcheck once joked in an interview: Rynecki, "In Search."

Page 203 **The Wall Street Journal** *reported:* Carol Hymowitz, "Crossing the Boss," *The Wall Street Journal*, May 20, 2008.

Page 205 Economist Linda Babcock hit upon a fairly simple

explanation: Linda Babcock and Sara Laschever, *Women Don't Ask: Negotiation and the Gender Divide* (Princeton, NJ: Princeton University Press, 2003).

Page 207 *Babcock's research helped spawn an industry:* Lois P. Frankel, *Nice Girls Don't Get the Corner Office: 101 Unconscious Mistakes Women Make That Sabotage Their Careers* (New York: Warner Business Books, 2004); Gail Evans, *Play Like a Man, Win Like a Woman: What Men Know about Success That Women Need to Learn* (New York: Broadway Books, 2000); and Lois P. Frankel, *Stop Sabotaging Your Career: 8 Proven Strategies to Succeed—In Spite of Yourself* (New York: Warner Business Books, 2007).

Page 207 *Babcock and Sara Laschever wrote their own version:* Linda Babcock and Sara Laschever, *Ask For It: How Women Can Use the Power of Negotiation to Get What They Really Want* (New York: Bantam Dell, 2008).

Page 207 *In one scenario, some colleagues:* Madeline E. Heilman and Julie J. Chen, "Same Behavior, Different Consequences: Reactions to Men's and Women's Altruistic Citizenship Behavior," *Journal of Applied Psychology* 90, no. 3 (2005): 431–441.

Page 208 *Perhaps the most dispiriting experiment was conducted:* Madeline E. Heilman, Aaron S. Wallen, Daniella Fuchs, and Melinda M. Tamkins, "Penalties for Success: Reactions to Women Who Succeed at Male Gender-Typed Tasks," *Journal of Applied Psychology* 89, no. 3 (2004): 416–427.

Page 209 *A few years later, Heilman came up with one:* Madeline E. Heilman and Tyler G. Okimoto, "Why Are Women Penalized for Success at Male Tasks?" *Journal of Applied Psychology* 92, no. 1 (2007): 81–92.

Page 209 *In 2011, researcher Hannah Riley Bowles:* Hannah Riley Bowles and Linda Babcock, "Relational Accounts: A Strategy for Women Negotiating for Higher Compensation," invited resubmission to *Organizational Behavior & Human Decision Processes*, 2011.

Page 211 *describes her own inept attempts at asking:* Mika Brzezinski, *Knowing Your Value: Women, Money, and Getting What You're Worth* (New York: Weinstein Books, 2011).

Page 214 *We know, from a long-term study of Chicago:* Marianne

Bertrand, Claudia Goldin, and Lawrence F. Katz, "Dynamics of the Gender Gap for Young Professionals in the Financial and Corporate Sectors," *American Economic Journal: Applied Economics* 2, no. 3 (2010): 228–255.

Page 215 Do women lack ambition?: Anna Fels, "Do Women Lack Ambition?" *Harvard Business Review* 9, no. 4 (2004): 50–60.

Page 216 perfectly articulated in a column by Michael Lewis: Michael Lewis, "How to Put Your Wife Out of Business," *Los Angeles Times*, March 6, 2005.

Page 218 This is an economy where single childless women: Analysis of Census Bureau American Community Survey data by Reach Advisors' James Chung and Sally Johnstone, "A Glimpse into the Postcrash Environment," *Urban Land*, March/April 2010: "When analyzing the incomes of single women in their 20s compared to single men in their 20s, women earn 105 percent of what their male counterparts earn in the average metropolitan market."

Page 218 I wrote a story in **The Atlantic:** Hanna Rosin, "The Case Against Breast-Feeding," *The Atlantic*, April 2009.

Page 219 since 1995, women have almost doubled the amount of time: Garey Ramey and Valerie A. Ramey, "The Rug Rat Race," Brookings Papers on Economic Activity, Spring 2010.

Page 219 a comprehensive 2006 study by the National Institute of Child Health: "The NICHD Study of Early Child Care and Youth Development: Findings for Children up to Age 4 1/2 Years," National Institute of Child Health and Human Development, January 2006. http://www.nichd.nih.gov/publications/pubs/upload/seccyd_051206.pdf.

Page 221 points out that a father's involvement is the critical factor: Sharon Meers and Joanna Strober, *Getting to 50/50: How Working Couples Can Have It All by Sharing It All* (New York: Bantam Dell, 2009).

Page 221 a massive Department of Education study, a child's grades: "Fathers' Involvement in Their Children's Schools," National Center for Education Statistics 98-091, September 1997, http://nces.ed.gov/pubs98/fathers/.

Page 222 memorable phrase "Don't leave before you leave": Sheryl Sandberg, "Why We Have Too Few Women Leaders," TED Talk,

December 2010. http://www.ted.com/talks/sheryl_sandberg_why_ we_have_too_few_women_leaders.html.

Page 223 "There was no having it all": Barbara Walters, interview with Jane Pauley in 2003, quoted in Pamela Paul, "For Anchorwomen, Family Is Part of the Job," *The New York Times*, December 9, 2011.

Page 223 as Fox's Megyn Kelly did: Back from maternity leave on August 8, 2011, Megyn Kelly showed a photograph of her baby daughter, Yardley Evans, to viewers of *America Live*. Later on the show, she blasted guest Mike Gallagher for having criticized the length of her absence on his radio program, *The Mike Gallagher Show*.

Page 223 Earlier she had squeezed her milk-enhanced boobs: Greg Veis, "She Reports, We Decided She's Hot," *GQ*, December 2010.

Page 225 none had quite the wistful tone of this recent one: Amanda Foreman, "Diana's Real Tragedy? She Married Too Young," *The Lady*, June 28, 2011.

Page 226 During that hiatus she wrote her best-selling book: Tina Brown, *The Diana Chronicles* (New York: Broadway Books, 2007).

Page 227 A recent McKinsey survey on women and the economy: Joanna Barsh and Lareina Yee, "Unlocking the Full Potential of Women in the U.S. Economy," McKinsey & Company Special Report, April 2011. http://www.mckinsey.com/Client_Service/ Organization/Latest_thinking/Unlocking_the_full_potential.

THE GOLD MISSES
ASIAN WOMEN TAKE OVER THE WORLD

Page 231 These rules were enshrined: Rosa Kim, "The Legacy of Institutionalized Gender Inequality in South Korea: The Family Law," *Boston College Third World Law Journal* 14, no. 1 (1994): 145–162.

Page 231 Park Chung-hee began to rebuild Korea's economy: See Sung-Hee Jwa, *The Evolution of Large Corporations in Korea* (Cheltenham, UK: Elgar, 2002).

Page 232 thirteenth-largest economy in the world: "GDP (Purchasing Power Parity)," CIA World Factbook. https://www.cia.gov/library/ publications/the-world-factbook/rankorder/2001rank.html.

Page 232 private "cram" schools: Margaret Warner, "In Hypercompetitive South Korea, Pressures Mount on Young Pupils," PBS *News-Hour*, January 21, 2011. http://www.pbs.org/newshour/bb/education/jan-june11/koreaschools_01-21.html.

Page 232 Korea climbed into the top five international rankings: "PISA 2009 Results: What Students Know and Can Do," OECD Program for International Student Assessment. http://www.oecd.org/dataoecd/10/61/48852548.pdf.

Page 233 made up 55 percent of those who passed: Choe Sang-Hun, "Korean Women Flock to Government," *The New York Times*, March 1, 2010.

Page 233 laws were revised: See Kay C. Lee, "Confucian Ethics, Judges, and Women: Divorce Under the Revised Korean Family Law," *Pacific Rim Law & Policy Journal* 4, no. 2 (1995): 479–503.

Page 233 the government abolished: Sanghui Nam, "The Women's Movement and the Transformation of the Family Law in South Korea. Interactions Between Local, National, and Global Structures," *European Journal of East Asian Studies* 9, no. 1 (2010): 67–86.

Page 233 about half of all women: Woojin Chung and Monica Das Gupta, "Why Is Son Preference Declining in South Korea? The Role of Development and Public Policy and the Implications for China and India," Paper presented at the annual meeting of the Population Association of America, March 29–31, 2007.

Page 234 In Latin American countries: Philip G. Altbach, Liz Reisberg, and Laura E. Rumbley, "Trends in Global Higher Education: Tracking an Academic Revolution," Report Prepared for the UNESCO World Conference on Higher Education, 2009. http://unesdoc.unesco.org/images/0018/001831/183168e.pdf.

Page 234 Latin American companies had fewer women in senior positions: "Women in Senior Management: Still Not Enough," Grant Thornton International Business Report, 2012. http://www.gti.org/files/ibr2012%20-%20women%20in%20senior%20management%20master.pdf.

Page 235 In Spain, some men have found: Albert Esteve, Alberto Del Rey, and Clara Cortina, "Pathways to Family Formation of International Migrants in Spain," XXVI IUSSP International Population Conference, October 1, 2009. http://iussp2009.princeton.edu/download.aspx?submissionId=92078.

Page 236 *Among the ten countries:* "World Population Prospects: The 2010 Revision," UN Department of Economic and Social Affairs, Population Division, April 2011. http://esa.un.org/wpp/Excel-Data/fertility.htm.

Page 236 *Divorce, still taboo in Asian society:* See "Asia's Lonely Hearts," *The Economist*, August 20, 2011. http://www.economist.com/node/21526350.

Page 236 *King Kong girl (a term invented by French feminist Virginie Despentes):* Virginie Despentes, *King Kong Theory* (New York: Feminist Press at CUNY, 2010).

Page 236 *"All that glitters is not gold":* Ahn Mi Young, "Poverty May Await S. Korea's Spendthrift 'Gold Misses,'" *The China Post*, August 15, 2009.

Page 238 *I may be a good employee:* Brian Lee, "The Disappearing, Desperate Working Mom," *Korea JoongAng Daily*, February 25, 2010.

Page 240 *"obsessed with having to excel in everything":* "Alpha at Work, Omega at Life: Korea's Superwomen," *The Chosunilbo*, May 23, 2008. http://english.chosun.com/site/data/html_dir/2008/05/23/2008052361016.html.

Page 244 *A research team at Harvard Business School:* Jordan Siegel, Lynn Pyun, and B. Y. Cheon, "Multinational Firms, Labor Market Discrimination, and the Capture of Competitive Advantage by Exploiting the Social Divide," HBS Working Paper 11-011, 2010.

Page 250 *Sixty-one percent of single Japanese men:* See "Single Japanese Men: Lonely in a Crowd?" *The Wall Street Journal*, November 28, 2011.

Page 253 *ideal of the attractive:* Virginie Despentes, *King Kong Theory* (New York: Feminist Press, 2010) p. 11.

CONCLUSION

Page 260 *In 2009, sociologists Carla Shows and Naomi Gerstel:* Carla Shows and Naomi Gerstel, "Fathering, Class, and Gender: A

Comparison of Physicians and EMTs," *Gender & Society* 23, no. 2 (2009): 161–187.

Page 262 "encouraging mockery of dads": Seth Stevenson, "The Reign of the Doltish Dad," *Slate*, March 26, 2012.

Page 262 The men want children more: Nick McDermott, "Now It's MEN Who Want to Settle Down Rather Than Women, According to New Research," *The Daily Mail*, February 14, 2011.

Page 262 "steeped in nostalgia": Leo Braudy, *From Chivalry to Terrorism: War and the Changing Nature of Masculinity* (New York: Knopf, 2004; Vintage, 2005), p. 6.

Page 263 story for Slate *by an American father:* Nathan Hegedus, "Snack Bags and a Regular Paycheck: The Happy Life of a Swedish Dad," *Slate*, August 31, 2010.

Page 263 The Japanese government has recently started: Felicity Hughes, "Ikumen: Raising New Father Figures in Japan," *The Japan Times*, August 30, 2011.

Page 263 "strong, almost hyper-romantic language to talk about love": Amy Schalet, "Caring, Romantic American Boys," *The New York Times*, April 6, 2012.

Page 264 an anthropological study of the worksites: Robin J. Ely and Debra E. Meyerson, "An Organizational Approach to Undoing Gender: The Unlikely Case of Offshore Oil Platforms," *Research in Organizational Behavior* 30, no. 30 (2010): 3–34.

INDEX

Page numbers followed by "*n*" indicate notes.

Accounting, 108, 117, 118, 124, 223, 276

Addiction, 45
  drug, 87, 88

Advanced Placement (AP) exams, 153

Affirmative action, 146, 147

Afghanistan, 42

African-Americans, 53, 94, 101, 147, 154, 156, 177, 178
  college-educated, 88, 94
  in manufacturing jobs, 88

Aggression, 171
  female, 168, 171, 174, 181, 183–187
  male, 172–174

Alabama, 91–92, 110. *See also specific cities, counties, and towns*

Alabama, University of, Huntsville, 176

Alexander City (Alabama), 79–88, 95, 96–105

Allen, Woody, 188

Alvin Ho (Look), 188

American Council on Education, 155

American Journal of Pharmaceutical Education, 119

American Psycho (Ellis), 171

Anal sex, 18, 27, 42, 43

Anderson, Sherwood, 128

Andrews, Steven and Sarah, 69–77

Apatow, Judd, 56, 138

Apple, William S., 133

Arab Spring, 151

Argentina, 28

Ark & Pancom, 241

Armstrong, Elizabeth, 21–25

Arnett, Will, 261

Arthur Colton Company, 127

Asian Debate Institute, 229

Ask For It (Babcock and Laschever), 207

Atlanta (Georgia), 81

Atlantic magazine, 14, 160, 218, 270

Attractiveness, 29, 30, 130–131, 253–254

Auburn (Alabama), 97, 103, 105–106, 106–110

Auburn University, 97, 105, 107–108
  Economic & Community Development Institute, 86

Austen, Jane, 114

Australia, 150, 165, 166, 243

Auto industry, 87
  Korean, 110, 202, 232, 247

Automatic Pill Making Machines, 127–128

Autor, David, 87, 125

Babcock, Linda, 205–206

Babies, sex preference for, 11–14

Bahrain, 150

Bangalore, 191

Baron-Cohen, Simon, 172, 258

Baum, Sandy, 158

Baumbach, Noah, 56

Baumeister, Roy, 37, 41, 42

Beauty premium. *See* Erotic capital

Beauvoir, Simone de, 1, 10–11

Belarus, 235

Belgium, 55
Bell Jar, The (Plath), 49–50
Bem Sex Role Inventory, 185
Bem test, 9, 16
Bend It Like Beckham (movie), 187
Benjamin Russell High School, 80,
    81, 95, 98–101, 105
Berkshire Hathaway, 81
Best Buy, 223
Better Angels of Our Nature, The
    (Pinker), 172–173
Beyoncé, 179, 187, 281–282
Bible, 75, 97–98
    Proverbs, 97–98
Bieber, Justin, 263
Big Sort, The (Bishop), 87
Birmingham (Alabama), 103
Bishop, Amy, 176
Bishop, Bill, 87
Black Widows of Chechnya, 182
Blue-collar jobs, 57.
    See also Working class
Bobbitt, Lorena, 176
Bogle, Kathleen, 20–21
Boomerang (Lewis), 200
Borghans, Lex, 135
Boushey, Heather, 48–49, 124
Bowles, Hannah Riley, 209–212
Brain difference, 159–160, 172, 258
    cultural factors in, 40, 165–166
Braudy, Leo, 262
Brazil, 5–6, 151, 235
Breadwinner wives, 7, 48–77,
    259–260, 261, 274–275
    and domestic responsibilities,
    53–55, 71–77
    and impacts of male job loss, 3–5,
    61–63, 272–273
    media representations of, 55–57
    versus traditional gender
    role-expectations, 62–69, 275
Breast-feeding, 75, 218–219
Briggs & Stratton, 108
Brin, Sergey, 192
Bristol-Myers Squibb, 170
Britain. *See* United Kingdom
Brizendine, Louann, 258

Brodsky, Alexandra, 18
Brooks, David, 86
Brown, Tina, 217, 225–226
Browne, Kingsley, 172
Brzezinski, Mika, 211–212
Buchmann, Claudia, 159
Buddhism, 45
Burger King, 177
Burns, James MacGregor, 197
Burress, Ashley, 156–157
Burt, Laura, 137
Bush, George W., 148
Business schools, 26–34, 33, 107–108,
    214, 217, 275. *See also specific*
    universities
Butler, Judith, 60

California, 92, 248.
    See also Silicon Valley
California, University of, 156
    Davis, 199
    San Diego, 185, 186
Cambridge University, 172
Canadian Medical Association, 68
Capone, Al, 176
Carbone, June, 87–88
Carnegie Mellon University, 205–206
Carroll, Jason Michael, 95
Carter, Jimmy, 91
Cassidy, Sukhinder Singh, 224
Census Bureau, U.S., 91, 153
Center for American Progress, 49, 124
Center on Juvenile and Criminal
    Justice, 19
Centers for Disease Control and
    Prevention (CDC), 19, 197
Central California Research
    Laboratories, 168
Chasing Stars (Groysberg), 201
Cheers (television show), 56
Chicago, University of, 182, 249
    Business School, 214, 216
Chicopee (Massachusetts), 177
Child care, 14, 15, 54, 216, 218–219,
    220, 221–222, 240, 260
    government options for, 241–242
    jobs in, 9, 118, 124

China, 5, 165–166
China Post, The, 236
Christians, 96–97
   evangelical, 91, 295*n*
Chung, James, 106–107
Chung, Vivien, 249
Citigroup, 202–203
Civil rights, 132, 148
Civil Rights Commission,
   U.S., 146
Civil War, 128
Clerical schools, 120, 129
Clovis (California), 167
Coal (television show), 87
Cognitive dissonance, 33
Cohen, Bernard, 68
Cold War, 152
Colombia, 55, 235
Colorado, 168
Color Me Flo (Kennedy), 65
Columbia University, 119
   Business School, 197
Comedy Central, 126, 143
Competition, 52, 171, 172,
   241, 244
   academic, in Korea, 230–231
   for college admissions, 160
   in traditional societies, 172,
      186, 187
Confucianism, 231, 232, 254
Congress, U.S., 203, 278
Cookie magazine, 11
Coontz, Stephanie, 51, 274,
   275–276, 277
Cooper, Hannah, 113–117,
   119, 123–124, 126–127,
   129, 141–143
Cornwell, Patricia, 174
Cosby, Bill, 90
Cosmopolitan magazine, 30, 39
Creal, Cameron, 155–156
Creative Korea party, 246
Crime, violent, 172–183
   against women, decline in, 19–20,
      174, 180–181
   committed by women, 174–178,
      182–183

Daily Beast, The, 217, 226
"Dancing on My Own" (song), 43
Dating sites, 52, 252–253
Daum, Meghan, 31
Delahunty, Jennifer, 158–159
Deloitte Consulting, 140–141, 223
Delta Kappa Epsilon, 17
Democratic Party, 148
Denney, Leandra, 88
Denny's, 177
Despentes, Virginie, 236, 253–254
Diana Chronicles, The (Brown), 226
Diary of a Wimpy Kid (Kinney), 188
DiPrete, Thomas A., 159
Divided Labours (Browne), 172
Divorce, 39, 49, 65–68, 94, 98,
   101, 265
   in Asia, 6, 236, 252
   of breadwinner wives and
      unemployed husbands, 51, 81
   and career opportunities for
      women, 152, 157
   custody of children after, 124
   financial impacts of, 67, 91, 294*n*
   murder as alternative to, 168, 170
   regional differences in rates of,
      91–92
Doctors, female, 59, 117, 132, 253
   specialties chosen by, 118, 139–140
Domestic violence, 13, 15, 168, 181
Drew, Ina, 200–201
Druggists' Bulletin, 128
Drug Topics magazine, 130–131
Duke University, 43
Dunham, Lena, 43
Dushane, Melodi, 177

eBay, 221
Ebony magazine, 88
Economist, The, 250
Ecuador, 55
Edge City (Garreau), 132–133
Edin, Kathryn, 92
Education Department, U.S.,
   161, 221
Ehrenreich, Barbara, 41, 63
Eliot, George, 163

Eliot, Lise, 160–161, 172
Ellis, Bret Easton, 171
El-Scari, Mustafaa, 89–90
Empowerment, 30, 37, 44–45, 187
EMTs, 260
End of Men and the Rise of Women (Rosin), 269–282
Engineers, 13, 54, 72, 80, 108, 150, 194
England, Paula, 24–25
Enlightened Power (Gergen), 197
Ericsson, Ronald, 11–13
Ernst & Young, 223
Erotic capital, 29–30, 36–37, 38
Esteve, Albert, 234–235
Evans, Harry, 225
Evans, Jenelle, 176–177
Ewha University, 230–231, 237

Facebook, 179, 193, 195, 212, 222, 228
Faludi, Susan, 9
Farber, Henry, 86
Farrell, Warren, 68–69, 72
Fast-food restaurants, female violence in, 177
Federal Bureau of Investigation (FBI), 174
Fels, Anna, 215
Feminine Mystique, The (Friedan), 279, 281
Feminism, 11–12, 13–14, 14–15, 21, 50, 60, 65, 75–76, 154, 180, 231
    accusations against, 160
    career opportunities and, 115, 124, 129, 152–153, 196, 212–213, 217
    changing cultural norms in response to, 172–173
    End of Men reaction, 270–282
    erotic capital and, 30
    in Iceland, 200
    motherhood and, 75–76, 92, 124
    power vs. powerless, 278–279
    realities (new) of, 271, 273, 279–282
    second-wave, 58
    sexual norms and, 37, 41
    Title IX complaints filed by, 17
    in views of murders by women, 176

"Fempire," 274
Financial planning, 118
Fiorina, Carly, 217
Fisher, Helen, 262
Flaubert, Gustave, 118
Flexibility, workplace, 140–141, 277
Florida, Lottery, winners in, 93
Florida State University, 42
Food and Drug Administration (FDA), 12
Food preparation, 118, 124
Forbes magazine, 203
Forensic pathology, 118
Fort Lauderdale (Florida), 81, 178
Fortune 500 companies, 81, 196
Fortune magazine, 203
Fox Television, 223
France, 117, 235, 248, 249
Frankel, Lois, 32, 34, 207
Franklin, Bernard, 154–155, 155–156
Friedan, Betty, 53, 279, 280, 281
From Chivalry to Terrorism (Braudy), 262
Fulbright scholarships, 253

G.I. Bill, 152
Gaga, Lady, 32, 187
Garreau, Joel, 132–133
Gates, Bill, 165
Gender equality, 14, 37, 67, 279–280
    lack of, 124, 275, 280
Gender role reversal, 137
"Gender segregation," 275
Generation Y, 140
Georgetown University, 147
Gerberding, Julie, 197–198
Gergen, David, 197
Germany, 248
Gerstel, Naomi, 260
Getting to 50/50 (Meers), 221
Gettys, Charles, 82–84
Gettys, Sarah Beth, 82–84, 97
Ghana, 232
Ghost Writer, The (Polanski), 187
Girl with the Dragon Tattoo, The (Larsson), 42–43, 188
Girlfight (movie), 187

Girls (television show), 43
GlaxoSmithKline, 170
Gneezy, Uri, 186
Godsall, David, 57–60, 69
Goldin, Claudia, 119, 130, 140,
    151–152, 193–194, 214, 276
Goldman Sachs, 221
Gold Misses, 236, 251, 254
Goler, Lori, 195
Goodstein, Eban, 158
Google, 191–192, 194–195, 224
Gordon, Claire, 18
Gorn, Elliott, 132
Gossip Girl (television show), 249
GQ magazine, 223
Grade point average (GPA), 147
Great Depression, 61, 152
Great Recession, 4
Greece, ancient, 10
Greenberg (movie), 56
Greenstone, Michael, 86, 125
Greer, Germaine, 65, 67, 278
Griffin, Phil, 212
Grose, Jessica, 9, 55–56
Gupta, Monica Das, 233
Gurian, Michael, 160
Guttentag-Secord theory, 39
Guyana, 150
Guyland (Kimmel), 40
Guys with Kids (television show), 280

Hakim, Catherine, 29–30
Hallmark, Gerald, 79, 97
Hamilton, Laura, 21–22, 25
Hanna (movie), 188
Harmon, Mark, 30
Harris, Tanner, 99
Harvard Business Review, 140, 215
Harvard University, 119, 224,
    264, 276
  Business School, 201, 243, 244
  Kennedy School, 196, 209
HBO, 43
Health-care industry, 118, 139–140,
    276. *See also* Doctors, female;
    Nursing profession; Pharmacists
Hearts of Men, The (Ehrenreich), 63

Hegedus, Nathan, 263
Heilman, Madeline, 208–209
Henderson, Darren, 89
Heriot, Gail, 145–148, 158
Hewlett Packard (HP), 217
"Hey, Soul Sister" (song), 122
Higher education, 94, 163, 275, 281
  gender dynamics of, 149–160
  See also specific colleges and
    universities
Hiroshima, atomic bombing of, 173
History Channel, 126
Hodge, Monica, 109
Home health care, 118, 124
Honduras, 81
Hooking Up (Bogle), 20
Hook-up culture, 17–46
Housewives, 65, 152, 170
  in Asian cultures, 236, 256
  role reversal fantasy about, 121
  in television shows, 47–48
Housing industry, collapse of, 87, 89
Houston, 81
How to Train Your Dragon (Cowell), 188
Huggies, 261–262
Humber, Gabby, 100
Hungary, 235
Hunger Games, The (Collins), 33, 188
Hunter-gatherer societies, 173
Hwang Myeong-eun, 238–239,
    240–242
Hyundai Motors, 202, 232, 247

Iceland, 5, 199–200
I Love Lucy (television show), 47–49
India, 5, 119, 182, 186
  traditional families in, 217
Indiana, University of, 21–22
Inequality. *See* Social inequality
Information economy, 5
Information technology (IT), 138
Institutional Investor, 201
International Olympic Committee, 247
Internet boom, 199
Iowa, 95
Iraq war, 173
Israel, 235

Ivy League schools, 26–29, 31, 145–146, 196. *See also specific universities*

J. C. Penney department stores, 97
Jackass 3D (movie), 143
Jacks, Margaret, 131
Jackson, Shirley, 168
Japan, 55, 236, 239, 250–251, 263
Jersey Shore (TV reality show), 176
Jews, 224
Job, The (Lewis), 120
Job loss. *See* Unemployment
Jobs, Steve, 165
Johns Hopkins University, 147
Jolie, Angelina, 187–188
Journal of Human Resources, 93
Journal of Personality and Social Psychology, 185
JPMorgan Chase, 200–201
Justice Statistics, Bureau of, 180

Kansas City, 89, 154–157
Katz, Lawrence F., 152
Keating, Charles, 176
Kefalas, Maria, 93, 95–96
Keith, Toby, 80
Kellerman, Barbara, 196
Kelly, Megyn, 223
Kennedy, Flo, 65
Kentucky, 92, 158
Kenyon College, 158–159
Kessler-Harris, Alice, 119
Khasi, 186
Kia automobiles, 110, 202, 247
Kim, Stephanie, 251–252
Kim, Yeeun, 229–230, 236–237, 255–256
Kim, Yongah, 243–244, 248
Kimmel, Michael, 40
King, Cisco, 108–109
King, Jacqueline, 155
King Kong Theory (Despentes), 253–254
Kinsey, Alfred, 41
Kipp, Peter, 230–231
Knocked Up (movie), 56
Knowing Your Value (Brzezinski), 211
Komarovsky, Mirra, 61–63

Kontz, Ann Miller, 170
KPMG accounting firm, 223
Krawcheck, Sallie, 203–205, 217, 224–225, 226–227
Kuziemko, Ilyana, 152

Labor Statistics, U.S. Bureau of, 117
Ladge, Jamie, 124, 197
Ladies' Home Journal, 3
Lady, The (magazine), 225
Lady Chatterley's Lover (Lawrence), 52
Laschever, Sara, 207
Las Vegas, 81
Latinos, 178
Lavin, Maud, 186, 187
Lawyers, 11, 28, 50, 51, 59, 74, 103, 108, 132, 218, 220
Leadership, 117, 123, 138
    charismatic style of, 29, 30
    corporate, 196–202
    in Korea, 256
    male, economic factors in collapse of, 97
Ledbetter, Lilly, 108
Lee, I-Sing, 68
Lee, Kirsten, 251–252, 254
Lee, Stephanie, 256
Lee County (Alabama), 106
Legal profession. *See* lawyers
Lewis, Michael, 199–200, 216
Lewis, Sinclair, 120
Li, Tianle, 170
Liberated Man, The (Farrell), 68
Liberia, 256
Lightdale, Jenifer, 184
Lonely Crowd, The (Riesman), 64
Longitudinal Survey of Young Women, 153
Los Angeles Times, 216
Louisville College of Pharmacy for Women, 129

Maasai, 186
Macho culture, 4, 55, 56–57, 69, 87, 160, 234, 256
    female aggression and, 179
    in workplace, accidents due to, 264

Madame Bovary (Flaubert), 118
Mad Men (television show), 195,
    204, 232
Mailer, Norman, 65
Majority in America, 278
Males, Mike, 19–20, 180–181
Manson, Charles, 176
Manufacturing, 108, 109, 258, 293*n*
    decline of, impact on men of, 2–5,
        81, 85–86
    jobs for African-Americans in, 88
    pharmaceutical, 130, 155
    steel, 155
Marriage, 18, 22, 23–24, 25, 39,
        91–92, 95–96, 98, 142,
        234–235, 251, 252
    age for, 24–25, 236
    in Asia, 6, 235–236, 253–254
    attitudes toward, 32, 36, 101
    births outside, 92–93, 96
    commuting, 122
    declining rates of, 81–82, 87, 91, 94
    delaying, 151, 153, 218, 234–235
    ending, 94–95
    expectations about, 7, 95–96
    "seesaw," 7, 47–77, 260–261
    sexuality and, 20
    See also Divorce
Maryland, University of, 198
Masculinity, 63, 262–265
    ornamental, 9
    post-feminist, 72
Massachusetts, 92
Massachusetts Institute of
        Technology (MIT), 86,
        87, 125, 199
Mass Career Customization, 140–141
Masturbation, 41
Match.com, 52
Maternity leave, 213, 223, 225, 228,
        239, 246, 270
Max, Tucker, 27
Mayer, Marissa, 191–192, 194–195,
        226, 279
McDonald's, 177
McDowell County (West Virginia), 87
McGowen, Meghan, 107–108

McKinsey & Company, 227, 244,
    247, 248
Median income, 87, 106, 107, 125,
    155, 274–275
Medical professions, 139–140.
    See also Doctors, female; Nursing
    profession; Pharmacists
Meers, Sharon, 221
Men's Health magazine, 30
"Men of Tears" groups, 5–6
Merck Vaccines, 198
Meritocracy, 124
Merkel, Angela, 32
Metropolitan Community College
    (Kansas City), 154
Mexico, 81, 234
Michigan, University of, 162
MicroSort sperm selection method, 12
Middle class, 66
    disparities between men and
        women in, 5, 39, 79–111
    norm of male breadwinner in,
        62–63
Mill on the Floss, The (Eliot), 163
Millett, Kate, 60
Million Dollar Baby (movie), 187
Miss magazine, 132
Missouri, University of
    Kansas City, 156–157
Miss Pharmacy beauty contest, 131
Mohler, Albert, 96
Mongolia, 235
"Monitoring the Future" study, 163
Montgomery (Alabama), 83
Moon Kook-Hyun, 246
Moore, Mary Tyler, 121
Mortenson, Tom, 150
Mount, Jeanine, 122
"Mrs. Carter Show World Tour"
    (Beyoncé), 281–282
Ms. magazine, 65
MSNBC, 211
MTV, 176
Mundy, Liza, 274–275
Murder, 171, 172, 180
    by women, 10, 167–171, 176,
        181–182

Murray, Charles, 93
Muslims, 183
My Life as a Man (Roth), 63–64
My Misspent Youth (Daum), 31
My Name Is Kim Sam-soon (television show), 254
"Myth of Male Decline, The" (Coontz), 274
Myth of Male Power, The (Farrell), 68, 72

Nakamura, Hitomi "Miki," 229–230
National Assessment of Educational Progress (NAEP), 161
National Crime Victimization Survey, 180
National Institute of Child Health, 220
NBC, 280
Nerds (Buckley), 188
Ness, Cindy, 177–178
Netherlands, 227, 263, 264
Neuroscience, 160–161, 172–173, 258
New Jersey, 170
Newsweek, 160, 165, 217, 226
New York, 92
New York, State University of (SUNY), 156
New Yorker, The, 195
New York Times, The, 86, 92, 158, 174, 176, 182, 200–201, 274, 278
New York University, 24, 208
Nice Girls Don't Get the Corner Office (Frankel), 32, 34, 207
Nightingale, Florence, 128
Nooyi, Indra, 212, 217–218
Nooyi, Rajkantilal, 217
Norma Rae (movie), 108
North Carolina, 170
North Carolina, University of (UNC), 156
Northeastern University, 124, 197
Norway, 150
Nursing profession, 2, 83, 87, 103, 124, 135, 154, 267
  men in, 9, 168, 258, 259
Nuttall, Roger, 169

Oates, Joyce Carol, 168
Obama, Barack, 86, 148, 196, 278
Obama, Michelle, 29
Office, The (television show), 15, 58
Office Space (movie), 136–137
Offshore oil platforms, 264–266
Offspring, sex preference for, 11–14
Oklahoma, 92
Opelika (Alabama), 106, 107, 109, 110
Oprah (television show), 240
Optometry, 118
Oral sex, 18, 26, 36, 42, 180
Organization for Economic Cooperation and Development (OECD), 66, 150, 245
  Gender, Institutions and Development Database, 234
Organization Man, The (Whyte), 64
O'Rourke, Lindsey, 182–183
Orwell, George, 114
Oslo stock exchange, 200
Out-of-wedlock births, 39, 49, 92–93, 96. *See also* Single mothers; Teen pregnancy
Ovesey, Lionel, 63
Owen, Karen, 43
OxyContin addiction, 87, 88
Oxygen network, 181

Panama City (Florida), 177
Pandit, Vikram, 202–203, 204
Pappas, Aggie, 178
Park Chung-hee, 231–232
Park Geun-hye, 256
Patriarchy, 10, 42, 135, 186, 227–228
  authority in, 58, 62
  criminal justice system in, 175
  girls' revenge against, in popular culture, 188
  middle class, 80
  power dynamics shift, 270–274, 277
  priesthood model of, 133
  in South Korea, 13, 231–233, 256
Patterson, James, 188
PBS, 279

Pell Institute for the Study of Opportunity in Higher Education, 150
People magazine, 12, 30
"People People" study, 135, 136
People skills, 64, 117, 119, 135
PepsiCo, 212
Perhaps Women (Anderson), 128
Pharmaceutical Era, 128
Pharmaceutical industry, 155, 170, 246
Pharmacists, 114–123, 124–139, 156, 276, 295n, 298n
Philadelphia, 92, 96
Philippines, 253
Piaget, Jean, 63
Pink, 178
Pink Brain, Blue Brain (Eliot), 172
Pinker, Steven, 172–173
Plasticity, 259
  sexual, 41, 42
Plastic surgery, 236
Plath, Sylvia, 49–50
Playboy Club, 29
Playboy magazine, 60, 65
Play Like a Man, Win Like a Woman (Evans), 207
Poisoning, 128, 167–168, 169–171
Polanski, Roman, 187
Polizzi, Nicole "Snooki," 176
Pornography, 19, 26, 28, 29, 40, 41–42, 43, 56
Portland (Oregon), 259, 264
Portlandia (television show), 260
Portnoy's Complaint (Roth), 44
Portugal, 235
Practical Academic Cultural Education (PACE), 178–179, 183
Premarital Sex in America (Regnerus), 39
Prentice, Deborah, 184
PricewaterhouseCoopers, 223
Pridgen, Abby, 98, 105
Pridgen, Connie, 84–85, 97–101, 105
Pridgen, Rob, 84–85, 98, 110
Princeton University, 86, 183
Prinz, Jesse, 173

Professions, 22, 58, 149, 223, 236, 245
  elite, 201, 214
  female-dominated, 4–5, 8, 275–277, 280, 281
  male versus female status in, 60–61, 152, 227
  marriage and, 72, 96, 252–253
  See also specific professions
Property crimes, 174
Pseudohomosexuality, 63
Psychology Today, 173
Publix grocery chain, 107
Push Comes to Shove (Lavin), 186
PyeongChang 2018 Winter Games Bid Committee, 247–248

Qatar, 150
Quarterly Journal of Economics, 199
Quenching the Father Thirst (Williams), 89–90

Rah, Theresa, 248
Raiders of the Lost Ark (movie), 165
Rape, 180–181, 253
  acquaintance, 19–20
Re-Making Love (Ehrenreich), 41
Real Housewives (television series), 48
Red Families v. Blue Families (Carbone), 87
Redhill, David, 135
Regnerus, Mark, 39
Remington typewriters, 127
Republican Party, 91, 149
Results-Only Work Environment, 223
Revolutionary Road (Yates), 64–65
Rice, Condoleezza, 173
Richer Sex, The (Mundy), 274
Richmond, University of, 145, 146, 158
Riesman, David, 64
Robyn (pop star), 43
Rogge, Jacques, 248
Roiphe, Katie, 67
Role reversals, gender, 137
Romney, Mitt, 278
Ronan, Saoirse, 188
Roosevelt, Franklin, 119

Rosin, Hanna, 269–282
Roth, Philip, 63–64
Routly, Chris, 262
Royal, Ségolène, 29
Russell Afternoon Center for
    Creative Learning, 110–111
Russell Corporation, 79–81, 88, 101,
    104, 105, 111
Russell Medical Center, 80, 81, 83
Russia, 182
Rust Belt, 87
Rwanda, 256

Safety 2000, 264–266
Saint Agnes Medical Center, 169
Saletan, William, 42
Samsung Electronics, 232
Sandberg, Sheryl, 195, 212–213, 217,
    222–223, 227–228, 271
San Diego State University, 185
Saudi Arabia, 150–151
Scarborough, Joe, 212
Scarpace, Katie, 137–138
Schalet, Amy, 263–264
Schmidt, Eric, 224
Scholastic Aptitude Test (SAT), 147
School, gender differences in success
    in, 160–166. *See under* Higher
    education
Schuster, Larissa, 167–171, 176
Schuster, Timothy, 167–171
Second Sex, The (Beauvoir),
    1, 10–11
Seoul (South Korea), 229–230, 245,
    248, 250, 251
Service sector, 5, 87, 88, 107, 293*n*
    in Korea, 247
Sex and the City (television show), 31,
    43, 249, 253
Sex at Dawn (Ryan and Jethá), 37
Sexism, 195, 245
Sexual abuse, 22
Sexual assault
    decline of, 19–20
    See also Rape
Shockley, Mary, 81
Shows, Carla, 260

Sickmund, Melissa, 175, 177–178,
    180–181
Siegel, Jordan, 245
Sigurdardottir, Johanna, 5
Silicon Valley, 192–195, 202, 218, 224
Silver Spring (Maryland), 122
Single mothers, 2, 49, 67, 81, 87,
    92–93, 275–276. *See also*
    Out-of-wedlock births
Sirleaf, Ellen Johnson, 256
16 and Pregnant (TV reality show), 19
Slate magazine, 42, 51–52, 55, 206,
    259, 261, 263
Slaughter, Anne-Marie, 270–271
Smith College, 152
Snapped (television show), 181–182
Social inequality, 279–280. *See also*
    Gender equality
Soft skills, 135
Solis, Bob, 167, 169
Sommers, Christina Hoff, 160
South Korea, 13, 55, 229–234,
    235–256
    Family Laws, 231
    Foreign Ministry, 233
    Most Admired Companies, 246
Southern Baptist Theological
    Seminary, 96
Southern California, University of, 13
Spain, 55, 117, 235
Sperm selection, 11–12
Spike TV, 40, 87
Sri Lanka, 182
Stanford University, 40, 194, 264
    Prison Experiment, 184
Stanton, Katie, 192–193
Stay-at-home husbands, 51, 53–54, 261
Steenbarger, Brett, 171
Steinbacher, Roberta, 12
Stevenson, Adlai, 152
Stop Sabotaging Your Career
    (Frankel), 207
Story of Edgar Sawtelle, The
    (Wroblewski), 114
Suicide bombers, female, 182–183
Summers, Larry, 86
Sumners, Joe, 85–86

Super Bowl, 56–57
Swank, Hilary, 187
Sweden, 19, 263–264
Swinger culture, 41
Switzerland, 55, 248

Taiwan, 236
Talk magazine, 225
Tallapoosa County (Alabama), 85
Tanenhaus, Sam, 176
Tanzania, 186
Target stores, 135
Tatler magazine, 225
Teachers, 9, 51, 71, 84–85, 99–100,
    229, 261
    and gender differences in students'
        behavior, 164–166, 256
    men as, 71, 84, 89, 119, 259
    Sunday school, 80, 83
    training of, 151, 155
TED, 222
Teen Mom (TV reality show), 19,
    176–177
Teen pregnancy, 19
"Telephone" (song), 187
Thailand, 36
Thatcher, Margaret, 173
Thelma & Louise (movie), 187
Things of a Man (Korean best seller),
    256
30 Rock (television show), 58
"Throwing Like a Girl"
    (Young), 187
Time magazine, 106
Title IX, 17, 18, 26, 147, 186–187
TMZ, 176–177
Toledo (Ohio), 177
Tomasdottir, Halla, 200
Too Many Women? (Guttentag and
    Secord), 39
Tosh.O (television show), 126, 143
Town Bloody Hall (documentary), 65
Twenge, Jean, 185–186, 188
Twilight (book and movie
    series), 263
Twitter, 193
Tyre, Peg, 160

U.S. News & World Report, 107, 145
Unemployed Man and His Family, The
    (Komarovsky), 61
Unemployment, 56, 62, 85, 89, 106,
    109, 116, 272
    benefits, 83, 123, 257
UNESCO, 150
United Kingdom, 4, 48, 117, 165, 181,
    183, 246
United Nations, 234
Up All Night (television show), 261

VandenHeuvel, Sarah, 138–139
Vassar College, 145, 158
Veterinarians, 276
Victimization, 20, 177–178,
    180–181
Victorianism, 133, 247
Video games, 40, 109, 157, 162, 183,
    215, 261
Vietnam, 253
Vietnam War, 152
View, The (television show), 240
Virginia, University of, 49

Wagoner, Lou Ann, 101
Walgreens pharmacies, 121, 133
Wallace, Emma Gary, 129
Wallace, George, 91
Wall Street Journal, The, 204
Walmart, 87, 103, 110
Walters, Barbara, 223
Washington, DC, 177
Washington Post, The, 204–205, 210
Wayne County (Indiana), 92
Weel, Bas Ter, 135
We Have Always Lived in the Castle
    (Jackson), 168
Weinberg, Bruce, 135, 136
Wertheimer, Albert, 134
What to Expect When You're Expecting
    (movie), 261
When Work Disappears (Wilson), 88
"Where I'm From" (song), 95
White, Emily, 193, 195, 213, 218
White-collar jobs, 129. *See also*
    Professions

White House Council on
Boys and Men, 69
White House Council of Economic
Advisers, 86
White men and 2012 elections, 278
Whitmire, Richard, 161, 162, 166
Whole Foods, 107, 194
Why Boys Fail (Whitmire), 161
Why Girls Fight (Ness), 177–178
Whyte, William, 64
"Why Women Still Can't
Have It All" (Slaughter), 270
Wilcox, Brad, 49, 93–95
Wilson, William Julius, 88
Winter Olympics (PyeongChang,
2018), 247–248
Wisconsin, 113–116, 137
Wisconsin, University of, 114,
116, 120
Women's reaction to *End of Men*,
270–274, 279, 281
Wonder of Boys, The (Gurian), 160

Working class, 1, 6, 24, 60, 71, 82,
87, 124, 270, 281. *See also*
Manufacturing
Working mothers, 9, 75–76, 140, 239,
240, 251–252
Working Mother's Guide to Life, The
(Mason), 75
Work It (television show), 55
World Bank, 233
World Health Organization, 236
Wright, Joe, 188

Yahoo, 279
Yale University, 17–19, 26, 44
Yamaguchi, Tsutomu, 173
Yates, Richard, 64–65
Yevlapova, Natalya V., 182
Young, Iris Marion, 187
YouTube, 177
Yuhan-Kimberly, 246–247

Zimbardo, Philip, 40

Hanna Rosin is a senior editor at *The Atlantic*, where she first reported on "the end of men." A founder of DoubleX, *Slate*'s women's section, she has written for *The New Yorker*, the *New York Times*, *GQ*, *The New Republic*, and the *Washington Post*, among others, and is the recipient of a 2010 National Magazine Award. She is also the author of a previous book, *God's Harvard: A Christian College on a Mission to Save America*. Rosin lives in Washington, DC, with her husband, *Slate* editor David Plotz, and their three children.